A FEW ANAGRAMS

Tan Mud Lord
Odd Palm Turn
Damp Old Runt
Darn Dump Lot
Land Turd Mop
Odd Rum Plant
Lord Pant Mud
Add Torn Lump
Dump Not Lard
Turd Nap Mold
Lord Dam Punt
Don Turd Lamp
Mad Plod Runt
Damn Rut Plod
Plot Mud Dam
Porn Dud Malt
Turd Pan Mold
Drum Told Pan
Lord Damp Nut
Old Dump Rant
Mold Pun Dart
Ant Lord Dump
Plant Mud Rod
Dump Tan Lord
Don Ald Trump

FUMPTRUCK

EDITED BY ANONYMOUS

DEDICATION

TO THE 45TH / 47TH PRESIDENT* OF THE DIVIDED STATES OF AMERICA

[* not a real president]

"Any form of art is a form of power; it has impact, it can affect change – it can not only move us, it makes us move."

– OSSIE DAVIS

CONTENTS

FUMPTRUCK

THE HOLLOW MAN

L.A. SPOONER

NUMB

ANONYMOUS

THE NIGHT BEFORE I watched the collapse of Everything,
everything I knew, a reality quickly ripped apart
Covered by blankets so soft I wished I could return
to Tomorrow, too afraid to see the dawn,
too afraid to lay my eyes upon that Crimson Sunrise
colored by self-destructions, old traits and hatred
descended from resentful gods whose wrath was
too grotesque for explanation;
I remained numb to the tedious truth that pragmatism was
murdered by mobs made real in the light of a new order,
and monsters were anything else,
couldn't be anything else
except that which we knew they already were;
everywhere and everyone around us.

BEYOND IDIOCRACY

ANONYMOUS

NEWSFLASH: CUBA UNWILLING
TO LIFT U.S. EMBARGO

President Cortas Chuevara said Cuba was "not willing at this time" to lift its embargo on trade with the USA. "The ideological differences are just too big, right now," Chuevara said, "and while we have empathy with the oppressed people of the United States, they really should put a government in power that implements Basic Income and Universal Healthcare, just like the rest of the civilized world. Morally, we cannot trade with such a backwards regime."

"We don't need no stinkin' handouts from stinkin' commies," US President Trump truthed. "People need to be smart like me and be born into a stinkin' rich family."

MEANWHILE, IN THE ALT-SOUTH

The worshippers went to Sunday church, cloaked and hooded in black, carrying pitchforks and sacrificial daggers. The church bells rang, but they were barely audible above the intro section of Slayer's "Hell Awaits" blasting from the geo-powered mega-speakers, as the crowd moved their fists in rhythm, pumping their energy to the invisible band behind the crooked cross.

Inside, the incense of smoked meat, bourbon, and pot was overwhelming. The worshippers gathered around fired-up barbecues—pews considered old-fashioned in the New Church of the Alt-South. Bourbon distilled with unholy water was being poured, while reefers imbued with the spirit of Satan were distributed.

"Welcome y'all," the satanic priestess said to her congregation as she raised her glass, "and obey the unholy rites of Our Lady Satan. Drink this bourbon, as it is the tears I shed at the injustice of this world."

"The injustice!" the worshippers answered in unison, then slammed their drinks ad fundum.

"Smoke this weed," she said, "as it is incensed with my anger at the state of this nation."

"The anger," the worshippers replied, then lit their tokes, and drew deep.

"Now, what shall we slaughter at the altar of sacrifice?" the satanic priestess said, pointing to the animals standing nearby, "a cow, a pig, or a bunch of chickens?"

"Slaughter 'em all," the crowd shouted, "nothing is good enough for Our Lady Satan."

Then, as the animals were slaughtered and their meat was distributed to the church's barbecues, the satanic priestess chanted: "Eat these ribs, as they are my ribs—"

"—that echo with the pain of the world," the congregation chanted.

"Eat these legs, as they are my legs—" the priestess chanted.

"—to give us the power to walk over the unbelievers," the congregation echoed.

"Enjoy these breasts," the satanic priestess howled in ecstasy, fondling hers, "as I enjoy mine."

"In lust is power," they chanted, "in power is lust."

"Finally, devour this steak, and put a stake through our enemies," she sang.

"Steady our minds and deliver us from libtards," the congregation shouted with unholy fire.

"See the light," the satanic priestess said, "and pledge your allegiance to Our Lady Satan."

Mercyful Fate's "Satan's Fall" blasted from the mega-speakers, drowning out the hydraulic whine of the cylinders that opened the retractable roof. Light poured into the church as the worshippers pointed their guns upwards and emptied their magazines. The shouts of "Lead for Satan and death to the unbelievers" were barely audible above the massive gunfire. Gun smoke mixed with pot smoke, smoked meat was served, and peaty bourbon was consumed with religious fervor.

"The service is now open to questions, "the satanic priestess said. "So let us hear your doubts."

"Why do our cloaks have to be black?" a woman asked. "It took me days to get ours repainted."

"The KKK was wrong," the satanic priestess said. "White is for god-botherers. True satanists wear black."

"Why don't we burn their churches?" an eager man asked.

"Because we're more evil than that," the priestess said, "as we refurbish their temples into ours. This hurts their medieval god more than just burning them down, and we sell it as 'environmentally friendly.' Double whammy."

"Why can't we all join the Sunday orgy?" an even more eager young man asked.

"Orgy privileges are only given to those who have our sterility implants," the satanic priestess said, "as procreation is only for the chosen. For a donation, followed by a minor surgical operation, we can provide that implant, which can be reversed if required."

"Three questions only," the satanic priestess said, "and now I must ask the non-implanted to leave so we can finish this service with our weekly orgy. And don't forget your donation."

"Naked. we shall face the Lady," the worshippers sang, and slid out of their black cloaks as one.

NEWSFLASH: PUERTO RICO TO ENFORCE THE JOHNSON ACT

San Juan, Puerto Rico: Mayor Penelope Carmen of San Juan announces the enforcement of the Jones Act. "It is with due regret that we must enforce the Johnson Act," Mayor Carmen announces at a press conference last Friday, "as our little island and community simply cannot absorb any more refugees from the American mainland. All shipping traffic to and from the American mainland is halted, effectively by now."

"While our robotized workforce and hyper-connected artificial intelligences are second to none in the Americas," she continued, "there is only so much they can do to guarantee a basic income for all Puerto Ricans. On top of that, we will not be able to grow enough food to deal with the ongoing deluge of émigrés. So, until further notice, we must enforce the Jones Act." Unable to withhold it any longer, she starts crying. "We are extremely sorry," she says between sobs, "but there is only so much we can do. In the end, it is simple math: three million can't take care of three hundred million."

MEANWHILE, IN THE ALT-SOUTH

"Time to make merry, young man," the old man said, lifting his glass of bourbon after taking a long drag from his toke, "and test the new batch'o'bourbon, smoke the new weed harvest, and then go-a-turkey-huntin'."

"But Dad, can't we just skip the huntin's part?" the young man said as a worried look crossed his face.

"No, m'boy, that's tradition."

"But last time we only hit one turkey—a tough ol' one—and killed a dozen of ourselves."

"Listen to our priestess' wise words: 'Sometimes the herd must be thinned,' she said herself."

"But our priestess's a satanist!"

"Well, son, Christianity was becoming boring," the old man said, "and this sharply-dressed and—if I may say so—devilishly handsome young priestess has re-invigorated our community."

"During her service we sacrificed animals," the young man said, voice echoing with despair. "Then she sodomized a volunteer with a black dildo, who then 'spoke with the voice of the Dark Mistress herself' all while a church-with-a-cross-the-right-side-up replica was burnt in offering."

"Church is more fun than it ever was," the old man said. "Attendance is up, and it feels so much better to worship a young horny woman than an old righteous guy. Now, prepare for the Turkey Huntin' tomorrow."

"But we'll shoot more of ourselves than turkeys."

"Which gives us the opportunity to engage in evil acts of heterosexual reproduction," the man said, relishing the thought.

"But all sex is allowed anyway, nowadays." The young man rolled his eyes in disgust.

"Only if it doesn't lead to reproduction," the old man said, "and that's why this evil, old-fashioned heterosexual dallying's become hot again. It's the forbidden fruit."

"You people are sick," the young man said.

"No, we've just taken the next logical step to our survival," the old man said. "By-the-by, didya know you look pretty damn purty when you're angry?"

"That's fucking incest!" the young man said in disbelief.

"It's non-reproductive," the old man said, "so allowed."

NEWSFLASH: A NEW GULAG ARCHIPELAGO; RUSSIA TO PUT AMERICAN REFUGEES TO WORK IN SIBERIAN OUTPOSTS

Moscow, Russian Federation: Cyborg President-for-life Vladimir Putin—now in its third decade in power—declares that Russia will be putting American refugees that enter Russian territory by crossing the Bering Strait to work in a network of Siberian outposts.

"I realize that life out there will be hard, "CP Putin said, "but it's definitely more humane than sending them back. Unless they refuse to accept their new Russian citizenship, in which case we will be forced—with great reluctance, I assure you—to send them back to Alaska."

MEANWHILE, IN THE ALT-SOUTH, IN A NEARBY PARK RANGER STATION

Somewhere in the Alt South, an animal rights activist was discussing—what he calls—dastardly acts with a park ranger, who didn't seem disturbed at all.

"They're shooting innocent creatures for their own pleasure," he said. "This medieval behavior must be stopped."

"They're so stoned and drunk that they only manage to hit one single turkey, and most of the time," she said, "there are more victims in their own ranks."

"They're becoming so dangerous they're killing humans," he said. "We should confiscate their guns."

"Confiscating guns from a trigger-happy satanic cult?" she said. "No, thank you. In this way, they're thinning their own herd and are distracted enough not to do real damage."

"But think about the turkeys," he said. "What about them?"

"Most of the turkeys they see are AR projections," the park ranger said. "We've set up AR sensors and projectors in the areas where they normally hunt. We lure them away from real turkeys and allow them to shoot one single one, the oldest of the rafter, who's led a long and happy life."

"That's still one too many."

"Unfortunately, they have to hit a real target once in a while, otherwise they might get suspicious," she said. "It's a small sacrifice, and the current numbers of birds can easily take that."

"But there's a principle at stake. We can't just let them behave like that."

"Their 'natural' conversion to satanism is the best thing that can happen," she said. "We've infiltrated their satanic sects with metalheads—who are laughing themselves silly, internally—and gently push them in the directions we want. For example, they still haven't noticed all their wild hunting parties are always during important elections—all except the Presidential, which is hard to obscure—so they forget to vote."

"What?"

"They're gradually losing seats everywhere—local, congress, and senate—and barely notice it because they're too busy worshipping satan."

"Too busy worshipping satan?" he said, incredulously.

"Our metalhead infiltrators keep them busy, alright," she said. "Hunting parties, satanic rituals, shows, and gigs (Slayer's 'Raised from the Dead' tour was a huge hit), barbecue'n'crowdfunding events. The whole scam pays for itself."

"I get it," he said, "the old 'bread and circuses' scam?"

"Bread and circuses are so last-millennium," she said. "Satan, guns, pot, and liquor is where it's at."

NEWSFLASH: MEXICO PRESIDENT KIDA FRAHLO ANNOUNCES BUILDING OF THE WALL

Mexico City, Mexico: Presidente Kida Frahlo announces the building of a wall on the Mexican-USA border. "We are a proud, innovative country, but even our resources are limited," Presidente Kida Frahlo said, "and while we wish to help our Northern neighbors as much as we can, there are three times as many Americans as Mexicans. The millions upon millions of Americans illegally crossing our border to take advantage of our Basic Income and

Universal Healthcare are putting a too high burden in our system."

"Unfortunately, we must think of our own people, first," she continued, "as the flood of illegal Americanos threatens to over-burden our system. While we will allow a selected group of Young American Dreamers to stay, we must stem the refugee flood by building the wall."

"With our fully automated robotic construction factories running at full throttle, it should take no more than a couple of weeks," Presidente Frahlo said, "In the meantime, we can only hope that the people in the USA consider regime change. Their future is up to them."

ARMAGEDDON SMILES

G.O. CLARK

WOKE up this morning
surrounded by zombies,
silent, smug faced zombies
not out for brains or slices
of fresh human meat,

but the peace of mind
of folks like me who have
fought against monsters big
and small, for seventy eight
years without rest,

like the guy across
the street, leaf blower in
hand, who greets me with a
toothy smile each day, dark as
a tunnel straight to Hell.

A SOMEWHAT LEVEL-HEADED RESPONSE TO THE RECENT ELECTION

STEPHEN KOZENIEWSKI

"STARING DOWN THE BARREL" (forgive the hackneyed cliché, but it seems more apt than ever) of a second, non-consecutive Trump presidency I am filled with conflicting thoughts, enough to fill a dozen novel-length collections of essays. I am fortunate, however, not to be filled with conflicting emotions. It would be apropos, perhaps, to use a second hackneyed cliché already here, that I am "dead inside," but that is not strictly accurate.

I am possessed of what is technically called a "flat affect," which is a symptom of the Post Traumatic Stress Disorder I was diagnosed with shortly after returning from the war in Iraq. What it means, in layman's terms, is that I feel very little. I experience neither great joy nor great pain; my emotional life is dreadfully gray.

Some of you reading this, I imagine, may envy my condition, as you are suffering in the depths of despair right now. I wouldn't wish a flat affect on anyone else, but since I have one I've decided to accept this cross between superpower and curse and simply use it for good as best as I can.

So.

A somewhat level-headed response to the recent election.

First, regarding that depression and despair you are suffering from right now? Wrestle with it. Deal with it as you see fit, or as best you are able. But be aware—be acutely aware, please—that despair is a weapon in the fascist arsenal, perhaps their ultimate weapon.

Make no mistake: Trump would prefer a fascist order in this country. He may not be able to achieve it, one hopes, but he would certainly prefer it, if for no other reason than that he is lazy and it would make his life simpler. He also underwent herculean efforts in his last administration to institute a fascist regime, or perhaps I should say he would have undergone herculean efforts to do so if he wasn't so goddamned lazy. Mostly his "efforts" amounted to firing people when they couldn't magic up a border wall or make the pandemic disappear, trying to cajole the military into shooting protestors, and attempting the most half-assed revolution of all time.

Fascism is, if not necessarily guaranteed, certainly the greatest danger we face right now from a Trump presidency. And the fascist wields despondency like a truncheon. The fascist convinces his enemies they are powerless to resist his depredations. Then the prophecy becomes self-fulfilling. Your despair is elixir to the fascist. The fascist licks your tears with his prehensile, vampiric tongue and draws his strength from them.

Despondency is fine for now, by which I mean it is an appropriate and human reaction, but it is only fine for right this very second. You will need to screw your head on right as soon as possible, and then gird your loins for the fight to come. We are going to need you. Which leads me to point two.

Second, the fight is not over. This sounds like an empty platitude, of course, reminiscent of Citizen Kane after he loses the governorship, railing that he ain't licked yet. Well, a platitude it may be, but whether it turns out to be empty is entirely up to us.

When I say "the fight is not over" I don't mean that we shall fight them on the beaches and in the fields and in the streets, although that's probably the appropriate attitude to take. I mean that if we throw up a few speed bumps and a few inconvenient traffic signals, they're probably going to get miffed, give up, and wander off.

During Trump's last administration his primary promise was to build a border wall. He couldn't accomplish it because, well, it was pretty hard and the logistics were a bit complicated. His secondary promise was to repeal Obamacare. Even though Republicans held both chambers of congress, he couldn't do that because it was pretty hard and the logistics were a bit complicated. I need not really go into infrastructure day, or any number of his other plans.

This man is a lazy, lazy fascist, my friends. So, while the idea of a second Trump presidency is terrifying, and he has promised some truly nightmarish things, a legal challenge here could gum up the works. An organized march there could shed some unwanted light on a particularly dystopian policy which Trump's regular voters dismissed as "serious but not literal" or some other bullshit justification. A wannabe dictator may think his word is the law, but the funny thing about a populist is that he needs the populace, and the funny thing about an administrator is that he needs the bureaucracy.

A third and final point on revolution and resistance. Every American, regardless of whether they're genuinely downtrodden or absolutely the wealthiest, most privileged fuck in the country, thinks they're Luke Skywalker. Perhaps it's the last thing that unites us?

You'll note that no one wants to be Luke Skywalker in the first third of the movie, but everyone wants to be Luke Skywalker in the final third of the movie. In the beginning he's oppressed, and in the end he has agency. What comes in between those two points is organization.

First, Luke comes together with an affinity group, all of whom are there for different reasons. One out of a sense of old obligations, one out of being a true believer, one purely for money, one out of friendship for the guy who just wants money, and two I guess who are robot slaves, which is not really a helpful metaphor, but kind of beside the point. Alone, Luke was worthless. Organizing with his friends he became capable of much more. Then when his cell further united with a larger force, they were finally able to strike meaningful blows against their enemy.

So, organize, goddammit. Imagine if we weren't just throwing up the occasional roadblock to Trump's plans but were flooding the zone with lawsuits and protests. Imagine if liberals in congress weren't just utilizing the odd procedural element that will be overturned by leadership a few hours later. Imagine if we were anticipating and predicting ways to tangle his whole administration up for years. (Realistically, we may only need two, right? It may only be two years of hell and not four if we flip congress in 2026.) What would the lazy fascist do if things became very, very hard?

He might just give up, go golfing, and take credit for whatever low-hanging fruit the conservative media says he did. "Egg prices went down ten cents? Sure, that was me. Don't worry about why I didn't get the twenty million immigrants deported. It's all happening according to plan."

The alternative is for us to give up and make things very, very easy for him.

BOL

USMAN T. MALIK

[translation of the poem by Faiz Ahmed Faiz (1911 - 1984)]

SPEAK, for your lips are free
Speak, for your tongue is still your tongue
Your chiseled, upright body still yours
This life still yours, this life still yours.

See in the blacksmith's forge
The flames turned fierce, the steel turned red
The padlocks' mouths gape open
And the chains spread their helpless laps.

Speak; this flicker of time is enough
Before the death of body and tongue
Speak, for Truth lives still. It lives.
Speak and say what need be said.

INCONCEIVABLE

ZOJE STAGE

Congratulations Angela S.! Your LifeDetect™ womb sensor has reported a confirmed conception. Your doctor has been notified and will contact you shortly with more information. Our records indicate that this is your first pregnancy.

Your LifeDetect™ womb sensor has now automatically linked with your multi-watch to monitor the vital health of you and your unborn baby. All data from your womb sensor and multi-watch will be forwarded to the Office of Reproduction Health for the duration of your pregnancy as a safeguard for the precious cargo in your womb. All communications will become part of your official Profile, including texts, emails, transcriptions of phone calls, and footage—as well as abridged transcripts—of in-person and video appointments. You may request copies of these communications for your personal records at any time— we're sure you'll want to document these precious milestones of your baby's earliest months!

Hi Angela,

We received the wonderful news regarding your conception! My name is Ellen and I've been assigned as your obstetric nurse and liaison. My job is to monitor the data received from your Life-Detect ™ womb sensor and multi-watch, and communicate with you everything you need to know as your pregnancy advances. I'll help you schedule appointments, and update you on all matters that pertain to the health of your baby. You're going to hear from me a lot over the next nine months, and I hope you'll think of me as a friend in addition to your nurse and liaison!

Our records indicate that your unborn baby is now six days

old. Conception is typically detected within twenty-four hours, but for the sake of certainty and accuracy most womb sensors send official notifications at about seven days. Lucky you—you got your notification a day early! The expected birthdate of your baby is August 12. That may seem far away, but you'll be surprised how quickly the weeks go by. And now is the time to optimize your body's health for the safe development of your child.

Attached you'll find our recommendations for helpful physical and mental exercises (including meditation and mindfulness practices), recipes for healthy eating, and a list of all the chemicals, foods, and behaviors you should eliminate from your daily routine. I've already signed off on your essential vitamins and they'll be delivered to you tomorrow morning.

I'm here to answer your every question, and as a first-time mom I'm sure you'll have many! If you contact me outside of my regular hours I'll be promptly notified. And if you experience any sort of emergency your womb sensor will likely detect it first—but feel free to call me or the office, or 911 if you fear your unborn baby is in immediate peril.

I'm thrilled to be going on this journey with you!

Your nurse and friend,

Ellen

TRANSCRIBED PHONE CONVERSATION: NOVEMBER 12

KAYA: Hey.

ANGELA: I'm pregnant.

KAYA: [*choking sound*] What? Are you serious? I didn't think you and Vic were planning to—

ANGELA: We weren't.

KAYA: How did Vic react?

ANGELA: Better than me, honestly.

KAYA: You sound pissed.

ANGELA: I'm not pissed about the ... [*audible sigh*]. I know I'm being paranoid, but I seriously think they fuck with the birth control pills. I mean, I take it at the exact same time every day, never miss a day.

KAYA: It's not a hundred percent.

ANGELA: I know, but ... [*audible sigh*]. We wanted to wait a few years. I haven't fully wrapped my head around it yet.

KAYA: Has your nurse liaison reached out to you?

ANGELA: About five minutes after I got the alerts on my watch.

KAYA: I know the timing isn't perfect, but ... I'm glad—we can go through everything together! [*Laughter*] That's a good thing, right?

ANGELA: It definitely helps. How are you feeling?

KAYA: Good, mostly. Still nauseous every morning and the anti-nausea herbal tea is a joke. But Charlotte keeps saying it won't be so bad once I'm in the second trimester.

ANGELA: Which must be soon?

KAYA: A couple of weeks. Hey, my mom will be here in a minute.

ANGELA: Just wanted to let you know.

KAYA: I'm excited for you! For us! Talk soon.

ANGELA: Love ya, bye.

TEXT [ELLEN – ANGELA]: NOVEMBER 18

Your blood pressure has been running a wee bit high. Should be manageable with diet and meditation. Be sure to avoid processed foods, that will help a lot!

TEXT EXCHANGE: NOVEMBER 20

ELLEN: Your first in-person appointment is scheduled for Dec. 2 at 10 a.m. Happy Thanksgiving!

ANGELA: Thanks, Ellen—but can we schedule for later in the day? I could be there by three-thirty.

ELLEN: Sorry! We're super booked. It'll only be once a month for now, and I'll try to do afternoons next time.

TRANSCRIBED PHONE CONVERSATION [CONDENSED]: NOVEMBER 22

KAYA: Hey.

ANGELA: Hey, how you doing?

KAYA: Good. How 'bout you?

ANGELA: Decent. They scheduled my first appointment without even asking me my preferred times or days.

KAYA: They *always* do that. I've learned from experience it's almost impossible to change them—they frown on changing them.

ANGELA: Why?

KAYA: Because [*speaking in higher register*] we have a lot of women to see and run a very tight ship.

ANGELA: Well it sucks to have to miss work and call in a substitute this early in the pregnancy.

KAYA: They make it hard to work and be pregnant—health of the baby, you know.

ANGELA: [*audible sigh*] I was just hoping to finish the school year without too many disruptions. Vic and I are talking about my not working next year—spend a full year with the baby before looking for daycare arrangements.

KAYA: That's great, Ang. Wish we could do that, but Bruno and I don't make enough.

ANGELA: Sucks they put all the resources into the forty weeks and nothing after.

KAYA: The unborn need the most advocacy.

ANGELA: Still, it's expensive as fuck to have a baby. You getting ready for Thanksgiving?

KAYA: Pie in the oven right now.

ANGELA: Vic's parents are coming—we haven't told them yet.

KAYA: I'm sure they'll be super excited. We're hosting both sides of the family this year, but everyone's bringing a dish.

ANGELA: That's a good way to do it. Talk again soon.

KAYA: Love ya.

IN-PERSON APPOINTMENT; TRANSCRIPTION EDITED FOR BREVITY: DECEMBER 2

DR. EMMERICH: How have these first weeks been?

ANGELA: Good.

DR. EMMERICH: Any health or personal issues, concerns?

[*Patient shrugs and shakes head.*]

DR. EMMERICH: You're established with your nurse liaison?

ANGELA: Yes, Ellen.

DR. EMMERICH: Ellen's great. Have you been writing everything down you've been eating?

ANGELA: No …?

DR. EMMERICH: I see Ellen advised you to eliminate processed foods?

ANGELA: Yes, but I don't eat that much processed—

DR. EMMERICH: Your blood pressure is consistently running a tad higher than we'd like. It would be best to get that under control now—we don't want you developing preeclampsia later on. If we can treat it without medication, that would be better.

ANGELA: I think I've just been a little stressed. The pregnancy was unexpected. And then my husband's parents stayed with us over Thanksgiving. A lot going on.

DR. EMMERICH: Sure, understandable. Do you have a target date for maternity leave?

ANGELA: Well, I teach—I'm a teacher, third grade. The school year ends in June, so I figured that would be great timing. Can I ask … What happened to my regular OBGYN?

DR. EMMERICH: I'm sorry, her caseload is really high right now. We felt my availability was better suited to the timing of your pregnancy. I'm going to have you talk to our dietician about getting your diet under control. I'll send Patricia in right after the exam.

ANGELA: I really don't think my diet is *out* of control.

DR. EMMERICH: Better to be safe. The unborn need the most advocacy—they can't speak for themselves.

TEXT EXCHANGE: DECEMBER 2

VIC: How'd it go?

ANGELA: They changed me to Dr. Emmerich

VIC: Why?

ANGELA: Dr. Moss is busy I guess

VIC: Did you like him / her?

ANGELA: Him. Not really. Everyone treats me like I'm stupid. I know what healthy food is FFS

VIC: Speaking of food—want me to pick something up?

ANGELA: I have to make all my meals. Whole foods. Low salt.

VIC: Blood pressure still high?

ANGELA: Marginally

VIC: I'll stop at the store

ANGELA: Thx. [*heart emoji*]

TEXT EXCHANGE: DECEMBER 9

ELLEN: Your food choices are looking good! Keep it up, girl!

ANGELA: Do I have to keep writing everything down?

ELLEN: Please! It's part of the baby's medical records. Any morning sickness? Concerns?

ANGELA: No, I'm fine

TEXT EXCHANGE: DECEMBER 18

BRUNO: Kaya lost the baby

ANGELA: OMG! I'm so sorry! Is Kaya OK? Are u OK?

BRUNO: She's taking it hard

ANGELA: What happened?

BRUNO: IDK I was working and got a call to go to the hospital.

ANGELA: I'm so sorry. Should I come by?

BRUNO: We're still at hospital. Heading home soon. I'll have her call you tomorrow when she's up for it. Wanted you to know.

ANGELA: Love you guys

CONVERSATION RECORDED VIA ANGELA'S MULTI-WATCH [CONDENSED]: DECEMBER 18, 11:09 PM

ANGELA: I feel so bad for her. [*unknown sounds—sheets rustling?*]

VIC: Yeah. [*coughing*] Bruno called and I didn't know what to say.

ANGELA: Yeah. Poor Kaya.

VIC: Bruno's freaking about the cost of the funeral.

ANGELA: They're having a full-on funeral?

VIC: No. I don't know. They don't have a choice. Burial or cremation, they have to pick one. [*coughing*] I don't know if they'll be inviting people, like for an actual service.

ANGELA: Well, it might be nice. If that's what she wants. Are you getting a cold?

VIC: I don't think that's what Bruno wants. Kaya wasn't that far along.

ANGELA: Yeah, but … It might help them grieve.

VIC: Maybe. It might just eat away their savings. They wanted to buy baby furniture, not a miniature casket. How's our little sprout?

ANGELA: [*laughter*] Stop, that tickles. She's fine.

VIC: She?

ANGELA: I think it's a girl.

VIC: What if it's a boy?

ANGELA: Then I'll use different pronouns. For now she seems better than it.

VIC: Fair enough. Good night, ladies. [*sounds of kissing*]

TRANSCRIBED PHONE CONVERSATION: DECEMBER 19

KAYA: Hey.

ANGELA: Oh honey ...

KAYA: [*audible weeping*]

ANGELA: How are you feeling?

KAYA: Like shit.

ANGELA: You're home?

KAYA: Yeah, we came home last night.

ANGELA: I'm so sorry.

KAYA: Me too. It happened so fast. Everything was fine and then ... [*audible sniffling*]. I just started bleeding, heavy. I was at the bakery and Tanith rushed me to the hospital. And ... that was it. There was nothing they could do.

ANGELA: I'm so sorry ... Vic said Bruno said you're having a funeral?

KAYA: We decided on cremation. It's cheaper. Not doing a service though. They tried to talk us into it at the hospital—like, aggressively tried to talk us into it. They sent the hospital chaplain to our room and started talking about our little boy's soul—it was a boy. We were going to find out at our next sonogram.

ANGELA: Oh Kaya ...

KAYA: We had to do a birth certificate—and a death certificate. We'd picked the name Bruno for a boy, but he changed his mind. He's still hoping we'll have a son someday.

ANGELA: Of course. So what did you name him?

KAYA: Adamo.

ANGELA: That's beautiful.

KAYA: Yeah.

ANGELA: You staying home for a few days?

KAYA: Just today and tomorrow. I know Tanith can handle it, but I like to supervise the younger bakers. And I can't afford to miss too many days.

ANGELA: Want me to come by after work?

KAYA: The weather's bad.

ANGELA: I don't mind. I can bring you something—what sounds good?

KAYA: Um … donuts?

[*laughter*]

ANGELA: You deserve a donut. I'll see you around four.

KAYA: 'kay, bye.

GROUP TEXT EXCHANGE: DECEMBER 19

BRUNO: Kaya's been arrested!

ANGELA: WTF?

VIC: Why?

BRUNO: For losing the baby

ANGELA: WHAT

BRUNO: They think she did it on purpose. Took one of those black-market pills

ANGELA: That's insane she wanted the baby!

BRUNO: They charged her w/ 1st degree murder

VIC: You need a lawyer! I'll get a referral from our in-house attorney

BRUNO: Thanks bro

ANGELA: Can we help w/ bail?

BRUNO: No bail. Locked up. This is so messed up! Guilty until proven innocent. The unborn need the most advocacy

ANGELA: Fucking nuts. Come over if u want. I'm just starting on supper

BRUNO: Thx. Yeah, might.

EMAIL: DECEMBER 20

Hi Ellen,

This might be a little beyond the scope of your nursing liaison duties, but I'm hoping you'll have some advice. My best friend was just arrested for having a miscarriage. She absolutely wanted her baby—it was a planned pregnancy—but they accused her of first-degree murder. I know she's completely innocent. And now she's recovering from her miscarriage while in jail.

Everything I've read online says there's no medical way to differentiate between a natural miscarriage and a drug-induced abortion—but Kaya absolutely did not abort her unborn child! I don't understand why she's considered guilty as the default—how can we help prove her innocence? We've been friends since the eighth grade and Kaya has *always* wanted to have children.

Please get back to me soon. We're all freaking out here.

Thank you,

Angela

CONVERSATION RECORDED VIA ANGELA'S MULTI-WATCH [CONDENSED]: DECEMBER 24, 6:54PM

ANGELA: One visitor a week? Why are they treating her like a serial killer?

[*background sounds: utensils scraping dishes, chewing, shifting in chairs*]

BRUNO: They keep telling us everything is standard policy, nothing personal.

ANGELA: This is *normal* for a miscarriage? I knew they'd ask her some questions but …

BRUNO: The Office of Reproduction Health will review her entire official Profile. All women who lose their pregnancies go through this, unless it's really obvious one way or the other. I guess it's some reassurance that this is standard.

VIC: How is it more obvious for some?

BRUNO: Like, if it's an ectopic pregnancy and it bursts.

ANGELA: What good does that do if they declare the mother innocent but then let her die? God, that's my worst fucking nightmare. That something goes wrong and they won't intervene.

BRUNO: They say that's why they monitor the mothers so carefully, to keep anything from going wrong.

VIC: It's not like they're God.

BRUNO: Anyway, once they determine Kaya is innocent they'll let her go.

ANGELA: How do they determine that? Everything I read online—

VIC: Angela.

ANGELA: What?

VIC: Bruno has enough going on.

BRUNO: A lot of it's based on character, I guess. Morality. Integrity. That's why they record so much, in case they need to see how people were acting. What they were saying to friends, family.

[*a pause in the conversation*]

VIC: The lawyer told you all this?

BRUNO: Yeah.

VIC: Can he help? Can we vouch for Kaya or something?

BRUNO: They'll interview her at least once. But mostly they rely on the recordings. He said it looks worse if families get lawyers involved—then it looks like they're guilty.

ANGELA: How is she?

BRUNO: Okay. She's allowed to call me once a day for ten minutes. Says the other women there are nice. Supportive. But they don't know what happens when women leave—are they going home, or to a real prison?

ANGELA: Why didn't we know about this? This is the worst standard policy I've ever heard of.

BRUNO: No one's supposed to talk about it. The press. Us.

[*a prolonged pause in the conversation*]

ANGELA: Spending Christmas with your parents tomorrow?

EMAIL: JANUARY 6

Hi Angela,

I was away for the holidays, but there isn't much I can tell you.

I sympathize with your anxiety over your friend, but the unborn need the most advocacy—and this is the type of situation where they need us the most. The Office of Reproduction Health tries to handle such cases efficiently and fairly, but I'm sorry to say they are understaffed in comparison to the workload. I'm sure you agree that it would be a tragic miscarriage of justice if even a single unborn baby's life was unaccounted for. We must protect the most vulnerable citizens in our society—and be their voice if anyone tries to silence them.

Happy New Year!
Ellen

TRANSCRIBED PHONE CONVERSATION: JANUARY 17

ANGELA: Hello?

RECORDED VOICE: This is a collect call from an inmate at the Women's Detention for Fetal Mortality. Inmate—

KAYA: Kaya

RECORDED VOICE: —is trying to reach you. To accept this collect call, press one.

ANGELA: Kaya! Oh my God! How are you?

KAYA: Hanging in.

ANGELA: Are you okay?

KAYA: Yeah. Sorry it took so long to call you—I've been using my bonus minutes to call my mom.

ANGELA: I understand. We're in touch with Bruno all the time. Are they treating you okay? Are you eating? Sleeping?

KAYA: It's basic. But clean. Crowded.

ANGELA: Are you allowed to read, or watch TV? Do they make you work?

KAYA: We watch TV. The only book is the bible. We're bored a lot.

ANGELA: You sound exhausted.

KAYA: Demoralized more like.

ANGELA: How long will you be there?

KAYA: It depends. They've questioned me twice already.

ANGELA: That's probably good, right? Progress?

KAYA: I dunno ... I'm worried, Ang. I was in my fourth month—second trimester. I'm healthy, the pregnancy was going well, totally normal. So they think that makes it extra suspicious.

ANGELA: A large number of pregnancies naturally abort. That was true long before we all had to get a womb sensor.

KAYA: They keep asking me about the morning sickness—was it worse than what I revealed to Charlotte; was it wearing me down. But the biggest strike against me seems to be money—both times they asked me a gazillion questions about our spending habits, our lifestyle. They already knew everything about us—how much

I make at the bakery, how much Bruno makes driving for UPS. They keep accusing me of *complaining*. I'm not a *complainer*, it's just a reality that we live paycheck to paycheck. And when I told them I was just stating a fact they were like, 'A fact could be a lie that hides the truth.' And I'm like no, that's not what a fact is ... I think they think I changed my mind—that I was worried that raising a baby would cost too much.

ANGELA: This is a fucking nightmare. If we had guaranteed healthcare or daycare or family leave—or didn't have to worry about the rising cost of food and housing and education. They don't give a shit what happens to the kid *after* it's born.

KAYA: Ang, a bit of advice? Don't swear so much. God help you if you're ever in my shoes, but it could hurt your record.

ANGELA: Good girls don't fucking swear?

KAYA: I'm serious.

TEXT EXCHANGE: JANUARY 28

ELLEN: Are you minding the mindfulness exercises? Watching your salt intake? BP still a little high.

ANGELA: High end of normal. And yes, minding and watching.

TEXT ALERT: FEBRUARY 10

Your LifeDetect™ womb sensor has reported an incident. Please call your obstetric nurse immediately.

TRANSCRIBED PHONE CONVERSATION: FEBRUARY 10

ELLEN: Are you all right?

ANGELA: I got a text to call you—what's wrong?

ELLEN: What happened? Where are you?

ANGELA: I'm at the park, ice skating with my husband.

ELLEN: Did you fall?

ANGELA: Yes, but I'm fine. It's nothing.

ELLEN: You *fell?*

ANGELA: I'm *fine.*

ELLEN: Angela, you do realize you're in your second trimester now? [*a pause in the conversation*] Hello?

ANGELA: Yes, I guess I am. A few days in.

ELLEN: You can't engage in reckless activities.

ANGELA: I wasn't. I know how to skate. A kid ran into me.

ELLEN: You can't put yourself in situations where you could get hurt—where the *baby* could get hurt.

ANGELA: Right. I'll be more careful.

ELLEN: I'll talk to Dr. Emmerich and see if we need to follow up.

ANGELA: The Pregnancy Police want me to go home and put on a flannel nightgown and sit my sorry ass on the couch for the day.

VIC: Is the baby okay?

ANGELA: The baby's fine, Vic.

VIC: Don't get pissed at me. I can't feel what you're feeling.

ANGELA: Neither can anyone else, and I'm *fine*.

VIC: Better to be safe—

ANGELA: Don't even fucking go there with the unborn need the most advocacy shit.

EMAIL: FEBRUARY 17

Dear Angela,

After careful review of your data, Dr. Emmerich has determined that it's in your baby's best interest for you to be on bed rest for the duration of your pregnancy. Records indicate that your pregnancy is High Risk. You can remain in the comfort of your home—provided you follow the Bed Rest Protocol. Should your womb sensor and/or multi-watch indicate that you aren't adhering to the BRP, you will be relocated to a Gestation Center with 24/7 monitoring.

Please don't hesitate to call if you have questions,
Ellen

TRANSCRIBED PHONE CONVERSATION: FEBRUARY 17

ELLEN: Hello Angela—

ANGELA: Why am I High Risk?

ELLEN: Let me bring up your file … [*audible sigh*] Your blood pressure is still running high. Your diet is questionable.

ANGELA: What's questionable about it?

ELLEN: You were going to pick up donuts for your—

ANGELA: I didn't pick up donuts. Kaya was arrested before I—

ELLEN: You've been driving in the snow—

ANGELA: It's winter.

ELLEN: You're a complainer, a malcontent. You swear profusely. And worst of all, Angela, you don't seem willing or able to use common sense. Your behavior is putting your baby at risk.

ANGELA: I can't stay home—I'll lose my job!

ELLEN: For the sake of your unborn child, we can't trust you to do everything to keep your baby safe. It's only six months—

ANGELA: What am I supposed to do in bed for six months!

ELLEN: Crocheting is a lovely hobby, adult coloring books—

ANGELA: For fuck's sake.

ANGELA: They contacted you too? This is bullshit.

VIC: They urged me to help you—to encourage you—to follow the protocol. Please, Ang. I know this isn't what you—

ANGELA: I'm basically a prisoner in my own home.

VIC: It's better than being an actual prisoner.

[*a pause in the conversation*]

ANGELA: How did we get here?

[*a pause in the conversation*]

ANGELA: It doesn't feel like it's about the babies. An embryo ...

VIC: I know but we have to be careful. Can I bring you anything?

ANGELA: A mini fridge? A microwave? I'm gonna be here awhile. You know ... I can't stop thinking now—about all the women I stopped seeing. Bailey never came back from maternity leave, we never heard from her again. We all talked about how busy she was with the baby and being a mom. But what if ... maybe something happened. And now I know why Sharna stopped teaching in her fifth month: it probably wasn't a choice. And the young women from the coffee shop, and the store, and the gym. They're making us disappear.

[*a pause in the conversation*]

VIC: I have some good news from Bruno—Kaya's being released on probation.

ANGELA: Oh my God! Thank God! Wait … what's probation?

VIC: Well, if she ever loses another baby … Once could be an accident, but twice … It'll be a mandatory twenty-year sentence.

ANGELA: But …

[*a pause in the conversation*]

VIC: Please, Angela—let's just get you through this pregnancy.

ANGELA: Then can I be a fully autonomous person again?

[*a pause in the conversation*]

ANGELA: Was I ever a fully autonomous person?

[*a pause in the conversation*]

PUT MY DEAD DAUGHTER ON YOUR BILLBOARD, I DARE YOU

SARAH READ

SHE WAS NEVER BORN, still
I mourn her.
I killed her
You say,
Murderer.
It was my time.
Should have been my time,
Mine and hers.
Not my choice, either way.
Choose life! You scream
In my face.
And I did.
I did.
I live.

A DIFFERENCE OF OPINION

MJ SYDNEY

I HAVE an immigrant grandmother who came to the United States with her sister from Brazil to make better lives for themselves.

You voted to have their naturalization taken away and to have them sent back to Brazil.

I also have family who immigrated from Ireland several generations ago. But maybe you think they get a pass because they look and sound white enough.

I have a Jewish family. My children grew up learning about the holocaust and about the survival of the Jewish people. They were taught that never again means never again—no matter who becomes the current target.

You voted for an antisemitic, Islamophobic man who idolizes Hitler and believes genocide and the extermination of an entire group of people is appropriate.

I have immigrant and migrant neighbors who are hardworking and successful roofers, landscapers, farmers. They have families, strong values, and contribute positively to society. They do the jobs you refuse to do and emphasize the family values you claim to want.

You voted to have them all (undocumented, documented, by birthright, doesn't matter) round up for mass deportation and for death camps (are we really still calling these holding camps?). You voted to round them up like cattle and treat them like criminals.

I live my life with a Black man who is both my life partner and my business partner.

You voted for a racist who believes in slavery and servitude. You voted against interracial marriage and racial equality.

I have a daughter with celiac and other health issues.

You voted against her health care and against her right to save her own life if she has complications from a pregnancy.

I have a transgender daughter and a transgender parent.

You voted to take away their rights to appropriate and gender affirming healthcare. You voted to put their lives in danger physically and mentally because you think these women are a threat to your daughters. All the while, the man you voted for actually is a threat to your daughters (and your wives and your sisters and your mothers).

I have gay and queer friends, many who are happily married, some with children.

You voted to invalidate their marriage and to put their lives in danger because you feel somehow it's your business who other people are spending their lives with. Or maybe you're just jealous that their marriage is happier and healthier than yours.

I have children who had special needs in school. I've worked with special needs children in early childhood education programs. I have friends with children that have special needs.

You voted to eliminate all of these programs and funding for children's education in favor of a ten-point program designed to indoctrinate children in the name of christian nationalism.

I see people on the streets, living in tents, desperate to feed themselves and their families, just trying to survive.

You see them as trash to be ignored and taken out of sight because it makes you feel uncomfortable.

I see mentally ill and drug addicted people roaming the alleys and parking lots in desperate need of mental health care and rehabilitation.

You see them as sub-humans who deserve their life circumstances and aren't deserving of help.

I see our planet being destroyed by air pollution, water pollution, soil pollution and the trash you throw out in the street. By greed and overconsumption, by wastefulness and a lack of concern for the environment.

You voted to dismantle environmental protections because you can't see climate change as an issue. You voted to completely destroy our natural resources and nature to build more 'affordable housing' that no one can actually afford.

I believe in freedom and human rights for everyone, regardless of sex, religion, nationality, ethnicity, sexual orientation, education level, financial status, immigration status. I believe in love and peace and equality and basic human decency. I believe in community and helping others. I believe in saving our natural resources and environment for the future.

You voted for a fascist dictator. You voted in favor of white christian nationalism. You voted for hate, racism, sexism, antisemitism, islamophobia, transphobia, homophobia. You voted for oppression, slavery, stripping away human rights, justifying the inhumane treatment of others. You voted for (rich) white supremacy. You voted for mass deportation and death camps. You voted for criminalizing the homeless and mentally ill. You voted for the indoctrination of our children in public schools. You voted for environmental destruction in support of corporate greed.

But it's just a difference of opinion and we should all get along?

No.

We tried that already and it didn't work out so well. So here we are.

We will not be friends. We will not agree to disagree. We will not be silent.

Fuck your opinion.

YOU CAN FEEL YOUR INSIDES MOVE

HANNAH REBEKAH GRAVES

UNSURPRISED,
But still somehow darkened
Like red wine spilt
On a beige rug

I can feel all of my insides moving
Like they're scrambling to crawl out of me
Like they're scrambling to crawl out of this mess
No one wants to be here

I could cut away my skin
Piece by piece
And I would still feel this
Terrible uncomfortableness

Fear?
I'm too tired for all of that
He's made me too tired to think
Too tired to get out of bed

Blood drips slowly down walls
Between my legs
Where I used to own acreage
Where decisions are now made without me

I curse
A hex made for the most awful
My ground bones put into a bottle
My every inch covered in soil

I will live in this world
I will die in it
Part of me is dead already
Body found the morning of

And when I sleep
I don't dream
I am given wholly into a void
Where everything is taken from me

Please make it all go away

THE ROT BENEATH THE SURFACE

RICHARD DEAN

I **DIDN'T VOTE** for Kamala Harris because I liked her as a candidate. You can have movie stars pump their fists, begging for the Hollywood vote, but Beyoncé doesn't resonate with struggling families in Oklahoma who can't afford eggs. Trying to cozy up to the Cheney's, literal butchers, may be appealing to some, but anyone with critical thought knows that "war criminal" should be boldfaced next to Dick Cheney's name. I didn't vote for Kamala because of her record as a prosecutor, where too many people faced charges that didn't add up, nor because of her support of a genocidal regime in Israel, which fills coffins in Palestine. I also didn't expect the working class to be a priority—because of party politics, American workers have lost opportunities for national projects that could create living-wage jobs, like building bridges and connecting our country with broadband.

I voted against Donald Trump. I have voted against him three times. Donald Trump brings out the worst in American culture. The cartoonization of our society took root with *Idiocracy*, and what was once a spoof of reality is now largely accurate. As a leader, Trump channels the most bellicose parts of us, encouraging our worst impulses. It's tough to admit, but women and minorities have suffered because the Democratic Party left the average American behind. By ignoring that most working people are just trying to do their best, they paved a path through hell, making deals with corporate interests instead of pushing for affordable gas or laws preventing non-American investors from driving up the cost of living. Your moral code may determine how you see friends and family who voted Republican.

The rise of Trump isn't just about one man's obsession with power—it's the manifestation of a deeper fracture in the American psyche. A society that rewards spectacle over substance, that values charisma over competence, is a society ready to crumble. This isn't about political ideology—it's about a culture that has normalized cruelty, corruption, and misinformation as part of the everyday. Look at the leaders we've chosen, not just in Washington but across the country, and ask yourself: Are these people the best we can do? Or are we simply looking for someone who can shout the loudest, distract the most, and keep us from looking at the rot within?

"There are very fine people on both sides." – President Donald Trump, on white nationalists in Charlottesville, Virginia.

Thanks to this poisoned handshake for America's soul, we've now licensed "bro culture" as the new norm, where progress isn't such a great thing. Trump is a mascot for the worst among us, and those same people will influence the future our kids inherit. Wanting better for the next generation isn't rooted in stupidity; it's a sadness for anyone who knows basic civics: tariffs don't help. They bleed the middle class dry, passing the cost to the consumer instead of the seller. Anyone who thinks a tariff will bring more American jobs isn't paying attention: corporations will always prioritize cheaper labor overseas.

But hey, Trump calls Kamala a "bitch," and people cheer. In Trump's first term, his presence was met with think pieces from both sides decrying his leadership. But as the party bends to the influence of its most divisive members, here we are—guys with "tell-it-like-it-is" podcasts dominate the culture, while millions of immigrants live in fear. Who do you think does the work white Americans refuse? That dinner you enjoyed was made by brown hands. Who do you think picks your fruit and mows your lawn? Remember that $20-per-hour wage I mentioned? Keep that in mind.

"You know, I'm automatically attracted to beautiful—[women's] legs, I mean, I don't even wait. And when you're a star, they let you do it. You can do anything. Grab 'em by the p**y. You can do anything." – Donald Trump, American President

The rise of Trump is built on the boogeyman that Democrats will invade your home in the middle of the night and eat your babies. The Christian Right, originally a product of Reagan's 1980s, was all about personal choice until then. Democrats have held the House, the Senate, and the Presidency multiple times in recent decades—enough to end homelessness, codify Roe v. Wade, wipe out student debt, and improve housing affordability. But they didn't. Instead, they created their own scapegoats, losing ground to appease corporate sponsors of war and middle-class values, expanding the pockets of the rich, and leaving an opening for Trump.

Be frustrated with America. The system isn't in your best interest—or theirs. Just look at cabinet picks like Mike Huckabee, Elon Musk, and Marco Rubio. Maybe next we'll get Joe Rogan as the Bad Hot Takes Czar. Democrats have no one to blame but themselves for failing to hold a primary and bending to their corporate gods, who extract every dollar they can from your wallet. Voters wanted something different from Sleepy Joe and cackling Kamala, and they got it. The next four years will play out like a reality show at the expense of the American worker, who doesn't know better in a system that only wants bodies for for-profit prisons and obedient labor to fuel a life they can't afford.

People expect the worst. Trump delivers. Slurs fly more freely now. Consequences? Not on this timeline. Cancel culture is dead; Tony Hinchcliffe is two-stepping on that grave. Democrats, scrambling to find their center, got pummeled by people sick of pandering without solutions. We should never idolize politicians as heroes—they're just doing a job to improve our lives. If a senator is getting richer by taking office, that's all the information you need.

The Donald will be on every media page, worldwide. His rule will be ugly, and values you hold dear could become criminalized because joy is a weapon in the world of grim realities. There's nothing wrong with wanting a bit of common sense in an upside-down world. But beware of who represents the worst of us, giving voice to the guy at the bar you avoid. That guy is now your senator, and he has plenty of opinions on women's bodies, who gets Medicare, and if Trans people should exist. The war machine will keep spinning, bombs will keep falling, school shootings will continue, and the earth will lose more years to corporate interests. The promises on the campaign trail? Some will come true; many won't—but all are ugly. So buckle up. This is America's decision: a failed businessman, rapist, and man who paid off a porn star is calling the shots and will name your next Supreme Court judge.

Now, horrific legislation will follow because, in this country, garbage in means garbage out. This is what we chose.

WARRIOR SONG

ANONYMOUS

I SHALL NOT COLLAPSE
Your weight
My defiance

Call me a whore
Tell me I'll amount to nothing
Tell me I'm dirty

Tell me more
I've heard it all
Your games

Words meant to destroy me
You push down these deceptions in hopes
They'll be consumed, in hopes they'll rot

The fighter growing, the rebel strengthening

He tells us things so we forget that we're legends
He tells us these things so that we will hate ourselves
He tells us these things so that we forget we are made of magic

Born of bloodshed and terror we survived
When our island was nearly cleared of adults and children
We survived

Words wound as hateful spells
I'll take that spell and dispel your myth
I am greatness bloodied and bound to this land

This was my home
This has always been my home
Will always be my home

Until my last breath

I'll pass it on to my children
We'll deny your incantations
We'll reject your slurs

No matter how many people you build up to destroy me
Battalions and armies
You cannot make me hate me

I will stand, as my ancestors stood
As my ancestors survived
They whisper to me to go on

There is no killing us
There is no driving us down deep
Seeds spring, sprout, grow

Babies are birthed
Legends are forged
We reject your hate

We come from kings and queens
Island breeze and palm trees
Bird song across treetops

There is no hate you can launch

That will ever deter me
I'm built of warriors

GUT PUNCH

DINO PARENTI

THE RUSSIAN STARES at me like he knows I have animal porn on my laptop, and time just stops.

You hear about this happening in moments of trauma, like some of my liberal associates right after the election. Or when one's been caught red-handed. Or maybe brown-handed in my case, but I shouldn't get ahead. Shouldn't take large bites. Like Warren Buffet said, don't look to jump over seven-foot bars—look for one-foot bars that you can step over.

As long as I have this frozen moment to collect myself, a few words on the Russian.

FIVE DAYS EARLIER.

When I *should've* picked the Chinese dumpling vendor across the street.

I was looking for a guinea pig. A pauper, ideally. Someone my uncle would've described as ambitious for an easy buck. And with the price of produce, milk, and eggs rivaling Bitcoin shares, who isn't ambitious for an easy buck these days?

This same man also said, "When chasing a buck, never slow down to watch the scenery. The scenery has eyes, and it stares back," so take his words how you will.

So the Chinese guy. Yes, his English wasn't exactly David Attenborough, and I had loads of nitty-gritty to lay on my potential subject. But he had this smile that stretched across the street and tickled. Spread widest whenever he stared at the sky, as if reading verse in the clouds.

Bottom line: malleable.

In the end, I rejected the poet for the practical: the guy dumping buckets of plaster into the cans under my stoop.

The Russian.

I'd seen him around. The Greek running the gyro shop on the corner told me he's a local handyman, living in a shelter. Slick at avoiding weekly ICE raids, though his skin is a bit lighter than the usual target, and his fake green card is supposedly exceptional work. But the Greek vetted his work ethic up and down. Last week he fixed my neighbor's basement window. His carpentry was supposedly excellent, but his English merely serviceable, and to be honest, I was fighting the clock. With *Le Grande Orange* back in charge and burning down regulations, I needed to make my move. Carve my mark deep in the bark while oversights are getting shredded like court transcripts.

Watching the top of his salt-and-pepper hair crown through a cloud of gypsum from my stoop, I asked the Russian, "Say buddy, you like coffee?"

He leaned back. Fifty or thereabouts, though like presidents, the indigent always look far older than their actual age.

"Why you ask?"

"I'm offering a taste test, and I'm willing to pay for the opinion of the average man-off-the-streets."

He leveled some serious side-eye, like drawing a bow, and his inventory of me curdled on his face in real time: young white busybody Millennial, blue sports coat, red-striped bowtie. All elbows and knees. A guy who side-sat a rail the way women rode horses in old Roy Rogers movies. It underlined my uncle's notion of what a blessing it was to rarely be able to examine yourself in your most relaxed, unwatched state.

The Russian's misgivings simmered. "You offer money … for *opinion?*"

"Your opinion and your time. Know anything about coffee?"

He straightened out the lapels of an old camel hair blazer that kept curling on him.

"Is expensive in your country, the coffee."

Aside from the simplification, his English was crystal-clear.

"Tell me about it. But I'll pay you to taste mine. Ten minutes of your time worth twenty bucks?"

We kept studying each other, me watching those ocular scales of his do their thing while I sucked at the corners of my cheeks. The cold sore I'd tongue-dueled with three days going raked barbs across my gums, and I had to squint to hold off the tears. Finally he shrugged and put down his buckets.

"I accept," he said.

I opened the door to my coffee-shop. Gut Punch. Opening day, a month away.

"Step into my office. Let's see if you've got the goods."

I DON'T, MIND YOU. Have animal porn on my computer.

But I am caught, hence the time-freeze. Caught by one who indeed has the goods.

"SO WHAT DO I CALL YOU?" I asked.

He was amazingly apathetic taking in the walnut paneling and chrome accents, the slate floors and leather seatbacks. As if he'd always known a swank little cafe lurked behind all the plywood covering the windows outside.

"I am Nikolai Komarov," he said. "But Americans, they call me Nikita. Nikolai, they say sound like …"—he fingered invisible frets with both hands—"… like disease. Like the Covid. Like, 'Hey, friend, you catch the *Nikolai* yet?'"

He grinned with teeth the yellow of old legal pads. I rolled eyes and gestured him along.

We passed through a long corridor narrowed by stacked burlap coffee sacks and into a small storeroom lined with rolling metal shelves. Except that one of these had a false drywall backing that when moved, revealed another door, this one opening to a flight of stairs to a basement not on any health inspector's notes.

Something else my business-savvy uncle once told me: Nobody succeeds by being 100% transparent.

Nikita followed. His confidence that I wasn't leading him to some torture chamber of horrors was downright spooky.

Rounding the corner at the bottom, he paused to run a finger along the spines of books piled on a makeshift bookcase of shipping pallets.

Think and Grow Rich.

The Success Principles.

Signed first-edition of *Think Big and Kick Ass in Business.*

My pièce de résistance.

Nikita scowled at my reads as if they'd slurred insult.

"Over here?" I gestured for him to walk ahead. I wanted to mark his reaction. Because the first time anyone sees my pets, they never know what to think. Part weasel, part raccoon. A fucked-up mutt of a critter any way you sliced it.

Two resided in a large cage in the middle of the basement floor, and they let out a collective croon the moment they caught Nikita's gamey waft.

Nikita watched them askance as they flashed fangs and scaled up the bars to the top of the cage, and I was glad to see his poise wobble. Nobody outside a president with a mandate or a sociopath had a right to be that cocksure.

"Loud little beasts," he said.

"That, Nikita, is the music of kopi luwak."

His pointy shoulders shrugged enough to scratch earlobes.

"Most people think the origin's a monkey, but that's the Parchment coffee from India."

"Origin of what?"

"The best coffee in the world, Nikita. The undisputed Bugatti of coffee."

Nikita's scrutiny came with an edge I'm sure animals could physically feel.

"They … find the coffee?" he said.

"Not quite, Nikita. They defecate it."

His cheeks bulged. "I no understand."

"They poo-poo it out."

Soon as I moved towards their cage, they immediately relaxed.

"Meet Bonnie and Clyde from Sri Lanka, Only *he* isn't a Bonnie. Fucking exporter promised me a breeding pair, and he sent me two dudes. Don't tell the church, right?"

Nikita dovetailed his daddy-longlegs fingers at his gut. "Sri Lanka no sound … legal."

I scratched Bonnie's golden-brown fur through the bars. He made a sound like a tea kettle set to blow. Before last month, Nikita would've been right. Before the White House shredded certain regulations during predawn votes. Now previously illegal imports short of fissionable material were basically okay, so long as they were *crucial* to one's business and could be tariffed up the wazoo.

"What's *legal* even mean nowadays? In any case, used to be only the Indonesian ones were importable, but I find their product somewhat washy by comparison."

Nikita nodded as if this was common knowledge.

"They're called palm civets, or toddy cats. They feed on jungle fruit and fermented tree sap, but what they really love is coffee straight from the tree. They gnaw off the husks, swallow the cherries whole. Once they steep in their belly juices, they're passed whole, get collected, then roasted."

"And you Americans … *pay* for this?"

I shot him a little cutting stink-eye of my own to counter the disbelief he'd dribbled on me.

"It's worth more per ounce than petroleum, so yes."

"And I am to … drink this?"

"Twenty bucks a shot. And, I'm doing it with you, so …"

His smirk could slice hairs. "Where I from, if asked to eat *poo-poo*, it is insult to pay … less than forty."

I should've snagged that Chinese vendor. Or some Chelsea hipster still depressed over an election fourteen months old now.

"Done," I said.

TWO FRENCH PRESSES. Four tiny paper cups that nurses drop meds in. That was my setup.

I filled two from each press, which I then separated and paired off in mismatched sets. I handed Nikita the first of the two promised twenties and pushed forward the first cup. He just stared.

"Relax, Nikita. There's no actual *poo-poo* involved. As I said, the civets pass the beans whole. Besides, the roasting process is hot enough to kill any bacteria three times over. They don't even sterilize surgical instruments with that much heat."

He took the cup with the delicacy of bone china. "So you say."

"I do say. In any case, you don't know which is which. Kopi luwak, or one of my basic Arabica blends. Just pick the better one. Look, start with the bouquet. By that we mean smell. You're looking for specific notes. Is it floral, earthy, fruity …"

But Nikita was already hissing through clenched teeth.

"Your lecture, no needed. Where I from, we once do with tea, we do with vodka now."

I smirked and took up my cup and put it to my nose to spur him on. One of the civets—Clyde—screeched as Nikita lifted the cup to his sniffer, and he braced himself for the punch of stinky. But once that good aroma took hold, he went full flare.

A few fast blinks later: "I say … *earthy*. Like tobacco."

"Not bad, *comrade*. And now we taste. Same as the nose— look for notes of fruit, spice, nuttiness …"

Nikita, waving me off again.

And once more, I sipped first to grease his wheels.

The moment the hot liquid hit his tongue and he realized no gooey floaties were imminent, he downed the rest. The alley sodium-vapor lights poured through the small window high on the wall, gilding his cappuccino skin bronze, and I spied for a moment the suave, hell-bent man under all the grime and circumstance.

When chasing a buck, never slow down to watch the scenery. The scenery stares back.

After a drawn-out swallow, he said, "Rich. *Nutty*. Quite nice."

I wasted no time hoisting my second cup.

"Number-two—no pun intended. Same as before: smell it, taste it, you know the drill."

Nikita was less apprehensive with his second taster, and this time he was done before me.

"Bah! Half the soul of first." And he held out a hand.

I palmed him the second twenty which, like the first, vanished unconsidered into his jacket.

"Well?" he prompted. "Which from the beasts?"

"Number one, of course. Told you kopi luwak was the best."

Nikita stifled a snort. "*Poo-poo*," he muttered.

I WALKED HIM BACK OUT to a sky the color of smelt. For some reason the lack of sun made the sore in my mouth scream.

"So the beasts," Nikita said. "They are, how you say … your *gim-mick?*"

"Those civets are my future. I have more in a ranch in Cuba, but right now I'm testing blends, trying to approach the kopi. Hard to match what nature can do though. And, I open in a month. Anyway, first-world problems and all. Thanks for the two-cents."

We shook hands, but Nikita held it a beat. I could tell by the way his eyeballs seesawed that he wanted to ask something, but needed the invitation first.

I offered quarter. "Something else?"

"My nephew Vadik, he send coffee from Santo Domingo. Every month. Very delicious coffee. If you want, I bring in a few days? You try?"

Yeah, I should have run. But then I remembered something Oprah said, about not putting ceilings on yourself, and I caved.

"If you like," he went on, "maybe I sell to you? How you say? Bulk rate?"

I chuckled. "Yeah sure."

Nikita smiled. Kept it full-bore as he looked across the street at the Chinese vendor flipping dumplings on his griddle, eyeing his pushcart as if something to be taken apart and reassembled.

THIS GETTING-CAUGHT MOMENT runs long, I know. But when you back the wrong horse, it takes time to sort things out, especially after said horse has caught you holding shit up to the light like Liz Taylor diamonds.

Relax, we'll get there. *Cope*, as I tell all the lefties pearl-clutching about the election.

IN THE INTERVENING DAYS while prepping Gut Punch, I forgot all about Nikita's proposal regarding his Dominican beans, so when he came knocking the following weekend, I was caught off guard, smothered in grime from slogging to get the place ready.

This isn't to say I'd forgotten about Nikita the *man* in the meantime, either his brass or easy-going spirit. Seeing him again with his spotty beige blazer and two Ziploc bags of coffee beans, my stomach soured at the prospect of kneejerk commitments with pushy opportunists.

"Nice coat." I gestured him in.

"A lesson about the poor," he said. "Vanity only luxury item that costs a man nothing."

I pictured all the rich slobs I knew as we headed downstairs, and decided he was probably as right as I would've been in declaring the opposite.

Upon smelling Nikita again, the civets uttered one screech apiece before settling down.

I ground his beans, then set up the French presses again. Soon as I returned with hot water, Nikita took over and I let him run with it.

"We do like last week, yes?" he said, pouring the mismatched cups. I just nodded. I was tired and twisted up over my looming store kickoff, and argument would've only siphoned more energy. "One cup, my Dominican beans. One cup, from the Starbucks."

Like last time, I went first, both smelling and tasting, and he watched me through buttonhole eyes from behind his cup.

The first cup was altogether wholesale. Safely balanced and one-note. Tasted mass produced.

The second cup though.

That second cup.

I knew old brew masters who would've lopped off their own yam bags to have achieved the transcendent richness of that blend. Jasmine and tilled earth at the nose. Freshly hulled chocolate with a truffle linger in the flavor profile. I'd never approached such Bordeaux-like evolution in the pallet. Not even Bonnie and Clyde managed such a symphony of complexity, and my first emotion was anger, followed closely by envy.

I won't lie. I went into this with the intent of succeeding or failing with my *own* ideas.

"Jesus-shit-Christ, Nikita," I managed before a second slow pull. "Did you sell your soul to Juan Valdez?"

Nikita swelled but didn't smile. "So you like." It wasn't asked.

I gawked for what felt like an hour. "What do you think?"

He conveyed apathy expertly just through stare and a lapping bottom lip before passing a hand across the table.

"So mine is *better*, yes?"

This time, it was most certainly *asked*.

"Does gobsmacked equal poker-face where you're from?"

He asked again: "So mine *is* better?"

The civets crooned together, as if they too demanded reply.

"Okay, Nikita. Yes. By leaps and bounds, yes." I picked up the cup and swirled the oily grit at the bottom. "How did you do this?"

He gave me the bottom of his palms. "Just like you, my friend."

Wait. He doesn't know.

"Come again?"

"Much like you, I ... *omit* ... information."

Some tiny but undeniable thing knocked loose in my chest.

"What information?"

"Roasting time. More important, *method* of roasting."

He *can't* know ...

"Method? What do you ...?"

And I think I turned and indicated more-or-less to where my Bunn machines were.

Nikita leaned across the table. That glint in his eye. Like twin universes birthing in miniature.

"Next time you give brother human a cup of your *own* poo-poo, please give warning first."

AND LIKE THAT, the getting-caught frozen moment spools out, and you have to face the music in real-time. Face the fact that you were caught dead-to-rights dumping a twofer onto kitty-litter, then picking through your own feces. Caught not only rinsing off your shit-drizzled beans, but then grinding and brewing them up into a hot batch of Joe.

Nikita lets me nibble air a while longer before twisting around and pointing up at the basement window.

"Should change clear glass to *frosted*. Like neighbors do. For security. For *privacy*. I can do for fifty dollars. *Plus* material."

Yeah, my window. Directly across from my neighbor's. Easy to peer into. Obviously it isn't grimy enough.

My impulse is to chew him out, but where's the sense in preaching fairness and honor when you've never really had the vocabulary for it yourself? The moment I involved him via clandestine delivery of my doo-doo into his mouth, my business became his business.

I picture him in the moment of question, one-eye gandering me through the high window as I squat over a tray of Tidy Cat, flipping through Howard Shultz's *Onward*.

The way to get started is to quit talking and begin doing.

So declared Walt Disney.

"Nikita, let me explain …"

He sighs and scratches the bottom of his chin.

"Look, my civets in Cuba, they're dying. Some parasite. Something, I don't know. And, and I open in a few weeks, and I read about this guy in Portland who tried to pass off his own digested beans as kopi luwak, but he got caught, and I was desperate, and this is my *dream* … you know? And I thought if I …"

But Nikita, he's already doing his quiet nodding bit. The ease with which his eyes deploy scorn and dismissal is sadistic.

"No sorries," he says, to my total shock. "You desperate. You … *improvise*. Want next tax bracket. Pay less. Your country, about opportunity. Make original? Not so much. Like you, I see opportunity, jump like cat!"

"How much?" I ask.

I think I blubbered it.

Nikita slow-frowns.

"I ask only for what is fair," he says, folding his hands on the table. "I suggest … *partnership*. This …"—he twirls a finger to the ceiling—"… your business, your money."

"A partnership?" I'd braced myself for some hard extortion. Then I think, no way the Chinese vendor outside would've pulled something like this. Nothing rings truer in that moment.

"I only request … twenty-five percent?" he says.

My teeth gnash. "What are you doing, Nikita?"

"You, like my nephew Vadik, are victim. Of *prosperity*. Three days ago, I have Vadik chew and swallow beans. As experiment. Vadik no want father to know he … kissy-kissy with the boys, so he do. His windows, also very clear."

I always keep them open. Bonnie and Clyde love the light.

"Too bad, his no good too. Vadik like you—bad belly, bad coffee. Then I think. I see. Good money make good health. Good health make tired acid in belly. Make tired roast. But me …?" He slaps his belly one-two. "No *snowflake* belly in Russia!"

And he guffaws and slams me a full platoon of piss-yellow teeth. A politico's grin.

Suddenly the idea that what I've just swallowed was first filtered through his colon sends my gorge shooting up the express elevator. I manage to spew it piecemeal in the form of swallowed micro-burps—and even muled in my hotfooting bile, the depth of flavor of Nikita's sloppy-seconds brew reminds me of re-birth, of opportunity, of dreams yet to be fulfilled, and just like that, I rediscover ambition.

As long as you're going to be thinking anyway, think big.

So said the commander-in-chief in his book. And now look at him. A skipped second term and shed of all prior convictions. Because mandates.

Nikita turns solemn on a dime, and after yanking down on his lapels, extends a hand.

"We have partnership, yes?"

I smack my dry lips and shake his mitt.

"Tell me something, genius," I say. "What're we gonna to do about volume? No way you can turn out the bulk we need."

Nikita flicks a wrist.

"I think much on this, my young friend. No worry yourself. But I do require company credit card."

A WEEK BEFORE OUR OPENING, I walk into Gut Punch and the wail of power tools.

It comes from downstairs, and when I reach the bottom step I find myself in a small plywood booth that wasn't there before. A moment later, Nikita opens a door, the seams of which are so tight I never would've noticed them.

"Ah, my young friend!" he announces. His blazer is flocked in sawdust that's nearly the same color.

"What the hell is this, Nikita?"

"Lobby," he says, and gestures me through.

The other side of the plywood is covered in foam insulation panels, the kind used in refrigerator doors.

"For odor," he says.

"What odor?"

He waves me along. We wind around towering pallets of kitty litter and toilet paper, then past several stacks of freshly imported Dominican beans before I see it. Along the entire length of wall below the basement window—the panes of which he'd frosted on day one—run a row of wooden niches, each about two-feet wide and framing a bench. In the center of every bench, a roughly ten-inch hole has been cut. Beneath each sits a litter box.

"Christ, Nikita, what have you done?"

"Latrines!" Nikita replies. "For volume problem. This the *dugout*. Like the baseball. I love the baseball."

I count twelve bays. Opposite them, a pair of giant flat-screen TVs. "And who do you propose is going to provide said volume? The Royals?"

"I know men. Dominicans, bribed out of deportation camp. You know, for the farm labor. No afraid of hard work. No like you *pindos*."

My hands crab into my face. "Nikita, are you out of your mind? You want to use illegals slated for deportation? We can't just ..."

"Why? They need the work. They have strong bellies! *Very* strong. You say yourself, I cannot do alone. I already taste the coffee. Better than mine, even! You will see!"

My testicles literally retract. "Oh god."

Nikita's enthusiasm flat-lines on the spot.

"Young friend, you speak with tongue of capitalist, but no the muscle. Do not pet like dog. Whip like horse! Do like Henry Ford do! Like president do!"

All my dreams and visions, all the hours of thought and anticipation, crushed into compost before my eyes, and all that loops through my brain is something Michael Dell once said: Ideas are commodity. Execution of them is not.

"Nikita, what did you do in the Russia?"

A bored shrug. "Many things. Teach English. Teach piano. Manage construction for government. Run many websites. Have degree in engineering. Fix problems. Make things from nothing."

At some point his smile had crept back, smug and ruthless.

WHENEVER I DREAM of opening day, I imagine applause and rampant toadyism.

I'm not ashamed to admit this. The current climate, if you don't practically cop to it, you're a schmuck.

And applauded I was. When I arrived at four to prep for the six AM opening, twenty people were already huddled in the Kansas City chill outside the door. By the time the doors opened, nearly a hundred jonesing souls were queuing, most clapping and chanting *kopi-kopi-kopi* as if it was some rock star politician about to stump.

By nine, the walls swell with coming-and-going customers, sniffing and sipping, smiling and mugging at a thing foreign and exotic. Some I overhear still think it's monkey poop, and they both turn up their noses and lick their lips at the lurid possibilities. I wonder how different they'd feel if they knew it was squeezed out of human anuses, and honestly, I doubt that would deter some. Given a hundred people in a room, each offered human meat to sample, you can count on at least five-to-ten takers, just to say they did it. Some people's bucket lists are more extravagant than others.

As the morning rolls and the registers pop, customers seek me out to both congratulate and commend the product, and it is, at least on the surface, what I'd always imagined.

Except I don't feel it. It's all smoke-and-mirrors. I'm a plagiarist, pushing some other mad genius's work as my own.

During a letup in flattery, Nikita sidles up to watch the crowd with me. We had an agreement that I would handle the front of the house, and he would run the basement. Lord of the Underworld, I wanted to call him, but stopped myself. Why build him up more than he was doing on his own? Standing next to me in that moment, he's the most pride-fat I've ever seen him. He'd even spiffed up for the occasion, snagging a shower and finding a cleaners with enough lye to sanitize his rancid coat.

"Our poo-poo making smiles," he says. "Making love."

Is that cologne I smell on him?

"Mingle a bit, why don't you," I say. "They should meet both ends of the business, don't you think?"

But I bolt before he responds. I huff it downstairs. Pushing through the antechamber door, my gag reflex all but clotheslines me, but onward I march.

At the back, all twelve dugout bays are occupied and raging. Dark-skinned men between twenty-and-sixty, all smacking the collective bitterness from their lips from having gnawed on the raw coffee husks before swallowing them. Like civets in the wild.

FOX prattles on the TVs. The latest prison contract in Missouri, a Montana wind farm being cut down for fracking fields, the president's latest notion of a healthcare plan since he slaughtered the ACA like a fat hog.

Insulin costs more than gold.

Everything we were promised, and yet nothing of it.

Bonnie and Clyde, huddled in the corner of their cage, eyes fully apertured, quivering at Dominican women in surgical masks and gloves sorting beans from fecal matter on a long work-table spread with cat litter.

Theory is splendid, but until put into practice, it is valueless.

Ah, good-old James Cash Penney ...

WE AREN'T ACTIVE three months before people begin citing a drop-off in quality.

Almost overnight, X, Facebook, and Yelp go from allies to turncoats.

They started off on fire, and now they barely fizzle ...
You get the feeling they literally started watering it down ...
Now it really is just shit in a cup ...

Bill Gates used to say that your most unhappy customers are your greatest source of learning, but these things always sound better on paper.

Two days ago, the first of the protestors showed up, accusing us of animal abuse. And the signs. Graphic, grotesque shit. One sign showed a bloody, mangy civet in a cage, riddled with self-inflicted bites.

Yesterday I was convinced the two women in the back corner all morning with shifty eyes and busy pens were from PETA.

I tell Nikita about it. He nods as if I'd mused on the weather.

"A man makes success," he says. "makes brother jealous."

"Except that our quality *has* slipped, Nikita. Have you tasted it lately?"

Nikita is working on the dugout schedule pinned to the antechamber wall.

"Yes, is true. Also, three sluggers, last night say *no mas*."

Sluggers. Nikita's euphemism for bean-shitters.

"We're paying them to do what comes naturally. Why are they leaving?"

"You think man poor, he no have ... proud? Half leave from shame. Other half, they poo-poo two, maybe three times, they get belly pain. Ulcer. Only four sluggers now. But other problem, too."

"What, volume issues?"

Here Nikita hesitates for the first time I can remember.

"A little. But problem worse. Three days ago, I test theory. I swallow and brew beans."

To be honest, I ignored this possibility, hoping it would not become an issue.

Or did I? Certain shit is starting to come into focus, and I don't like what it's threatening to show.

"And?"

Nikita presses his lips till the color drains from them.

"Well, like sluggers, you have money, food more healthy. Poor want to live, too. But coffee, it go ... weak."

I stare at all the cross-outs on Nikita's schedule, which is starting to resemble a de-classified government document with all the black Sharpie lines. "So you're saying we're toast."

His head rolls in meticulous thought.

"No, no. Problem have solution. Find new source. Also, no more cat litter. Chemical in litter change flavor. Affect acid. Maybe woodchip better. No worry yourself, young friend. Niki-tata Komarov solve. I spill with idea."

Of course he does.

"You know what you are to me sometimes, Nikita? That cold, probing finger of water that shoots up your bum when you plop one of those dense little turds into the bowl."

He caps his pen and smiles.

"The bad are remembered better than the good, yes?"

THE CHINESE HAVE A SAYING: Drinking a daily cup of tea will surely starve the apothecary.

I had to look up apothecary. In any case, I think you can substitute coffee for tea easily enough. I've seen the average morning commuter snarl for their daily fix of mud with the grit of crack-heads, though admittedly, I've yet to see one suck dick for a cup of fair-trade Kenyan.

Point is, if you make it good, they will come, and within two months of reshuffling our blend and reducing kopi luwak to an occasional, verifiably sustainable reserve blend to keep the animal nuts at bay, the bad press stopped and we were top-of-the-coffee-heap once more.

Nikita came up with the name of Triple-C for our new roast, described on the pouch label as a blend of Columbian, Costa Rican, and Cameroonian beans.

It's in the basement one day that I discover the true nature of Triple-C.

I wander down to check in on Nikita. The shit stench, stronger than ever, karate-chops me in the throat, and when I make my way to the back I behold his latest line-up change.

Eight skin-and-bone Asian men are on deck, groaning their payloads onto fresh litter, only it isn't litter and it isn't woodchips. Nikita had kiboshed his own suggestion when he realized that shredded paper is the less tannic, cheaper alternative.

I'll learn later that day that he's been shredding my books for this purpose, but I won't care. Seeing earlier all those lowly, hungry Chinese women handling and separating the beans from stringy, shit-smeared paper pretty much relegates the importance of my precious library to the back of the line.

Nikita stands by the last dugout, holding the hand of the slugger, sweet-talking him along as if coaching a wife through labor. And like an expectant mother, the Chinese man strains, teeth clenched. The smile tips me off. That amazed, goofy grin that he gives the sky between flipping dumplings outside.

His *Make America Great Again* shirt, sopped with sweat.

Are these tears I feel?

When chasing a buck, never slow down …

Fuck off.

Nikita will later explain that the rancid fish and rice mixture they were fed in route to America produces magnificent coffee. He'll also say, in what I'll take to be his first overt stab at sarcasm, that calling the blend *Cargo Container Chinese* is bad branding.

All fake news …

Fuck off.

Still reeling, I ask why the TVs are off.

"When president talk, make poo-poo ... stubborn to come," Nikita replies

But her emails ...

Fuck off.

She's for they/ them. He is for you.

Fuck off.

ALWAYS LOOK for the fool in the deal. If you don't find one, it's you.

Mark Cuban was so right, and a month after the release of Triple-C, and of our profits nearly doubling, I gather my things into a couple of bags and leave my downtown loft. On the main service counter in the dining area, I leave Nikita a note.

She's your baby now. Good luck with her.

I put the keys on the note. This is my uncle's building. He owns dozens like them. He gave it to me when I turned twenty-one. To start whatever business I chose to someday. My dad didn't approve. Thought it omitted crucial maturation steps towards self-discovery.

I replied with something I never thought myself capable of thinking: Yeah? Look at the good old U.S. of A.

Maybe he was right. I'd lost the stomach for it, if I ever had it at all. Thirty-six hours later, I'm back home at my parents' in Miami, crashing in my old bedroom.

THE NEWS HIT eight months after I'd left Kansas City: Local Russian entrepreneurs, arrested on charges of human trafficking and running an unsanitary eating establishment.

Nikita had conned others to run the business while he remained the silent ideas man, and they took the brunt of the rap.

Still, he was sentenced to two years.

Since hightailing it back to Florida, I scrapped the civet farm in Cuba and sold Bonnie and Clyde to a pot farmer in Oregon. I'd quit coffee altogether. Tea, too. All things brewed or steeped.

But Nikita keeps weighing on my mind, and after he got pinched, I was sure the feds would come crashing through my folks' door at any moment.

AN HOUR AGO, two GOP senators who'd finally grown a pair publicly announced possible impeachment. The third one for *Le Grande Orange*. Naturally, X explodes within minutes. Loser-chumps, they're called. *Traitors*.

Back to regularly scheduled programming, and there's Nikita on my TV.

He'd lost some weight, but otherwise he's the same rest-less-eyed schemer, always working angles.

He still wears a blazer, though a nicer tweed one.

After eighteen months in prison, he's now free and hocking a book. A combination self-help/business-start-up / memoir tome he wrote at Rikers Island called, *My American Experiment*.

The blonde bubble-head running the interview is eating up Nikita's victim narrative, how he became an unwitting pawn in a cycle of exploitation and degradation while struggling to achieve the American dream.

"*Success,*" he says, "*is art of convincing man to do what you want and let him think his idea. I learn in Russia.*"

And he goes on a litany of hard-won wisdom.

"*If one can find his gift, all walls grow small.*"

That smile. A gesture undoubtedly seen as gratitude.

"*Idea that stay on vine should be picked and replanted by man willing give it water.*"

All I see is the mockery between the sprockets of his teeth.

"*God does not make mistakes. He makes opportunities.*"

The con is on.

TYRANNUS TRUMP

KAREN POPPY

FED ON A DIET OF ORANGE-faced rage,
Word salad, *covfefe*. We tried to laugh,
Protest, donate to causes, otherwise engage.
You a buffoon: *Make America Great Again*.
Then reality kicked our teeth in.
All we can think about is the children.
Children in cages, families torn apart.
Child who claims you spread her legs apart,
Raped her at a party, a 13-year-old girl.
Children massacred, gun violence rampant.
Our own children. We fear for them.
What we have is great: Our collective rage.
No one can sing rage like the mother goddess,
And the father god, and all who love children,
Gods and mortals, and the Almighty God.
Separation of Church and State a sad hoax.
Religious organizations contract, build the cage
For the Almighty dollar. Lock up our children.
You want to debase the weak and the mighty.
Immigrant poor, Hillary Clinton—
Lock them up! Lock her up!
Who are these people who chant for you?
Who are these morally bereft?
Ironically, the very weak and the very mighty.
I've been told, "Try to talk to them,
Compromise, find some common ground."
But I can't talk to them, compromise my morals,
And there is no common ground
Where there is no common decency.
I will stand, in one big NO to it all.
Our voices united, together, until you fall.
For the only right thing to do is to stand.
Stand against you. Stand for our democracy.

To insist that morality and common decency
Remain our country's majority. Stand,
Stand, and together we rise, until you fall.
You think that you are king of it all.
"President for life … maybe we'll have to
Give that a shot one day," you joked,
But there is truth in every joke, you
Admiring dictators, as blatantly
You push to become one, destroy
All checks and balances, place
Us all into a cage, we who wonder
How we ended up here, a crumbling
Infrastructure nothing compared to
A crumbling democracy. Autocracy.
You, Tyrannus Trump, with your
Small hands and flaccid body,
But we have to take this seriously.
You weren't even supposed to take power.
Electoral College, not majority.
Here we are, and we refuse the cage.
Wouldn't those sweet children refuse it too,
If they could? What good is it to rage
When we're not even allowed within range
Of lending a helping hand, granting freedom?
What good is it to rage when children die
Anyway, shot full of bullets, going to school,
Or because of their beautiful brown skin.
You have given people permission to hate.
You have given people permission to hurt.
You have given people permission to kill.
You have given people permission
That most of us will not take—

We who still believe in this country.
We will stand as its moral majority.
Stand together until you fall.
We will stand for the good of it all,
Our sweet land of liberty. Freedom
To sing or speak our minds or engage
Silently. Some of us take a stand by
Taking a knee. Some of us enrage
You with our speech. Some of us try
To just simply live and get by, knowing
That to speak is too dangerous, even here.
You don't understand free speech or care
About our First Amendment. Incite
Violence, tear our nation apart, invite
The divide of our people. Fake news
The new norm because who cares for truth?
We do—and don't you know, we will fight
For it. You will not be our *forever president*.
We will fight for freedom, truth, our own
Democracy. You will be but a shadow in history.
Like Hitler, you know, and do you admire him?
You keep praising the dictator of North Korea.
You praised Putin, and deny collusion.
Do they have golf in Federal Prison,
Or will you be off to North Korea, Russia?
Will one of your so-called friends
Take you and your family in?
The house guests that nobody wants.
Oh, but justice is sweet and I love being a seer.
Watch you standing there, thick-tongued
Bumbler. Tweet, Tweet, Tweet.
Then off you go—to who knows where!

ORANGE LIES MATTER

PAT R. STEINER

ORANGE
LIES
MATTER

AN OPEN LETTER TO YOUR WHITE SAVIOR COMPLEX

SUMIKO SAULSON

AS A PERSON who is both African American with ancestors out of slavery (my grandparents' grandparents) and Ashkenazi Jewish with relatives who died in Auschwitz (my grandmother's aunts, uncles, and cousins), I would love it if a bunch of you allies would stop traumatizing the crap out of me by posting shit about how people like me can hide in your attic or escape through your underground railroad.

91% of Black Women voted Democrat. That's a higher percentage than any other group. Yet somehow now people are fantasizing about us as the disempowered and in need of rescue.

Harris didn't win and now overnight you're acting like instead of being out there running for President and stuff we're gonna be back enslaved like our ancestors. How are you supposed to be *helping* us by fantasizing about our being disempowered so you can be the heroes?

I don't want to live in your attic while you live out your white savior complex. Because a bunch of your relatives voted for Trump. What kind of Boxing Helena nonsense is that?

It reminds me of back in 2016 when a bunch of you were threatening to leave the country, promising to "keep us safe" yet … leaving the country. How are you keeping us safe by fleeing the country?

Last time, most of you actually stayed in the country. And voted him out in 2020. So what happened this time?

A bunch of you *did not vote*, or you voted third party, and acted completely dumbfounded by Trump becoming President. Many of those of you who did vote for the Democratic Candidate ran around talking some "lesser of two evils" crap then wondered why your kids were apathetic and did not vote. Some of you ranted about how a Black Woman couldn't become President in this country instead of trying to get her elected.

But we need to wait for you to hide us in your basement? We're not there at all yet, and minorities aren't helpless.

You say you want to "hide your political activities" on your socials now so you can "leverage your white privilege for good" by setting up a fictional place for me to live in your basement instead of *telling your racist trumpster siblings to fuck off?*

And some of you didn't bother voting because the DNC candidate wasn't a white man, but you want to offer us a hiding spot in your attic?

Stop *gaslighting* us with that bullshit and go volunteer for a telephone bank, rock the vote, take back Congress in two years, publish political zines, wear a T-shirt with a pertinent political slogan showing the world you're pro-choice. You know, basic, effective, non-glamorous shit.

Anne Frank died, you insensitive prick. No one saved her. Most of the runaway slaves died. They didn't make it to Canada. They were hunted down and died. If you had a basic understanding of Critical Race Theory you'd stop traumatizing marginalized people by bringing up our genetic trauma just so you can stroke your own ego about how you'd have been one of the Good Ones in Nazi Germany or The Antebellum South.

Minorities don't exist for your self-aggrandizing inspiration porn.

Stop dreaming up scenarios where we can't fight for ourselves while we're still fighting back.

FUMPTRUCK

MICHAEL BAILEY

[a rap]

VERSE 1

So, I'm ridin' shotgun, seein' Trumpf in his fumptruck,
Spoutin' bullshit, yeah, this 'rump-guy outta luck,
World's fed up with this dumb(ass) fuck,
This mad mogul got no game, he suck.

Actin' all tough, but he just a plump chump,
Duckin' facts like a coward, high on his stumpf,
Spittin' out lies, just like his junk, straight trash,
Watch this fumptruck burn, skid out, and crash.

CHORUS

Fumptruck, stuck, he's a fucked-up chump,
Runnin' on fumes in that rusted dump,
Blowin' smoke, but it's weak as(s) shit,
Watch him fall hard … this is it.

VERSE 2

Got his ear "blown off" like he somethin' hardcore,
Fake blood for the press, now he thirsty for more,
Poor kid's dead, played out like a sad movie scene,
Just for fame 'n dress-up on that damn TV screen.

Talks big, dog-bark, like he's somethin' tough,
But he's soft as a pillow, actin' all rough,
He's full of bluff, but this fumptruck's stalling,
We're here to spit truth, watch him go fallin'.

CHORUS

Fumptruck, stuck, he's a fucked-up chump,
Runnin' on fumes in that rusted dump,
Blowin' smoke, but it's weak as(s) shit,
Watch him fall hard … this is it.

VERSE 3

Check that combover, fake as his chin,
That bleach-blond buffoon wrapped in orange skin,
Lookin' like a Cheeto on a power trip high,
With a mess on his head: half comb / half lie.

Tryna look sharp, built more like a clown,
With that bozo hair-flop draggin' him down,
Thinkin' he's oil-slick, a damn political joke,
Oranged-faced wannabe, 'bout to go broke.

VERSE 4

Speakin' at hate rallies, spinnin' his shtick,
Dancin' arms held high, double-pump, sick,
Wavin' round nazis, swastika flags a'flyin',
And it's not all show, this phony-man a'lyin'.

Movin' side to side, with that goofy-ass stance,
Fingers curled, double-handjob parody dance,
Talkin' fate while the crowd screams loud(noise),
But he's lookin' like a fool to the insane-proud(boys).

VERSE 5

Racist / rapist, always duckin' allegations,
Turnin' his back on a whole damn nation,
Just a prick, deceiver, with a longlist of felonies,
Got big pharma-talk, but ain't got no remedies.

Stacked with charges like it's all just a game,
Pointin' fingers while always dodging the blame,
Red-dirty hands flappin', a past he can't shake,
White house of lies, watch it faulter and quake.

CHORUS
Fumptruck, stuck, he's a fucked-up chump,
Runnin' on fumes in that rusted dump,
Blowin' smoke, but it's weak as(s) shit,
Watch him fall hard … this is it.

VERSE 6
Man's illiterate, four-letters or less in his stash,
Spoutin' single-syllable-gibberish word-mash,
Repeats himself, stu-stuck on constant replay,
Lips leakin' "best" / "I the best" / "um … okay."

Vocabulary small, got nothin' to say,
Big words for him just get in the way,
Tryna sound "big-smart" yet it's all a mess,
Watch his fumptruck rollin', nothin' but stress.

OUTRO
So next time he rolls in his fumptruck shit show,
Step back, let that ego deflate and blow,
Wheels fallin' off, it's a sad little dumpf,
Watch the fumptruck crash hard—peace out, Trumpf.

CHORUS [fading, like him]
Fumptruck, stuck, he's a fucked-up chump,
Runnin' on fumes in that rusted dump,
Blowin' smoke, but it's weak as(s) shit,
Watch him fall hard … this is it.

PEARLY GATES

JEFF STRAND

"**WELCOME, WELCOME,**" said Saint Peter. "Sorry to hear about the car accident. At least here in the afterlife, your heads are back on. Anyway, you both died at the same time, so I'll just go ahead and process you together, if that's all right."

"Of course," said Mr. Tensil, looking around in awe. "So this is Heaven?"

"Almost. Got to get through these expensive-looking gates first."

"I can't wait," said Mrs. Tensil. "We accepted Jesus into our hearts long ago, and now we'll reap the reward."

Saint Peter opened his spiral bound notebook. "Let's see. You do go to church every Sunday like good Christians. You don't run any dogfighting rings. And ... uh-oh ..."

"What's wrong?" asked Mr. Tensil.

"Found a 'Whoopsie!' on your record. Looks like you're Trumpers."

"Well, sure," said Mrs. Tensil. "That's how our Lord and Savior Jesus Christ wanted us to vote."

Saint Peter stared at her for a moment. "I've processed millions of your kind, and it shouldn't keep surprising me, but ... are you for real? How did you look at that cartoonish parody of a villainous buffoon and think, 'Yep, he's the guy for me!'? You should hear God when He's gazing down, watching you MAGA wankers, questioning His whole free will experiment."

"What's so bad about Donald Trump?" asked Mr. Tensil.

"No, no, no. Don't play the '*Goodness gracious, what could be problematic about Mr. Trump?*' game. Are you seriously trolling a saint?" Saint Peter sighed. "Look, if you want to support a lying, racist, sexist, xenophobic, gross, reality-denying, whiny little beeyotch, that's fine, but don't pretend you were following Christ's path."

Mr. and Mrs. Tensil exchanged an uncomfortable look.

"To ascend into the Kingdom of Heaven, you're going to have to take a quiz. It's only one question. Are you ready?"

"Yes."

"Name one aspect of the teachings of Jesus that is evident in the words or deeds of Donald J. Trump."

Mr. and Mrs. Tensil just stood there.

"Uhhhhh ..." said Mr. Tensil.

"Uhhhhh ..." said Mrs. Tensil.

"Um, uh, you should ... uh ... hate trans people?" asked Mr. Tensil.

A cloud trapdoor opened underneath Mr. Tensil and he dropped out of sight, screaming.

"Anything?" Saint Peter asked Mrs. Tensil.

"Abortion!" Mrs. Tensil shouted. "Jesus hates killing babies!"

"And what is Donald J. Trump doing for the unwanted babies after they're born?"

"Uh ... worrying that they might be trans?"

Mrs. Tensil also plummeted through the trapdoor. She and her husband screamed until their throats were raw, finally making their landing in Hell. Their eyeballs melted in the sockets and their flesh sloughed off the bones, but that did not spare them further agony—goodness no!—because their skeletons felt pain, too.

An eternity of suffering awaited them and those of their ilk. Some, as their skeletons vomited up molten lava a million times a day, questioned why they'd thrown their support behind a man who was way more like Hitler than Jesus, while others comforted themselves with the belief that their Lord Trump would issue a pardon to commute their sentence in Hell.

"I don't get it," said God. "Look at that guy. He's one of my most ridiculous creations. I made him as a joke. I want to just crack the planet open like a walnut and start over."

"There's still goodness to be found in humanity," said Saint Peter. "Acts of kindness and decency abound. Yes, there are plenty of douche nozzles out there, but plenty of others try to be compassionate and genuinely good people."

"Yeah, I know." God gazed down at the earth. "But, Jesus Christ, dude. Jesus Christ."

LOBSTER IN CHIEF

PEDRO INIGUEZ

THE CROWD WAITED with bated breath
as the first neurologically-enhanced lobster
elected President of the United States
clambered toward the podium.
The lobster hovered over the microphone,
clamped its claws and rubbed its antennae.
A storm of neurons fired inside its
ganglia, and its mandibles burbled out
a rousing acceptance speech.
The men whooped and hollered
at the significance of the moment,
while the women, relegated to years of
waiting for their turn, clapped tepidly

OATH OF OFFICE

JG FAHERTY

"MR. PRESIDENT, they're ready for you in the briefing room."

Mr. President. How good it was to hear those words again. So long, yet it seemed like yesterday.

He waved a final time to the packed plaza outside the Capital building, let the thundering cheers wash over him, and then turned and followed the Secret Service agents up the stairs and into White House. In the temporary war room, televisions and laptops showed the post-inauguration festivities, while talking heads on the various news channels endlessly discussed what the country could look forward to under the new POTUS.

The decision to run had been an easy one; he had unfinished business after his last term. The years since then had been particularly galling. A woman had succeeded him; in some ways, that was worse than having one of *them* in the Oval Office.

He'd be so close the last time to accomplishing everything he'd wanted. Thanks to the laws he'd put in place—another brilliant move on his part, stacking the Supreme Court—he'd emerged unscathed from his scandals, like the one with Vlad. Or the riots after he'd kicked out all the illegals.

But it was all part of the greater plan, the one that would prove to the world his true genius. And now he had his chance to finish it.

Truly, he was God's chosen messiah.

And although he hadn't planned on it happening this way, his repeal of the two-term limit on being elected president had ended up being the very thing making his return to office possible.

As he'd expected, he'd coasted to an overwhelming victory, riding tsunami waves of rose-tinted nostalgia and fervent optimism right into the White House, exactly as he and his advisors had planned.

Of course, considering the super-liberal the Democrats had thrown against him, the only surprise was that he hadn't captured all fifty states.

They remembered me and the country yearned for what I represented: keep the immigrants out, the crime low, and stop spending peoples' tax money on helping the poor.

God bless America and me.

Taking his seat at the table, he looked at his advisors. He'd chosen differently this time, because the days of being nice were over. Some of the best minds in US history sat there. Seasoned political experts and military hawks, all ready to begin a new age in American ascendency.

"Gentlemen. As you know, for the past few years I haven't had much to do, so I've had plenty time to think about what this country needs. And I came to the conclusion only one thing can save us. Shaking reform, a strong military presence, and a return to our place at the top of the political food chain. Food chains are good, the best. That's why you're all here. Have you read the materials I provided?"

A smattering of affirmative responses and nods. He had expected nothing less. If there was one thing his forced retirement had given him, it was the opportunity to concentrate on his goals and strategies without distraction.

"Good. It's not a plan I would have considered during my other terms, but after watching the mistakes my VP made, and then being forced to sit back and say nothing that loud-mouthed woman, I can't even call her a woman, I mean, those dresses she wore, simply awful, piled failure on top of failure and tried to reverse all my hard work. I realized then that drastic times called for drastic measures.

"The world looks at us and sees a cowardly, weak nation where once a military giant stood proud. It sees a country where hard work and success are punished with high taxes while the poor and lazy get everything handed to them. Other countries used to respect us. Now they laugh at us and send their criminals over the border to rape our beautiful women. Like my granddaughter, she's beautiful like her mother. They would love to have her. And do you know what that all means?"

Without waiting for an answer, he held up his hand, his thumb and forefinger less than an inch apart. "It means we're this close to rolling over and playing dead while China and the Middle East take over the whole damn world. Well, I'm not gonna let that happen. God has spoken to me. Some people said I didn't know what I was doing the last time. Well, look at us now. Are we better off than we were then? Of course not. We need to get tough. Times have changed, and so I have I."

The twelve men gathered at the table smiled or chuckled, appreciating the shared joke. They'd all changed, mentally and physically. But that was okay. Sometimes, change was what the world needed. On that, they all agreed.

He motioned to his Chief Advisor. "Is everything ready?"

"The moment you give the order, sir."

"Time to get the wheel rolling, then." The President stood up. "Gentlemen, let's go make a new world. A better world. The world I was meant to create."

EVEN THOUGH IT HAD BEEN YEARS since he'd last given a State of the Union address, the President felt supremely relaxed as he stepped up to the podium. *Like coming home again,* he thought. *This is where God wanted me, and by God this time I'm going to finish what we start. I am the greatest leader this country has ever seen. Who else has done what I have? Nobody!*

The teleprompter came to life in front of him. He gave it a glance and then looked up. He didn't need it. The words were emblazoned in his brain. That was another unexpected benefit of his unwanted imprisonment. His memory was clearer, he was more focused and prepared.

"Ladies and gentlemen of the press, citizens of the United States. I know it isn't typical to address you in this manner less than a day into my presidency, but these are serious times we live in and I don't have the time to waste on celebrations or niceties. Quite a surprise, coming from me, right? When I took my oath of office this morning, I swore to many things. One of them was to uphold the safety of this country. We are not safe, we haven't been for years. I intend to fix that. That's why I stand before you now and announce that together with these great people around me, the greatest military minds ever, and the agree with me, I've initiated actions to end our country's economic, moral, and military challenges within forty-eight hours."

He held his hands up for silence as the gathered reporters clamored for attention.

"Listen, people. Listen to what I have to say. It's important. Very important. Ten minutes ago, right before I came out here, I gave the order for our military forces to saturate the atmosphere over the United States with a combination of a highly-lethal, rapid-acting toxin and the reanimation virus."

Hundreds of voices filled the room, and he had to raise his voice to be heard over the shouting and screaming. "My people tell me that close to seventy-five percent of our population will die, die just like I did in that jail, and be re-animated. And when that happens, a new America will be born. Things like government-subsidized health insurance, food services, and welfare will no longer be a burden on our economy. See that? No more worrying about money! I told you I would rebuild our economy if you gave me a chance. And that surplus of funds will all be used for the military. Casualties of war will become a thing of the past. Our country will return to its rightful place as a global power, free from the threat of terrorism, economic disaster, and dependency on foreign countries."

The President glanced at the teleprompter, and then decided to end his speech early. Judging from the mass exodus occurring among the press corps, no one was likely to hear it anyway. With a smile and a nod, he waved to the stationary cameras with both hands. "Thank you, God Bless, and Make America Great Again!"

ACROSS THE COUNTRY, as the President's decaying, mold-encrusted orange face faded from television and computer screens around the country, the living looked to the skies in terror at the sound of the approaching jets.

And the reanimated cheered as one.

IF THE ARTICLE 'EVER FEEL LIKE YOU'RE LIVING IN A COLLAPSING SOCIETY' WAS A POEM

TONYA LIBURD

WHAT'S THAT? Oh, just Society Collapsing.

If you feel like you're living in a collapsing society
Bad news: it's because you are
If you are feeling powerless
Bad news: it's because you are

People need globally distributed COVID vaccines
But whitey jetting to the moon and Mars.
Apathy, Resignation, indifference
We fall into these after raging,
Retreating to our cocoons,
Retreating to what little comforts
We're allowed.

It's where Gen X falls
After the despair
And feeling a black hole rage
Instead of singing about a black hole sun

Because we know
Deep in the core of our beings
That the systems of
Capitalism
Patriarchy,
White supremacy
Can barely be moved.

There's:

Black hole rage
At this fact
Black hole rage
At the futility we feel

Black hole rage
At the meaninglessness of
Younger lives wrecked

Black hole rage
At the worthlessness
Of it all:
Vanishing economic opportunity,
Shit jobs
No futures.

Black hole rage
At all that was stolen:
From the young, the old,
From the planet,
From every democracy,
From the future.

Facebook and Instaculture
So engrained in the fabric of our culture
That it takes a whistleblower
To make undeniable
Like a pustule,
The rot within
And
The rot and harm it perpetuates without.

But no one apparently cares
Because it's not affecting
The demographics that matter:
White
Older males.

Everyone knew
Where the people at the top
Hide their money.
An open secret
That no one can do
Anything about.

Which leads back to
Apathy, resignation, indifference.
Great moral sentiments
Encompassing our age …
A defense mechanism
That can spell our end

20-30 years of US economic
Stagnation
Bringing forth fascism upon the world
That like pond scum
Floats at the top

Of course we feel powerless
One person cannot do this
The point is to make change
As a collective.

We could act together
We could take the power back
We could call out and together
Pressure things to change
For the better
But I won't hold my breath.

MIND CEMETERY

RICH DUNCAN JR.

ON ELECTION DAY, November 5th, 2024, I was filled with hope. Support for Kamala Harris and Tim Walz seemed to be surging nationwide while Donald J. Trump and JD Vance's rallies appeared woefully attended and rumors were swirling that his campaign seemed resigned to a Harris / Walz victory. I was one of the first voters at the polling area where I lived and emphatically cast my ballot, voting Blue across the board. For me, it was an act of defiance. See, I live in New York—a historically Blue state—but in a small, rural community far from the bright lights of New York City. It's one of the many communities that has overwhelmingly shown support for Trump.

Flags emblazoned with his name and campaign slogans are flown proudly in front of homes, which is normal for supporters of a political candidate. But then there are some of the more unhinged flags I've personally seen. Ones that depict Trump as some sort of Rambo-esque savior of America, with the phrase "No Man, No Woman, No Commie Can Stump Him" emblazoned underneath. Or the similarly designed flags that seem like an '80s action movie rip-off cramming every American stereotype you can think of into it—tanks, rippling American flags, explosions and screeching bald eagles. But the one that sticks with me the most—the one that perfectly encapsulates the man that Donald J. Trump is—is the homemade banner I saw stretched between two trees on the side of the major road on the way to a neighboring town. It was just a plain white bedsheet with the words "DEMOCRATS ARE TERRORISTS" spray-painted on it. That sign is just one of the many representations of the larger fabric of the America in which we all now live. Ironic how they also rail against some Democratic policies, like "healthcare for all" or other similar programs, as radical socialist ideology that needs to be stopped at all costs, but have no problem with the free meal program started by the Democratic party that allows our school to provide meals that feed their children who might otherwise go hungry.

Later that night, as I was checking some of the early results, Harris and Walz were down and my eight-year-old daughter said, "No! Not Trump!" I'm familiar with the so-called "Red Mirage," so I wasn't overly worried.

"Don't worry kiddo," I said. "It's still super early. They have a lot of states left to go. I'm sure things will turn around soon. It will be okay."

When I woke up on the morning of November 6th, 2024, the first thing I did was grab my phone and check the results of the election. I was instantly filled with a boiling rage and sense of despair. Why? Because I lied to my daughter. Things are not okay. On Election Night, a vast majority of Americans decided that their vote was best cast for a man that was convicted of 34 felony counts, has other convictions pending, and who was impeached twice. Almost immediately, swarms of MAGA voters hit social media and began bombarding women with appalling messages.

"Your body, my choice!"

"America has spoken. Get back in the kitchen."

"Women threatening sex strikes like LMAO as if you have a say."

Women have been dealing with this sort of disgusting behavior since the dawn of time. But make no mistake—and I am addressing everyone who cast a vote for Donald J. Trump—his victory allowed these people to think that this sort of behavior is acceptable as a society. Now, in the off chance there are Trump voters reading this, I know you're already feeling that first hint of anger beginning to bloom in your gut. That anger that pretty soon is going to flare up and start working its way through your body. You're going to want to fire up your electronic device of choice and go on the defensive—or maybe even the offensive— as you draft some kind of hate filled message to send me. Good. I want you to sit with that anger for a minute. Allow me to share some snippets of a transcript Penn Bullock of *The New York Times* provided—on the eve of Trump's first election—of a tape many of you may have forgotten about:

> "It's like a magnet. Just kiss, I don't even wait. And when you're a star, they let you do it. You can do anything."

> "Grab 'em by the pussy. You can do anything."

Hearing those words—straight from the President-Elect's mouth, I might add—is it any wonder the people running rampant all over social media feel comfortable saying the very real quotes I provided? Now, let's get back to that anger that I asked you to hold on to. Are you angry because of the words I wrote about Donald J. Trump and the MAGA voters who feel emboldened to spew hatred or are you angry that your convicted felon President-Elect holds these kind of abhorrent views? Because if it isn't the latter, make no mistake, you're part of the problem. Not the immigrants he tells you to fear, not the schools that he tells you are indoctrinating your children—it's you and people like you. Knowing that he said those words, I genuinely ask you to look at the faces of your wives, your sisters, your daughters, your nieces, your granddaughters and honestly say you voted for that man because you thought he was the type of leader that would provide a better world for them.

The quotes I shared aren't posts taken out of context or fabrications, they are real and indicative of the very real attitudes people within that movement carry. I've experienced them firsthand. I was debating a Trump supporter and called them out when they shared an ignorant opinion about the transgender community. They questioned my love for my country and I responded to them by saying I loved my country so much; I was willing to speak out against people who promote bigotry and hatred. Their reaction to me standing up for the transgender community? They told me they couldn't wait until the day a man followed my daughter into the bathroom while I cried "I love my country!" They actively, and with pride, wished for a day where my daughter would be assaulted. So yes, these are real attitudes that real people carry with them and not fabrications or the work of bot accounts.

A lot of people who vote for Trump when confronted with proof of his misogynistic and racially charged views, react with some form of "it doesn't affect me personally." They say they're worried about their neighborhoods and their school districts. They may even say "Yeah, he's an asshole, but he's going to fix the economy!" or some other variation that focuses on a different issue. Being worried about your neighborhood and school district is important and an admirable trait. Setting aside the fact that many of Trump's policies—particularly his plans to implement tariffs—have been largely panned by experts and that many of the issues people place at the feet of Biden are patently untrue, why does it have to be an "either or" proposition? It costs absolutely nothing to treat people of different races, genders, sexualities, or backgrounds with dignity and respect. And yet, time and time again, Trump continues to spew talking points that can be construed as misogynistic, racist, and sexist. Casting a vote for him sends the message that those kinds of viewpoints are acceptable in society, whether that was your intention or not.

Trump's success is driven by the cult of personality that he's been able to cultivate over many decades and the very real lack of media literacy a vast majority of Americans possess. I'm a trained journalist, so unlike a lot of armchair pundits who like to bleat "FAKE NEWS!" every chance they get, I actually know what I'm talking about. People are quick to dig into their favorite news source and the information they receive from them is treated as gospel. Now, there are news outlets that are biased for a variety of reasons, including corporate interests and editorial-style programs that push talking points over fact-based reporting. That's why consuming news from a variety of sources, being aware of those biases, and fact-checking are so important. Trump and Vance exploit the fact that most Americans don't do that.

Remember back when Trump claimed the Haitian migrants of Springfield, Ohio were "eating the pets of the people that live there"? He made that proclamation despite officials telling him there were no credible claims of that happening. Subsequent reporting not only proved those claims were untrue, it told a story of migrants who were in the country legally, just trying to find a way to make a better living for their family. Not only did they find it, they helped revitalize a once struggling town only to have a man born with a silver spoon in his mouth claim they came in "and destroyed the place." JD Vance was confronted with the facts that disproved Trump's proclamations and do you remember what he said? He gave an answer that in part said he felt the need "to create stories so that the … media actually pays attention to the suffering of the American people."

During his debate with Walz, Vance grew heated at one point, and complained that the rules were supposed to be that the moderators were not going to fact check. MAGA voters love to claim that the reason Democrats keep losing is because they treat them like they are stupid or talk down to them. The reality is that is *exactly* how Trump and Vance treat them. Vance's quote about manufactured stories and his complaints about fact-checking prove this. What he's saying in both instances is that he knows none of this is true. That as long as they control the narrative, their zealous followers will swallow the bullshit they are being fed without question and will actually thank them for being "truth-tellers" and "speaking their mind." Where is that outrage from MAGA supporters at their elected leaders for treating them like children that need to be told what to think?

People also like to point to Trump's strength as a reason for voting him into office, but the reality is, he's not strong. He's weak and he's a coward. People like to point to his relationship with Vladimir Putin and other world leaders and that his strength has eased tensions in certain regions. But the reason for that isn't respect, it's because they know Trump is a man who is fueled by his massive ego and that his reliance on adulation makes him easy to control. Throw the man a few compliments and they're much more likely to be able to steer him to the outcome they want because he'll think they respect him. Just look at how many people have been replaced in his own administration. It wasn't because they weren't a fit for the job, it's because they wouldn't kiss the ring and do what he said. He clearly can't stand being told "no."

Vance is also a coward. Remember 2016, back when Trump was running for president the first time? Vance publicly called Trump an "idiot," "reprehensible," and at one point compared him to Adolf Hitler. But guess what? When it became clear Trump had a stranglehold on the Republican Party and Vance saw a way to fast track his way into the political elite, he knelt at Trump's feet and kissed the ring. Because he's a man who lacks conviction, lacks a backbone and only serves himself and his interests.

I'm a cishet white man that has a well-paying job and as such, I understand that I have an incredible amount of privilege. Privilege a lot of my fellow Americans don't have. I wavered on whether or not to submit this piece anonymously and the more I thought about it, I decided to publish it with my name attached for that very reason. For far too long, many Americans from under-represented groups have had to bear the brunt of fighting for their rights with little support from those that benefit the most from the power structures of this country. As a cishet white man, I fall into that group, and I think it's past time that more of us openly speak up and push back against all forms of hatred that seem to be driving this country when we see it. I'm making it clear right now that if I see or hear any of that behavior, I'm calling it out. I don't care who you are and I promise you, you will not intimidate me.

I don't say this looking for a pat on the back. These communities have been fighting the good fight for many, many years and understand the struggles they face better than I ever could. I say this as someone that is open to listening and someone who is willing to lend my support and my voice where it's needed. I pledge to stand up for you and protect you from hatred without question, whether we know each other or not. Women, LGBTQIA+, BIPOC and anyone else who has ever felt persecuted for being your authentic self, I'm sorry this country failed you, and I'll support you always. Because that is the America I want to see and the America I want my daughter to live in. And to Donald J. Trump and JD Vance, I mean this from the bottom of my heart—fuck you.

COFVEVE: A TRIO OF PROSE POEMS

EUGEN BACON, ILLUSTRATED BY ELENA BETTI

A COSTLY LEGACY

authority is total the way it's gotta be
   black lives matter cofveve how about bleach
     a bad grouping of tornadoes cast doubt on facts
       about what imperilled the world's agenda
     how fraud paled the troika laundromat
  and what's with turkey's gas for gold
a new variant of virus?

the dirt scandals a hand overplayed
   violent deadly incompatible with law
     arrogance racism antifa done it
       senators forsook a scene of crime
     shaking heads at find some votes
  everyone there saw what happened
the world not there gasped it happened.

bonnie and clyde make this go away
   is it constitutional who's fake news
     but nobody's asking where the ventilators
       it's pinocchio's nose dead right it is
     a plan is close let's go back to the regular
  but a question for scholars is it just politics
a vote is all it takes or a secret pardon.

UNFINISHED

Survival reduced to pickets wakes me at night. Walls painted in stench, each day the beginning of my last. A siren of coppers chases rioters waving placards about paradigm shifts. Faces of my dead friends break out from the wind, imprint on each uniform's head, sketching shapes with colourless lips. Hearts weeping, bones humming. I exit by an alleyway, words raining like a president's bisque full of grime. I duck into cold roads of the city, walls pissing unfinished graffiti: I. Can't. Brea ... A hobo with an umbrella hands me a parcel of dreams. More sirens—is there a better life? I take each folded dream and its prosthetic limbs, flick it to immortality. Text is your legacy! I call to the drifter losing himself in the brolly as I flee. Eat it! Lest the world murmurs oaths buried in your manuscript.

Illustration by Elena Betti

IN A CAFÉ ...

by the rampage, all the chairs are carved in limestone
because granite and alabaster cost too much.
Attendants are picked for lasting—more than
sandstone sounds just right. They float on teargas
without coughing, but their skins are full of burning.
Clientele are the ghosts of Mau Mau, John Lennon
and Pussy Riot. It's not the likes of these that sashay
with guards or inmates in the know, but they walk on
water. Today's talk is on the meander of time in a 6
by 8, steel or brick walled, no angling for parole as
you flirt with quarter worms slipping off stale crusts.
There's a depth beneath each brow, eyes full of
whispers that float in clouds above activists with soft
bodies falling like feathers. But the crowd is a
meniscus, fully cushioned and evened out, unyielding
to line of police officers swallowed in masks. I see
oceans, la-di-da, a shimmer of hope in a new
yesterday, but today's a long way to the sea. I'm a
blind fish without a name and, right now, I can't
breathe.

Illustration by Elena Betti

THE CANDIDATE

HARRISON DEMCHICK

BROOK STARED WIDE-EYED AT THE TELEVISION screen, fingers cupped around her lips, as she sat on the ratty old living room sofa. On the other side of the screen the screams were tinny, muted, uncoordinated. The camera operators had run, mostly—she could see the cameras themselves on the periphery of the stage, misdirected and abandoned—but she felt the trembling of the one who remained by the herky-jerky movements of the screen as it zoomed in from the balcony back toward the candidate.

"Mom," Brooke said in an unsteady warble. "Mom, you need to see this."

After a moment, her mom walked in from the kitchen rubbing a green, plaid-patterned dish towel against a chipped yellow plate. "What's he saying now?" she said, but then grew fixated as well.

The candidate hovered on his knees over the moderator's stomach, his weathered, chunky fingers digging between the torn-apart bloodstained buttons of the once-neatly-pressed white cotton shirt, deep into the chunks of flesh and entrails. He tore out another dripping handful and raised it up past his dangling red tie to his cracked lips, chewing and slurping and leaving asymmetrical streaks on the flecks of flesh-pink TV makeup.

Screams and shouts carried as the auditorium emptied. The camera shook. Brooke didn't understand why the studio hadn't cut away.

"Hm," her mother said. "Huh." She pressed the dishrag distractedly into the plate.

The moderator spasmed. The candidate swallowed.

"Well," said Brooke's mother. "At least he's not a Democrat."

With that, she turned and walked back into the kitchen. Brooke heard the clatter of the dish as it settled into the pile overwhelming the sink. But as the water flowed and the dishrag scrubbed, and as the screams faded into the air, all she could do was sit there on the edge of the cushion, again, and stare helplessly into the screen as the ground shifted beneath her.

TRUMPY TALK (SUNG TO THE TUNE OF "HAPPY TALK" FROM SOUTH PACIFIC)

ELIZABETH MASSIE

CHORUS
Trumpy talk, keep talkin' Trumpy talk,
Lyin' 'bout all the folks you screw,
You've got fake it big,
If you don't fake it big,
How you gonna make 'em think it's true?

VERSE
Talk about a guy,
Carpenter by trade,
Helpin' to support his wife and son,
Talk about ole Trump,
Hiring on this man,
Then not paying him for work he's done.

CHORUS
Trumpy talk, this is just Dumpy talk
Talk about those you treat like dirt,
You couldn't give a shit,
Why would you give a shit?
You don't feel a thing when others hurt.

VERSE
Talk about a gal,
In a pageant show,
Talented and smart and lovely, too.
Talk about ole Trump,
Letchin' on this gal,
Laughin' that there's nothing he can't do.

CHORUS
Trumpy talk, such fucked-up Punky talk
As president, you think you're God,
You think you own us all,
You'd love to own us all,
But think again, you reckless worthless clod.

VERSE

Talk about a child,
From a foreign land,
Praying that she'll find a brand new start,
Talk about ole Trump,
Callin' her a risk,
Sayin' she's a terrorist at heart.

CHORUS

Trumpy talk, it's goddamn Schlumpy talk,
Your "I'm the savior" cover's blown,
We know your dark desires,
Your greedy, cold desires;
One day we'll have you off your gilded throne.

If you just talk Trumpy,
And you lie and cheat and screw, In the end the
one you'll screw … is … you.

INMATE #4547

THOM ERB

"OH, LITTLE DJ AND E-ROC, please shut your pie holes, daddy's workin' here."

"Sorry, Daddy," the two boys said, hiding in the room's deepest shadows.

The obese man, the strangest shade of Cheetos, stood naked—save for the over-sized Russian-flag boxer shorts that reached the tip of his black socks—as he stood before the floor-to-ceiling mirror before him.

The smarmy host, who looked like a combination of Howard Walowitz from *The Big Bang Theory* and a satanic Howdy Doodie, sounded like a prepubescent teen on helium and too much cocaine.

"Hello, I am Cucker Tarlson and we're back to the *Big Show*. Well, Mr. President-Elect, to continue the topic of your first thirty days once you're sworn in, please tell our salivating viewers more about your 'Five-Thousand-A-Day' plan you touched on before the break." The smarmy host's voice cracked.

"Well, Cucker, I've been the best, the most *successful* president of all time. Best POTUS in the galaxy, by a biggly amount. Even better than that all-time leftest loser, Reagan." Big Daddy spoke into the large, hair-spray-clogged brush, assessing himself in the large mirror. "The Great Communicator had nothing on your Dear Leader!"

"Daddy," came the squeaky voices from the shadows."

Big Daddy grumbled and forced a smile into the mirror and stomped his flat feet, hoping it would shut up the annoying voices.

"Ah, yes. Reagan was nothing but a tiny shadow to you, sir. So, Mr. President-Elect, moving on. I'm sure you're beyond excited for your second glorious term to begin, with the very affable and well-done JD at your side. I have to humbly assume, however, that you have a special cabinet position for yours truly?" the host said with a slobbering and slight taint of begging.

"Daddy. Daddy! It hurts!"

The two annoying voices came from Big Daddy Donnie's feet.

Those damn boys. Shut the hell up!

Donnie stamped harder on the floor.

"Uhem. Moving on, Mr. President-Elect," Cucker continued. "The lame-stream media is all up in pearl-clutching arms over your alleged connection with the much-bandied-about Project 2025, put forth by the most moral and honorable Heritage Foundation. What can you tell our beloved viewers about this to help quell all this insanity and lay it to rest once and for all?"

"Well, as you know, the crooked leftist media is out of control. And in my new adminis—"

"Daddy! Daddy! It's hurting us. Help!" The shrill boys' voices were like dragons' nails on a chalkboard, causing Big Daddy Donnie to snap and shout, his angry voice echoing.

"God*damit*, you little fuckin' shits! Where's your mother? Oh, she's golfing. So, if you don't pipe down, I'll have the Hulkster make a very personal visit again!"

The air and all went silent. Only the heavy breathing from Big Daddy Donnie could be heard, bouncing off the cold, cement walls.

"Your feed is breaking up, Mr. President?" Cucker's panicked voice rang in Big Daddy Donnie's ears as the big man fell to his aching knees. "Can we get someone working on the connection?"

The droning boys' cries pounded in Big Daddy Donnie's ears. Cucker's panicked voice rung in Big Daddy Donnie's ears, as the big man fell to his aching knees. "We *told* you, Daddy. It hurts. It hurts so much. Please. Please help us!"

An unbearable burning pain erupted from his feet and, like horrific dominos, scorched all the way up his support-stockinged legs and to his bum and exploded like a Soviet-made missile, causing Big Daddy Donnie to scream out in unbearable agony.

"I'm sorry, Mr. President-Elect, but we are going to have to cut your feed. Hopefully we can get you back on soon." Cucker's words wavered, as if a million miles away.

Another burning blast of pain filled Big Daddy Donnie, and he fell over into a bright light.

"We *told* you, Daddy. It hurts." Junior and Eric cried.

"INMATE 4547, time to get up and out of the rack. Your conjugal visit is over."

The harsh, sarcastic guard's voice shook Big Daddy from his sweaty, heart-pounding slumber; that, and his body being violently rocked back and forth.

"Wha ...What?" Big Daddy strangled his worn, tear- and blood-stained Hulk Hogan doll.

The burly guard laughed mockingly. "Day One, *Mr. President.*" His words were curt and mocking. "Enjoy your tyranny. Your dream is over."

Big Daddy slowly came back to consciousness with a sudden burning pain in his backside.

He looked around and fought desperately to find the source of the agony, and once he got to his wobbly feet, he saw the blood on his mattress and suddenly his bone spurs didn't hurt so badly.

The large, muscular, and overly-tattooed man with two gold teeth smiled at him. "Hey, when you're famous, they let ya do it!" He winked and slapped Big Daddy Donnie on his naked throbbing red ass and then left the cell with a bitter chuckle. "See ya tomorrow, Mr. President."

The one-termer wept into his sweat- and tear-stained MyPillow.

YOU ARE TRAPPED IN A COMA

HOLLY LYN WALWRATH

FAR TOO LATE than is comfortable to admit, you realize comatoseness is not consciousness. Like a plant, you are now purely reactive. To have consciousness, an organism must be able to learn. When the new nurse struggles to turn you and you fall off the hospital bed, growing bruises like mold on your hip and your shoulder, you cannot react. You cannot process the operant conditioning that would teach you to move away from that nurse in the future, to call for help, to beg for someone, anyone else. When your mother comes to sit by your side, rewarding you for once in your life for all the times you showed up to Baptist church functions with the requested casserole dish, for mowing the yard, for watching your little sister, you cannot reap the benefits of that reward. You can hear her say goodbye into your ear, telling you that she's moving away, but you can't see the expression on her face. Image-based consciousness is the theory that humans map the data that comes into the brain. What we see defines who we are. But you cannot open your eyes. So are you really alive if you cannot see the card your niece left on the windowsill, or the person who shares the room with you beyond the thin curtain? You can't sense the danger outside the room, how the oceans are rising and the forests are burning and the moon is crashing into the Earth. You don't know who won the election. You can't feel anything, maybe a little vibration—it could be a passing bus or a meteor. Like the tree in the forest, you are not yet realized. The world could be ending—or it could just be a dream. You are Schrodinger's coma patient. Living in a constant re-pondering of the question: Will I ever wake up? But the question you're refusing to admit is: Would I even want to?

THERE'S NOTHING WRONG WITH YOU

HOLLY LYN WALWRATH

YOU ARE A PART OF THIS big, strange, wonderful world and there's nothing wrong with you. You belong here, body and soul, from your tiniest toe to the top of your head, from your fingerprints to the end of your hair—you are supposed to be here and now. Maybe not in this exact here and now, maybe you need to move or change or grow or retreat, god, let it be okay to go backward every once and a while, let a mistake be something you can come back from, let just existing be allowed. Licensed even. Because there are enough terrible laws in this place. There are enough terrible dictators trying to take you're your rights, they want to shoot you, but they can't find you in here. There's enough pain and enough suffering to last for a million years. So you can sit on the couch and watch something soft; you can pet your dog while it rains outside; you can make a tea and watch the bag steep. You can do all these things without having to be wrong because there's nothing wrong with you. You don't have to fit into all their puzzle pieces and feel broken all the time because there's nothing broken about you and if you have to be their kind of right then maybe right is wrong too. They don't know how to deal either. They haven't caught on to the fact that we are all just beautiful stardust floating through a mystical dream—and maybe we're all some collective hope, a matrix of understanding that's anything but broken. Here's what I'm trying to say: You are human, and there's nothing wrong with you.

UPPER CRUST

MICHAEL PAUL GONZALEZ

BACK IN COLLEGE, I ran in some good circles. Not the best. I always wanted to be in the best. *Now*, I'm in the—I was looking for a fraternity, because you know it's *who* you know that gets you ahead in the world. I wanted to know the important people. Only the best. My father, when he sent me off to Wharton, he told me, I don't give a shit what you learn or what your grades are. I care who you meet. *That's* where the important lessons are. Know *who* to know, and *what* you know becomes second place.

One night, I'm at a rush party for Delta Kappa Epsilon. Lot of good people in that—Gerald Ford, the Bush Family, you see where I'm going—but this is obviously before any of them were president. I'm at this party looking at a goddamn oil painting of my great grandfather, he pledged so many years—but even legacies have to earn their spot. Out of nowhere, I feel something slide into my pocket. I look down, and there's this hand—silk glove, red silk, sexy as hell and—good party when someone's reaching into your pants before you've finished your first drink, right?

I turn, and there's this woman behind me, just *painted* into this silk dress. Everything red. Hugging every—I mean everything, the curves and her nipples—she just smiles at me, extends her hand, and says, "Ursula Dupree." Just like that. So I kiss her hand, and she flicks a finger toward my pocket, turns, and walks away.

In my pocket there's a little engraved business card. Gold. Sharp as a razor. Still got it here somewhere. You can see the stains from our meal on the—we'll get to that.

TANNER STEED – YOU ARE CALLED

SEPTEMBER 14, 1964

10PM

FULCRUM

ANWEALD · FEOH · WEALDAN

FOLLOW YOUR GAZELLE

Gazelles! That's what they called them … anyway. And you've seen the Fulcrum logo on my desk. That's usually covered by the first dollar I ever "made," nobody gets to see—but I have to show it to you tonight. And you've seen it, so now you have to—my father sent me there to meet people. Fucking is meeting, right? You don't pass up opportunities.

So, I followed her to this big ballroom, and everyone's eating dinner. We sit, she says, "Don't eat, you'll be eating later tonight," and she slides a finger up her thigh and gives this little shudder, and I'm—well, you get the idea. But she eats! Seven courses. Clam chowder, oysters Rockefeller, escargot, poi and sashimi, mustard potatoes, lamb with mint sauce and jelly, and a pineapple upside-down cake for dessert. I remember all seven, it comes back later. I'm just supposed to watch her eat? But the way she did it was— she could do things with that mouth, and—so we're talking, small talk, and then the last course comes, the waiter sets this little silver dish down, lifts the lid, and nothing's there.

Ursula stands up, and I swear, I don't know how they cut this dress, but it slides open across her thighs, and there, eye level, *pow*, her pussy, right in my face. Just a long enough flash that I can see how neatly trimmed, and she says, "Dinner was delightful. Are you ready for dessert?"

You're thinking what I'm thinking, right? She walks away. Up this spiral staircase in the corner of the room. There's these two guys standing right at the top of the stairs, like big stone—these were, one of them was probably Samoan, I mean huge—and the guy just looks at me and says, "Card." Just, *card*.

And the other guy has his hand out, gentle on my shoulder, but like a granite—so I give them the card, right? I pull it out from on top of my money clip. Back then I was like you, stupid, thinking that power came with showing wealth—anyway, showed them the little card she gave me, and they melt. Big, soft teddy bears. They step aside, backs to the wall, but like I said, big guys, so I still have to squeeze between, and then this door slides open a few feet away.

Maybe she's a prostitute, right? That's what I'm thinking, these were her bodyguards, they saw the money, they thought I—anyway, I step inside, thinking it's a bedroom, but it's an elevator. The door closes. She's not there. Small elevator. Red lights. And I can't even feel it moving, I'm just waiting for five minutes to move and—the doors open, and I'm on another floor. Basement. Way down. Didn't know it at the time.

I step into this waiting room. Two benches, one along each wall, look like they were from a museum. Like they'd been there since the 1700s, and that's because *they were*. Immaculate condition because people only sat on them once every four years. That's how lucky I was to—anyway, one wall, four ladies sitting. Four silk dresses. Red, purple, blue, and green. Other wall. Three guys. Not even college guys like me. One of them was my age, the other two were older and—they don't matter.

I stood by them. Here's a little secret. If everyone's sitting, you stand. If everyone's standing, you sit.

The walls are covered, floor to ceiling in these small oil paintings, little two-foot-tall portraits of men, great men. Didn't know it at the time. That's another secret—most of the truly powerful men, you never know their names, because there are positions. Roles. Some people are behind the scenes, some people, like me, are destined for the stage. So. We're just looking at these ladies, and they're not talking, just sitting there looking as hot as—and then these two big double doors open.

And the ladies stand, and this is where it gets good. This guy, this little butler, comes out wheeling a cart. On top of the cart, four leather collars, each attached to a chain. Without a word, the ladies stand up, unzip their dresses, and slide them off. You've never seen anything like—I mean, they all had underwear on, same color scheme, red—I guess Ursula had just put them on—

and blue, green, purple, somehow that was even sexier than if they'd been naked—each one puts on a collar, walks over to us, hands us the leash. The butler gestures us through the big doors.

Inside, there's a—I'm not supposed to talk about the room, but you're going to see it soon enough, so I'm not really spoiling anything—like a courtroom fucked a brothel. Best way I can— there's a big, tall judge's stand. Big podium, three chairs way up high. On one side, a jury box. Sits twelve people. On the other wall, nothing. Well, almost nothing. Two little iron loops that I didn't notice when we—I'll get to that.

In the middle of the room, where the lawyers would normally go—a small table, like we're here to play poker. I don't know what the hell's going on, I just know I have Ursula's hot blonde ass on a chain. I'm up for anything. The butler claps, and the ladies lead us to a chair. High-backed, satin cushions, and the cushions match our ladies' clothes. My chair's red, guy next to me is blue, the— you get it. You understand. The ladies pull out the chairs, we sit, and they stand just behind us.

The butler claps again and says, "Judges." Two more doors open. Twelve guys in robes file into the jury booth. Then the butler rings this little bell. And it gets quiet. A door opens behind the podium, three men walk in, and they have full hoods on. Can't see their faces. They sit up high. The Triumvirate. You'd know their names. You've read about them in history books. They have done great things—a history you only get to learn if you pass tonight.

They sit, and I figure this is it, we're being hazed into the fraternity, right? Couldn't be more wrong. The Triumvirate, as one, they raise gavels and tap three times. The one in the middle says, "Dinner is served."

The butler leaves and comes back, with—get this—a pizza. A fuckin' pizza margherita. The most boring—cheese, tomato slices, some marinara. Smelled good, but I mean, *this* is what you dragged us down to—and nobody else reaches for a piece, so I don't either. I don't know where this is going.

"Gentlemen," the butler says. "This is the gathering of the Fulcrum. You've been carefully selected to begin the process of advancement to an echelon of society known to your fathers and their fathers. Every four years, we open our chambers around the world so that men can prove themselves worthy of joining the ranks of the Fulcrum. Is the Triumvirate prepared?"

The guys behind the podium gavel in turn. They go in order, left to right, saying Secundus, Primus, Tertius.

And Primus bangs his—god I wish I was allowed to tell you his name, you'd die, you wouldn't believe—anyway, he bangs the thing and gives us this speech.

"We are the playwrights of society. We control the stagecraft of the world. This is not an honor, it is the highest achievement a man can strive for. In the Fulcrum, there are no individuals. Behind these doors, we are many. In the world, we are one. If one of us succeeds, it is shared victory. If one of us is slighted, we are all wounded. This is your opportunity to join us. *Sacrifice* is a word greatly misunderstood. *Power* is a word greatly misused. *Fortune* is a word whose meaning few people truly grasp. Tonight, you will sacrifice. You will understand what is required to obtain fortune. With fortune comes power, responsibility, money, and no need to sacrifice again. To show your willingness to move to the next phase, you must break bread together. *La Festa dei Burattinai*. Will you take a bite of the food before you to show you are willing?"

That's all they wanted? I check the competition. They each grab a slice. Me? I do it big time. Slide a knife under a piece, guide it up to my plate with my fork. Cut a slice, the right size, not too big. I pick the guy across the table, the first to grab a slice. Unbroken eye contact while I chew. I look at the next guy, same thing, keep chewing until he looks away. I swallowed before I had a chance to look at the third guy, but he got the idea. It wasn't the best pizza I've ever—and then, after one bite, the butler whisks it all away and another guy brings in a different pizza. This one has sausage. Hot peppers. Like really hot, the ghost kind, we don't know from—and then the Primus says, "The world presents resistance. Can you push through hesitation, work through discomfort, withstand the heat of the forge?"

This time, maybe they're on to me, they're really testing my resolve, because all the cutlery goes away. I have to pick up the slice with my bare hands like these other chimps. We take a bite, and it's hot, really fuckin'—I mean, we need water, and we're laughing at this point, because we can see this coming. Spicy food, gross food, whatever, we're pledging, getting hazed. Same drill again, one bite, butler goes out, new guy comes in with a new pizza. This one is covered in black crickets and live earthworms.

"The world is rife with poor, simple creatures. The mechanisms of society are infested. You must consume them. Their bodies exist to nourish and sustain you."

And here, of course—I mean, fried crickets, yeah, that's disgusting, but live worms? But then again, it's fraternity life, right? So one of us, not me, I'm not ashamed to admit, goes first, big bite, and then we all dive in. Not as disgusting as I thought. Tastes like dirt. Cold and soft, though. Like a dead lady's lips. I figure once they stopped squirming it would be—but they never really stopped. I could feel them moving in my stomach for—probably a lesson in there somewhere.

"People are the salt of the earth. Though it may turn your stomach to mingle, you can, and must. Farm them, nourish them, consume them." Right as the Primus says this, the butler's back in with another pizza, tomato and cheese. Big slices. And behind him, another guy's pushing a cart with small cardboard boxes.

We hear this scratching. Pecking. *Peeping.* Our ladies open the boxes and pull out these fuzzy chicks. Little baby chickens. Without a hitch, they take the chicks, and *krick-krick-krick-krick*, break their tiny legs. They set them on a slice, and these little birds are

... not fluttering, vibrating. The wings are moving so fast and their eyes squint from the pain and—and the primus says, "Sacrifices will always need to be made. Vermin and pets alike. You consume them all, those you revile and those you adore. Increase their suffering or end it, but the suffering is not the matter. Our nourishment is. The door awaits."

We stare at each other. Hazing is one thing, but this was ... and Ursula leans down and whispers–and I can still feel her juicy lips brushing my ear when I think of this, gives me goosebumps—she says, "Do it. For me." I don't know what the other ladies were saying, and I didn't care, because this time I was first. If only one of us was going to win this game, it had to be me. I rolled the little bird up in the pizza slice, cradled it with the head pointing at my mouth, because I figure, you break the neck and then—and it was a clean bite, I have strong jaws thank god, and it was ... it didn't taste like I thought. Crunched like ... and the beak just felt like an unpopped popcorn kernel, if it was stuck in a cottonball soaked in blood, and ... I saw the other guys going for it too. And the butler, thank god, tells us, "You may spit."

The ladies give us a chalice, and we spit out the mess, and just stare at each other. It was the act, not the eating, you understand? Ursula gestured to me. I had this little piece of gristle and a tiny feather stuck to my lip.

The Primus says, "The game begins. Woman. The ultimate tool of resistance and persuasion. Her fortitude is incomparable. Her service to you is irreplaceable. Her greed will push you to greatness. Her guile will bring down those who would seek to hurt you. Uncontrolled, her fury will consume you. Choose your tools wisely."

The butler brings out the next pizza. A plain ham and cheese. Each woman rotates to the next man at the table. Now I've got blue next to me. They plant their hands on the table and snort. I mean, big, phlegmy ... and they start spitting on the pizza. Just greaser after greaser. Big, green shiny … coating the whole thing. Then they fold their arms and stare at us.

After the birds, this seemed like nothing to me, so I grabbed a slice and took a bite. I mean, I had plans to bury my tongue in Ursula's asshole, what's a little spit? We all take a bite. The women rotate again. They put our slices on the floor. The butler gives them sneakers. Each announces where they walked from to get there. "I took the train from Shitburgh to blah blah blah," you get the idea. They made it clear, these shoes had been through spook neighborhoods, or immigrant shitholes, whatever piss-stained, dog-shit-encrusted sidewalk you could think of. And they stood on the slice. Really smeared their foot in there. Then, without lifting the shoe up, they took it off, carefully slid a hand underneath, flip it, and served the piece to us, like the shoe was a plate.

This one made me hesitate. You know me and germs. Eventually the other guys ate, so I had to.

The Primus says, "Four courses: The women will weed out the weak. They will serve until two remain. This will comprise the end of the second chapter. If all four pledges remain, the women are deemed to have failed. Fortune does not accept failure."

A new pizza comes in. Cheese only, nothing else.

The Primus says, "Sauce."

And two of the ladies squat over it and piss all over the—soaked it—and this was where things got weird.

The Primus says, "Toppings."

You know how sick a woman can—the lady in blue says, "I'm menstruating." Drew out the word to scare us. Reaches into her underwear and pulls out this fat, brown piece of cotton.

The butler comes over with a silver tray and she sets it down, gets out a scalpel, and carefully cuts it into little pepperoni slices, putting them on the pizza. She says, "Who wants a fresh one?"

I figured if I got it while it was still warm, I could—and you know, it tasted—have you ever had a bloody nose? Sort of like that. I meant the cotton was ... it wasn't easy to chew. But thank god, the butler clapped again and we were allowed to spit that into the chalice too. So far, we're all in.

Ursula though, what a bitch, brings out this small plastic box with a picture of her dog on it. And she says, "This is Mopsie. She's a purebred Pomeranian." I hated that dog, by the way, so glad when it died. Little worm-infested—always chewed up my— anyway, she opens the box. "Mopsie eats only the finest cuts of meat and pure vegetables. Mopsie made this for all of you."

She takes tongs and sets down one perfect little roll of Mopsie shit on each piece and stares at us. Like little tootsie rolls with rice noodles embedded in—dead worms, you see? And win or lose, eating this means a trip to the doctor's office. You can't succeed without eating a little shit. That's what my father always told me.

It was too much for the guy across from me. He pushes the plate away. The first failure. He starts to curse the Triumvirate, ask them what the hell they thought they were doing, if they knew who he was, who his father was, and in come the Samoans, you know, dragged him out and things got quiet.

The Tertius stands at the podium, and points a finger at the guy's lady. She's dressed in the blue, right? And he says, "NAME?" nice and loud, and I swear I saw a little squirt of piss shoot down her leg. And she says, "Savannah."

"Expendable."

The Samoans are back. One grabs her arms, handcuffs her. The other puts this ball gag in her mouth, and then they chain her neck to the iron loop on the empty wall. Put a big spotlight on her.

"That's a sight," I say. Got the Primus to smile at that. Always try to make friends. Read the room.

"Three remain," the Primus says. "Crimson has proven her breeding. One woman can be a worthy ally and a fierce adversary. A group of women can be insurmountable. Where Crimson leads, the others will follow. Present the next challenge."

And I'm thinking, wow, I got the good one, right? She won, she gets to go again. And the other two women look nervous. Like maybe they're all playing a game too, and Ursula's on the brink of winning their end or something?

"Dinner tonight was splendid," Ursula says. "Seven delicious courses." The butler brings out another pizza, this one just bread. Nothing else on it. But it's deep-dish style, right? It looks like a giant bread bowl almost. Our women move back to us and sit in our laps. And even with everything we'd been through, feeling that ass in those silky panties on my—anyway, they sit.

"Our compliments to the chef," Ursula says, and she sticks two fingers down her throat, and everything she ate earlier that night comes back. Chowder, some pineapple cake chunks, the oysters Rockefeller, escargot—whole fuckin' snails, the poi thing, man, the smell of that, and sauce, wine, she stops and pumps her stomach again—like a cat with a hairball— I mean this was Chicago-Style. Just *gallons* sloshing and—I'm just feeling her ass clench every time she retches and watching her ribs expand and lurch as she pours it all out. And it was almost sexy. Almost. I think she's done, but no! The potatoes, more wine, the lamb with mint sauce and jelly like green chunky toothpaste, and all of it's in this perfect cone on the pizza, and then to top it off—how did she do—a perfectly whole pineapple ring from the cake. Like she saved it just, *bam* on top.

And the smell?

The Primus looked at me and said, "You shall begin. The next man to eat may allow his woman to add to the feast. The game continues."

Ursula looks at me, just … the other women, they're all over their guys, right? Rubbing thighs, shoulders, nuzzling their ears—I mean, they all got a shot of mouthwash first, but—they look like they're pleading for their lives. Not Ursula. She's got this gaze of steel, just looks at me and says "Do this. You will do this now."

Her eyes are wet and wild, like she's somewhere between crying and orgasm, her crotch is like a dripping furnace sitting there on my thigh, and she's just *animal* and I dove in. I can't explain it, and I know she looks a little tough now after all the surgeries, and who cares, you don't worry how the car you sold twenty years ago looks now—I mean, back then, she was *something*. I don't know how to—and I mean, it's just food. That's all I thought. It's all just food.

I swallowed. Tried not to chew. Terrible. It was like chili. The bile made it taste like old sausage—but the other two guys, it took them another five minutes to even start. I thought I won, for the longest time, I thought, this is it, Steed, you win. But then another guy, the guy across from me, chows through a bite. So his woman gets to puke on the pizza too, and now it's down to the third man. That's all they ever wanted us to do, right, just a bite. That's the big thing. The hesitation. They want you to get over the—but the last guy, he couldn't do it. He went to push the plate away, got some of puke on his fingers, and then *he* puked, everywhere. Bam, in come the Samoans, *boom* out he goes.

"NAME," the Secundus, this time, stands up. And the woman, this is the lady in purple, she says, "Posey." And she looks so sad, like a pale little flower. That was the first time I felt sad that night. She's crying right, because same thing, here comes the Samoans, the handcuffs, then they force a piece of puke pizza into *her* mouth, then the ballgag, and *bam*, chained to the wall.

"The game continues," the Primus says. "When your competitor falls, it is up to you to utilize his assets."

I don't know why it was worse to know a man's puke was part of this soup now, but Ursula did this thing with her palm, like cupping my—you know—and instant, I mean *instant*, like Viagra has nothing on—and so I took a bite. Unbroken eye contact until I swallowed. And the other guy whispered, called me an asshole, and he took a bite too.

It's just me and him. Eyes watering, trying not to lose it. Ursula in red. His woman in green.

The Primus smiles and says, "Blood and money are the finalists. Names?"

"Ursula," Ursula says.

"Amalie," the lady in green says. Pretty name, I'd never heard it before. Usually you hear AHM-uhlee, but she was AM-alee. Cute girl. Great ass.

"Tanner Steed," I said, offering the other guy my hand. I guess I can tell you, it was Colton Northcutt. Remember him, ran for president a few years ago? Anyway, he goes to shake, and I did this thing, you know my trick, pump twice, and pull them in. Got his whole forearm in that puke pizza. He knew who was in control. You have to break them.

The Primus says, "Loyalty and Ambition will provide *il corso principale.*"

The big guys come in, real careful, and take that table out. Didn't spill a drop out of that puke-soup pie. They bring in a new table. White marble, unfinished. That's when I noticed the walls for the first time. Same white marble. Like big tiles, all with these abstract color designs on them. Reds and browns. A year inscribed at the bottom of each one. Little plaque with a name—a woman's name, I would later learn. You see where this is—Ursula in red and Amalie in green sit at the table, staring at each other. The butler sets two empty wine glasses next to a new empty pizza. New pizza, new table. Thin crust. No toppings. No plates. Not even a pan under the pie.

"The gentlemen will pour," the Primus says.

The butler hands us these knives, like little syringes. Or funnels. Like big tubes of … and we couldn't figure out what to do with them, but the Samoans come back, and they unchain the two ladies from the wall. Savannah and Posey. Bend them over the table, yank back on their hair, their necks are just hovering above the wine glasses. They're panting through those ballgags, just frothing and moaning and crying. And the veins on their necks jump up and, just coated in sweat, and you know they're in their little underwear, and this whole thing is kind of sexy until the one Samoan holding Savannah looks at me and his eyes go to the weird knife-funnel thing, and he says, "Sir, will you pour?"

He tapped a finger on the vein in her neck.

I looked at Colton across the table. Looked at Amalie and Ursula, but they only had their eyes on each other. I push the needle into the side of Savannah's neck and—have you ever popped champagne on New Year's? You know? Just ... everywhere! Sprayed everywhere! Everything's red, Ursula and Amalie in their little underwear, just soaked and the Samoan is kind of helping me, right, guiding my hand, keeping the funnel pressed in so that I fill up one wine glass with Savannah.

And Colton, in for a penny, in for a pound. They didn't—and see, this is the thing with power, they didn't even have to explain to us exactly what we were playing for here, it just made sense—so Colton pops Posey's neck, and she—maybe she's dehydrated, she's not a squirter like the other one, and she pours out, one glass, and the Samoans grab the ladies by the nape of the neck, haul them out of the room, like meat. Empty boxes. I thought they were taking them out back to ditch the bodies, but—can you believe it—I actually saw Posey at a function a few years later. She couldn't really look me in the eye. Fucks like a rabbit though, little—anyway—they're gone, right? Now, it's the big deal. Colton and I toast each other and take a sip.

The Triumvirate stands. The butler announces, "The game will conclude!"

The jury stands, and shit, I'd forgotten they were there this whole time. The judges have their hoods off. And they all start saying their names, full names, names you'd know! Cereal companies, newspaper barons, cattlemen, oil magnates, you name it.

Fortune. They said their name followed by a woman's name. Not the women they married. Not a woman I'd ever heard of. You'll see in a minute.

"Appetizers have finished. Each woman has hidden a gold ring. The game concludes when an entrée is prepared and served and the ring is found," The Primus says. God I wish I was allowed to tell you his name, it's gonna blow your—anyway.

The butler lays a sword on the table. A real, god-damned ancient … I mean not like a big broad—just like a little curved— an Egyptian dagger thing. I'm standing on one side of the table, Colton's on the other. Ursula to my left. Amalie to my right. The big Samoans are holding them with a short leash. All of this in an eyeblink, mind you, I see their stomachs, bare skin, I see the veins in their necks, smell the sweat, and I just get it. Dinner. It's my job to serve.

So I go to grab the sword, and Colton realizes it too, but I'm faster. All he can do is watch. I swing for the fences, just *hi-yah!* right into Amalie's midsection. Cut it wide open in one—like a piñata! But instead of a bunch of little spic kids running around grabbing candy, it's just me and Colton watching Amalie *literally* spill her guts onto the table. And the Samoans help. White glove service. They're just delicately guiding her large intestine out onto the blank pizza pie, piling it like spaghetti, and it's just—you can see what she ate *moving* in there, right? Even after the puking! Still so much food left. Pulsing and squeezing, and they just keep feeding organs out. Liver, kidney, spleen, stomach and this is a *mess* I tell you.

"The ring is presented!" the Tertius shouts. "Claim your prize."

And the ring—they said she hid one, remember? Way down in her intestine, I see this hard little outline, kind of round on one side, flat on the top. She swallowed it this little film canister thing, see? The ring has the seal of—well, you see it here on my finger. I can't tell when Amalie died. Maybe it was fast. Probably. I mean, her head was rolling back and forth, mouth open, eyes like glass. You get disemboweled, you can't really scream. It was like bad opera. Embarassing. That was the—I can't describe it. I saw her soul leave, and whatever was left was staring at me, and all I thought—and I said this out loud—was, *I deserve this.*

"Will you serve?" the Primus asked.

I took the sword and cut a piece of pizza. I don't know when they led Colton out of the room, but it's just me at the table with Ursula, chewing this other woman's guts. Ursula had to eat too. They all ate. All of the jury, the Triumvirate, they all came down and took a bite, like this is the best buffet they've ever—And they're all applauding us, and Ursula's crying like Miss Fucking America, covered in blood, and shit, and filth, and she takes my hand, and I'm—I mean normally I'd tell them to take this bitch out and give her a bath, but this was a *moment*, you understand?

I took her hand, and I looked her in the eye, and I kissed her. And I swear if the challenge would have gone further, I would have sat her bare ass in that pile of guts on that pizza and fucked her, right there, that's how happy I was. Because I understood everything.

But it didn't come to that. I don't want you to think I *actually*—Anyway. That was my dinner that night. That was my entrée into fortune. The *Festa dei Burattinai.* These days, they make fun of me in the press for eating bland food. Steak and ketchup. Simple things. They have people working at restaurants. They test you. They slip in little pieces of things sometimes. And if you're eating fancy food, you might miss it. I want the flavor to stand out. The sacred organs. Liver. Kidney. Hearts. Guts. It reminds me who I am and what I'm capable of. The flavor of life.

You have to meet the right people. And you have to eat a little shit. I told you it takes guts. Didn't say whose. Your job, your only job tonight, is to come back here with my daughter on your arm. Full, and happy, and content. Fortune favors the bold.

THE ORANGE MENACE

MATT PANFIL
[woodcut]

LEADER OF THE FREE WORLD

MATT PANFIL
[short film]

FETAL ATTRACTION

AMANDA WORTHINGTON

RONNIE WAS CONCERNED WHEN IT HAPPENED the first time, devastated when it happened the second, and only mildly surprised when it happened the third. They were on the 10th administration and Liz was pregnant again. It was kind of their thing now, to create life as death creeped in at the edges of their miserable existence. She was done after this one; she'd said so herself. Securing Trump's blessing was no longer enough.

The lone shelf in the room started to shake. It held not books but a long series of participation trophies, signifiers of the Immortal One's undying gratitude for her sacrifice. There were nine of them now and soon, gods willing, there would be a tenth.

There had been ten Trump administrations in the way that there were five oceans. It was really one continuous thing divided up so that our brains could comprehend it, something infinite made measurable. Because if you could still account for space and time, there was hope. It was always the unfathomable that defeated you. If it could be measured, then perhaps it could be tamed, and if it could not be tamed, then perhaps it could be bargained with.

"Ronnie! Did you hear me, you fucker? I said, it's *time!*"

Liz's screeching voice tore him from his reverie, and he took a deep breath, collected himself, and then said calmly,

"I'll call the Collector at once."

TRUMP HAD HEARD THE RUMORS of the Liminal Fuckspace. Of course he had. As far as he was concerned, it was a kind of euthanasia, a hospice for the sex-starved losers who welcomed defeat. He was a winner though, had in fact won more than any other human in the history of winning. Even the flies that buzzed expectantly around his head thought so.

Thwap. Agent 29 killed another of the buggers with a well-executed swing of his swatter. He's have been a good ball player in another life.

"What would I do without you, 29. Say, is the shipment here yet? I'm ravenous and does my face look tight enough to you?" The statement ended in a petulant question the way it always did.

"Well, Sir, there's a bit of sag but I think it should hold."

29 swallowed deep. He always felt on edge when he spoke the truth. Trump turned to him and smiled grotesquely.

"What about now? Is it more noticeable?"

Something writhed underneath, like trapped worms desperately trying to surface.

"I'll see to your breakfast at once. Some of the tributes will certainly have arrived by now. Any special requests?"

Trump had taken to playing with one of the squirming things in his cheek like a child with one of those motor learning toys with the fish inside the gel.

"Fat and fully formed. One of the loud ones. I suspect the steak a few weeks back was a quiet preemie. It didn't go down easy, and I had a weird rash for a week."

29 bowed and nodded. "Of course, Sir."

"THIS ONE IS PERFECT. Liz Monroe of Apple Valley's baby, you say? She always does good work. I'm not sure how she makes the money last for four years. We've got women with offerings every nine months. But good on her. They're always solid specimens."

The collector smiled wanly. "Monroe is one of the good ones. As you know, Marie is her sister from the before-times. She's asked if we might pass along a note to her." The collector withdrew a small, folded square of paper from his pocket. "I've checked it already for compliance. Could you see that she gets it?"

29 hefted the fat baby. It had to be nine or ten pounds. Its mouth rooted uselessly for milk and it banshee-screeched in protest. Marie Devereau would make quick work of it. He smiled, took the folded paper in his free hand.

"Of course."

THE BABY WAILED from its place in the waiting basket next to the knives. Marie stopped its mouth with a small plum from the fruit bowl, and then she read the poem that graced the page.

Sweetest sister from the Long-ago
Trump shall taste my tribute and be too moved to speak
Raise his glass of blood merlot
Yearn for more of the precious meat
Cut and roast, with me in mind
Heap in the spice, pure as mother's milk
Nobly serve the lord my final crop refined
I'll see you soon at the fort we built
Now burn my words, along with your pain
Every promise, no matter how long ago made ... will be fulfilled

TEN LINES. An ode to the tenth election, the outcome of which had never been in doubt, not even for an instance. A final offering. A message of hope from a sister that had always jokingly called her the Silencer of Children, first for her older-child tendency to shush, and then for her affinity for comfort, and now. Now she supposed she silenced children to keep women fed. Progression.

Marie caressed the packet taped to the underside of the paper. One thing was certain in this world of unknowns. She would treasure these words for all the days still left to her.

TRUMP SMILED and the worms shook in fear as the dish was placed before him.

"It screamed almost nonstop. I also received word that the mother was very miserable while pregnant, nightly begged God and Satan both to take it out of her, wrote in her dream journal of bashing its head in," Marie intimated with a tight smile.

"Unwanted babies are simply divine. I can't wait. Thank you, my dear. You can go." Trump waved her away and turned his full attention on the plate before him. It was heaped with fragrant meat and peppered eggs, fresh bread with butter rendered from the tribute's fat. It smelled like resurrection. The things under Trump's skin were pressed flat as his skin firmed, cementing them in their temporary prison. There they waited. There were not enough babies to sustain him forever. Soon they would have the space to wriggle again.

At first 29 thought it was just another quake. They were common enough these days. The shelves did not tremble though. The other furniture in the space was stable. The only shaking was coming from Trump's body convulsing on the table.

"Mr. President!" he cried, springing into action. He grabbed his phone from his belt.

"I need a medic *stat!*"

29 turned his attention to the kitchen. Marie. Loyal, efficient Marie. How could she?

"Marie!"

29 thrust the doors to the kitchen open and found the space abandoned.

THE RATS WERE BACK in droves. Ronnie had brought it to her attention that they had apparently gone through their stores of the toxic powder that kept them away. The dead amassed in the streets and the vermin grew fat and fearless and now they shared space with the Monroes.

Liz accepted their cohabitation with a weak smile. They couldn't eat the things and expect to live to tell about it. They had the rancid meat of the street-corpses in their teeth still. Ronnie had taken the intrusion worse, went out looking for cats some-times. Like anyone had seen one in the last decade. It was a fool's errand, but it made him feel useful. Men needed to feel useful. They couldn't birth bartering chips as women could. Liz bore his mounting insanity with amazing dignity, she thought.

But the time of bearing children and men's ineptitude was coming to an end.

There had been a dead rat wedged beneath the door today. That happened sometimes. That was not the noteworthy thing. The noteworthy thing was the letter beneath it.

She had loosened the page from beneath the dead thing with an effort, opened it up on the kitchen table.

The text that greeted her was like coming home at long last.

> Congratulations. You have been accepted into the Liminal Fuckspace! You don't want the same old missionary action. No god ordained this penetration, but it's what you need. You need someone who can find the holes that don't yet exist, not really. But they'll exist someday, and the artful lover can find them, knead at them, find a way inside parts of you you can't even fathom.
>
> We're really into you, Liz. Or rather, we'd like to be. What do you say?
>
> Sign below to reserve your spot now. Act now and bring one friend of your choice!

Liz signed quickly, folded the page and shoved it into her pocket. Then she headed for the meeting place.

Somewhere her president spasmed in pain. Another temblor rattled the house. A different kind of trembling overtook Liz. Looking down, she saw that she was wet.

Liz smiled. And then she stepped out of the wretchedness of her old life and into the promise of a death filled with pleasure.

UNNAMED

DOMINIQUE HECQ

YOU LISTEN to the black dog in your sleep speaking of dreams-capes of peril. It lists litanies of murderous melodies that make your blood boil. The is a fist of kindling scraping your veins running away from blood clots and / or fleeing the nightmare's crumbling teeth that cripple your mouth. You wake tight-jawed to a wagging of no no no that's all there is to contain time.

You limp through murderous alleys, each step marking night's forgotten scars down to the underpass where the dog turns to wolf. Cinder rain pours from eye-sockets. Coats inaudible words. Your feet walk you past numbered urns to the back of the grave-yard where garbage collectors, roofers and hooligans wild as the new weather stand next to tiny white crosses with scattered dates from memory lane. Sleeves rolled up, they tell you how the dead were born from their blood and bones.

Qué calor la vida. The stink of it.

Now you can see it, the wall. It is crimson and dripping.

THE FREEDOM FACTION

GORDON LINZNER

IN HIS TODT HILL BASEMENT, Arnold Trent called the Freedom Faction meeting to order. A handful were there in person; scores more attended on an oversized zoom screen.

"We have a single priority," he growled. "Our leader, Ronald Boldfinger, though still running for President, is in the Tombs prison, awaiting trial. The woman responsible, Auntie Evie Franklin, whoever—whatever—she is, must be stopped."

"Agreed!" shouted Dan Grogan, loudest of the attendees. "That witch interferes in everything we stand for. Benny lost an eye, attempting to bomb that synagogue and blame the Moslems. Jerry tried convincing a group in Harlem to start looting when he vanished, we still don't know where. As for Alex ..."

Grogan never used one word where twenty would do. Tortoni wished mute buttons worked in person.

"Minor quibbles. This Auntie person is undercutting all our programs. The question is, what do we do about her?"

"That's what I said," Grogan interrupted. "Add that fiasco at the high school, and ..."

Tortoni threw a ballpoint pen at Grogan. Not as effective as muting, but still satisfying.

"I was about to say," Tortoni went on, "we have our answer. Professor Spanopokis, zooming tonight from New Rochelle, is an expert in the mystic arts. He spent weeks studying Franklin's activities. I now turn the platform over to him. Full screen."

Grogan started to open his mouth.

"I will also mute our computer mics. We want to, need to, hear what the professor has to say."

Few attendees understood the professor's words. Tortoni gave a simplified summary afterwards. Spanopokis claimed Franklin's powers came from an amalgam of mystical endeavors, reaching back to ancient Egypt and early China. Mixing bits of Catholicism, Protestantism, Islam, Jewish studies, et al—in short, all of the world's religions, exact opposite of what the Freedom Faction hoped to accomplish—she refined her abilities.

Though it pained them to do so, the Faction would need to work together against these elements.

"With our help," Tortoni concluded, "the Professor can confront Franklin directly."

"How? Have our people call her people?"

Tortoni ignored Grogan's comment. His own grin filled the screen. "We create an event she can't ignore."

THE FREEDOM FACTION collected over fifty protesters to rally in Columbus Park, near The Tombs. Despite every bent rule Boldfinger's supporters used to protect their candidate, Evie Franklin's powers had gotten the man confined, awaiting trial for embezzlement, power abuse, sexual assault … a long list.

Despite which, he still might be voted into office.

Outwardly, the Freedom Faction appeared to simply protest the candidate's arrest, but they wanted the attention of a particular person. Their hand-made signs contradicted each other; the group's chants made little sense.

"They Had it Coming!"

"Go Back to Home!"

"Blue Lives Matter!"

The latter was directed at the police standing beside barricades erected to keep the crowd under control. The officers were not impressed.

No one—not protestors, police, curious onlookers or resentful neighbors—noticed Franklin slip through the barricade into the park. The woman in black was not visible, until she was. Her cold blue eyes glared down from the balcony of a pavilion at the park's northern end.

The chants faded.

Police tensed.

"Look at yourselves!" Franklin did not shout, yet her words

resounded through the park and down nearby narrow streets.

"You protest the imprisonment of a man who did evil acts! Who shows no remorse. Who brags about his crimes to his fellow inmates. His punishment may serve as a lesson to the world." Her voice lowered. "Your own, not so much."

The protesters grumbled.

"Disperse. Go home. Think about what you do."

The crowd shifted, allowing Professor Spanopokis to step forward and confront the woman in black.

"Your tricks will not work on us, Auntie Franklin," the professor countered. "We are true believers. We will not be kept from doing God's work. I trained these warriors to resist your power, turn it against you. This day, you shall die."

The surrounding police officers stiffened at the death threat. Still, the crowd appeared weaponless, milling about rather than assaulting the tall, heavy-set woman on the balcony. Her own attitude said 'wait and see.'

"My policy is to give but one warning," Franklin replied.

"And our policy to give none!" shouted Tortoni, joining the professor. "We end this charade now! Fellow Factioners ..."

"I thought we were Factionators," whispered Freddy Grogan.

"The minds of half a hundred of us now work together, to stop you forever!" Tortoni screamed.

Auntie Franklin felt the balcony tremble underfoot. She stepped back, her cloak swirling about, black against black.

Fifty minds, and more, sought to overwhelm her own.

Fifty untrained minds.

Fifty very stupid minds.

Franklin shook off their combined energies as one would an annoying fly, to reclaim her position on the balcony.

"I offer a history lesson," she announced.

"She's not dead!" Tortoni looked at the Professor. "Why isn't she dead?"

The Professor shrugged, mouth agape.

"This area was the site of Kolch Pond," Franklin continued. "The English colonists anglicized it to Collect Pond, their main source of fresh water on Manhattan Island."

The police and onlookers stepped back, leaving a gap of several yards around the Freedom Faction.

"Now," the woman in black concluded, "the long-drained pond shall live up to its name."

Concrete pathways cracked and shattered, blocking the protesters. Water bubbled up from the gaps.

Most of the crowd sank beneath ground level, with barely time to scream. A few near the edges tried to swim free.

A giant serpent rose from the depths, quickly ending that.

The event lasted under a minute; the park quickly returned to normal. As a side benefit, litter had been cleared away.

"They've dispersed?" the Police Captain asked no one in particular. What occurred was so fantastic, so quick, even those observing could not believe it. They put their own, rational, spin on the events.

"They have been dispersed," the woman in black acknowledged, confirming the onlookers' version.

Auntie Evie Franklin leaned against a pillar, eyes shut, hood drooping forward. Until today, she'd only encountered such heartless humans singly, or in groups of four or five at most. Dealing with half a hundred fools at once was exhausting.

She gave a thin smile. This should at least give pause before the next such situation. She could use the rest.

She did not expect to relax for long. The world held no shortage of hateful stupidity.

SCARS

TEEL JAMES GLENN

THE HOLE INSIDE

My soul
That hollow, writhing
Spot
Was torn and twisted
Out of me
By life, luck
And a lot—
Too many lies and
Long goodbyes
And traitor loves
Who stabbed
Me
So why I still have
Hope in me
Is a mystery
To ponder
As through this fucked up life
I continue on
To wander.

I AM NOT AN INCUBATOR

JO KAPLAN

MY BODY is not an oven for your dinner. My body is not a refrigerator for your leftovers. My body is not a vessel for you to possess or a tool for you to use or a thing to be exploited.

My body is not a toy for your pleasure. It is not a cocoon for your transformation. It is not soil for your seed. It is not an object for your amusement.

My body is not land for you to conquer, dominate, subjugate.

My body does not belong to you or to anyone else.

I am my body.

I am more than my body.

If something unwanted begins to grow inside you, what do you do? Is your body no longer yours to command? Do you let the growing thing consume you, or do you excise it before it metastasizes? Just because something *can* grow in my body does not mean I have to allow it. You do not get to force me to host a parasite, nurture a tumor, or accept another being using me without my consent. No one is allowed to use another's body without their consent. You may not come in if you are not invited. In this way, vampires may be considered the most cordial of men.

My body is not a house for you to furnish or demolish at your whim.

You ask, what is a woman? A woman is many things, and she is more than her body, what her body does, what her body can do. You may as well ask, what is a person? What is this curious combination of mind and matter that creates a single identity? We are all miraculous, living, thinking bags of meat. The details may differ but the architecture is the same. I am more like you than I am unlike you.

My body is not a puppet to be manipulated into dancing for you. My body is not a water balloon for you to toss until it breaks.

You have long suffered this desire to control that which is not yours. What selfish cruelty drives this? What cowardice? The belief that if you do not conquer, dominate, subjugate, then you will be conquered, dominated, subjugated? Does that make you feel small? Does that make you want to do anything to feel large again? Is that why you hate me with such ferocity—because I make you feel the way you have made women feel for thousands of years?

I am not evil simply because I don't want to use my body the way you think I should. I am not deranged simply because I've decided to live my life how I like, in a way that does not conform to your stunted understanding of value and purpose. I won't shrink myself to fit the expectations of smallminded men.

I have no desire to control your body. Do me the same courtesy.

Your body is not mine.

My body is not yours.

SELF-PORTRAIT

STEVIE L. MORLEY

[acrylic]

ALL ABOARD THE TRAITOR EXPRESS

LINDSEY GODDARD

SO DAWNS THE HOUR WHEN WE ARRIVE at a station
Between two tracks. Where they lead, we can't see.
And each man with a hope or a dream for his nation
Must board a train toward his chosen destiny.

A horn softly bleats; a whistle moans, as if crying,
As an old train to your left is starting up.
Truth be told, as it starts, it sounds more like it's dying,
Its rattly engine like dice in a cup.

Some folks boarding this train look in need of a meal,
Holes in their clothes and pain etched on their brows.
You imagine this pain will take a long time to heal,
And you'd rather feel relief right here and now.

The conductor announces as he leans out,
"This train needs a tune-up, and its track, some repair,
But each passenger who rides will pitch in, no doubt,
And fix things together until we make it there.

The place we are going is a safe space for all,
No matter their gender, abilities, or race,
But the track may be broken, and the engine may stall,
So we don't plan to get there with haste."

A horn to your right drowns out this man's voice
With its blaring, beseeching, boastful call,
And you turn away from the left (not a difficult choice),
For the train to your right has it all.

You can tell lots of money was spent here—a ton.
Not a speck of rust shows on its parts, all brand new,
And there are not people waiting to enter this one
Who appear so awfully different from you.

ALL ABOARD THE TRAITOR EXPRESS

The passengers seated in its gleaming cars
Are well-groomed, well-off, and wear a smile.
And though it seems too picture-perfect, your intuition ran afar
When you chose the well-worn path of denial.

So you climb aboard the ritzy train to your right.
The door slams shut, and the lock clicks behind you.
Suddenly your stomach flips at the unnerving sight
Of every set of eyes turning to find you.

I guess you didn't know this train was built for the elite.
Reservation only, its members never change.
You'll soon discover that there's rarely an open seat
And they eat sheep like you for meals aboard this train.

Alas, progress scares you. It has moved too quickly,
Reshaping the world, by which you can't abide,
But these mouths are watering, as they lick their lips, sickly.
For it's the biggest smiles which have the most to hide.

DAMNATIO MEMORIAE

BRACKEN MACLEOD

I WANTED TO FORGET. That night before bed, I'd counted on the wish that tomorrow we could all begin to release him from our minds. A psychic cleansing. I imagined him retreating to Truth Social and Fox News and never standing at the Bully Pulpit again. No utterance of his ever reached my comprehension with my consent, and I *needed* the sound of his voice saying all the vile things he'd uttered with such confidence to wither and fade as distant soundbites from history. Testament only to his untrammeled arrogance and unfitness to serve. I had gone down into sleep fearful from experience, but naïvely hopeful. Dreaming the better angels of our nature would prevail.

I don't believe in angels.

The next morning, I awoke and checked my phone before even climbing out of bed. There I saw a single small emoji sent at five a.m. in a group chat we'd begun the night before and *knew*. Yellow circle, round black eyes, no mouth. The memetic distillation of horror in its simplest form. The feeling that tiny collection of pixels inspired should not have been so overwhelming. It's an emoji—an un-language that speaks without nuance. It's hard to convey sarcasm or irony in a text, so we supply it with sunny derangements of Harvey Ball's 1963 ideogram. This time, there was no "Have a nice day!" implied. No reassuring tone of *I'm only joking*. This face had no mouth, and I must scream.

In 2016, pundits said he'd grow into the office. That the guardrails of our institutions and the separation of powers would hinder him from the worst of his impulses. They'd meant he'd mature into the role of statesman and leader. Instead, he grew into the office like a tumor, a corrupting presence in the body politic emboldening the worst among us. He grew into the role like a stochastic cancer, sickening our discourse and withering decency. He gave license to a viewpoint long chased away into the shadows where it could be dismissed as a fringe extremity—*not who we are*. He shone like a hot sun exposing that lie. This is who we are. It's who we were in Charlottesville and at the Capitol. It's who we've always been, though we'd locked it away for a while, telling ourselves we're better now. Kinder, gentler.

To the contrary, he's made us all a little meaner.

Even the look of him challenges my convictions. Vulgarity oozes from his smug expressions, his mocking gestures. Invective spews from lips that purse like the core dimple on the underside of an orange rind (a much kinder simile than what I really think). I remind myself his derision and bodily mocking are things he *does*. I can hate them with a clear conscience because it is a contempt of substance, not appearance. And yet, I can't stand the sight of his stained face and dyed hair and his poorly tailored clothes, unbefitting a man of his means. He is a book whose cover is a perfect realization of content and quality.

Part of me wants to think I don't know how there are people who don't see that. How is it the faces of the people who adore him, who stand in the rain for hours, in humid airport hangars and sweltering arenas to behold him, are rapt with admiration? They look up and beg to be fed by the embodiment of everything antithetical to their professed faith. The truth is as long as he says the things they think in their darkest moods, hates the same people they do, they swell full. What had once been a bewildering "How was that not the end of it?" now seems that they'd been waiting for someone to come give them license to be their worst selves. They know him for who he is and choose to defy the disinfecting power of sunlight and stand openly in the day, resplendent in his corruption.

Having seen that emoji, I knew I needed to resist the obsessive urge to read every single news report. The same need overwhelmed me September 2001, after the Boston Marathon in 2013, when Dobbs overturned Roe in 2022. Doomscrolling until the day is gone and I've forgotten to look up at the faces of my wife and son. Faces that need to connect with mine, to see we're all here together, and we'll get through this somehow because we have no other choice. But how does one look away from the horror? It's not fear of missing out, but a fear of being caught out, unprepared for what's to come. I had to recharge my phone at midday and again at bedtime. Same the next day.

I was so heavily invested in forgetting. I desired the damnation of memory. Done with his face and name and that fucking voice. I wanted more than anything else to let go of how it feels to lose faith in all the things that were once sacred to me as a young lawyer with dreams of slaying dragons. The Supreme Court. Congress and the Presidency. The integrity of the law itself. All poised for ruin in the slouch toward slaking the insatiable thirst of one man for attention, power, wealth, and the debasement of everyone not himself.

To forget is to prove how hollow campaign slogans really are.

And yet she persisted.

I'm with her.

We won't go back.

It's the same privileged luxury as believing this is not who we are. This *is* who we are. And we must be better. Failing that is abandoning the values and ideals, and most importantly, the *people* we profess to love. While I do not believe in gods or angels, I believe there is somewhere in us a better nature, if we don't forget to be each others' angels.

ADDRESS ON THE MALL

INDRAN AMIRTHANAYAGAM

IT'S BRAVE, my friend, the weave.
where it has led us. We've got
the sheep ready to be fleeced.

The shepherds are dropping
their staffs and picking up
knives and cutlasses. This

is going to be a rich red
feast unlike any other since
Biblical times. And these

my friend are truly end
of game preparations.
We're going to celebrate

the greatest offering the Mall
has ever consecrated, a sea
of red on red, bigger than

the Red Sea and bigger
even than the crowd
in 2017. Sweet liberty

friends, sweeter revenge.
and I am lost no more.
I am found: Y. M. C. A.

CONFESSION

INDRAN AMIRTHANAYAGAM

I CONFESS I am Catholic
and I did not vote for
the sexual predator for president
who stacked the Supreme Court
with Catholics and catholic lovers.

I confess. I erred in my reading
of the pulse. I thought to decide over
one's body was a human right not one
for only God to decide. I am deeply
sorry for my sin, my inability to follow

the indirect of the Pope, God bless
his blessed soul, may he pronounce
again if the new president who
wants to heal the nation decides
to send Mexicans and Haitians,

and me, my valid passport
notwithstanding, across
the Rio Grande, Red River,
for those who don't
speak Spanish.

TACO TRUCK

NICK KOLAKOWSKI

SHE DOESN'T LOOK LIKE MUCH, Jesus sometimes mused, but she gets us through.

Under his baby's dented hood roared a Chevy 350 V8 capable of zero to sixty in a blistering twenty seconds, provided you pointed her down a steep hill. Inside the kitchen, the exhaust fan hacked and wheezed louder than a lifetime smoker running a marathon. But the electrical system kept the fridges under the prep counter running without a hitch, and the griddle could fry up pork and chicken like a champ, and that was good enough for Jesus.

Today's lunch spot: a mall parking lot in scenic Duke County, Kansas. As he propped open the taco truck's customer window, Jesus scanned the storefronts, half of which stood empty and boarded up. A big blue box store to his left spat customers every few minutes, their arms heavy with plastic bags. No fast-food places in sight meant more hungry patrons meant more money for gas, food, supplies. Enough to get them to the next state, at least.

Beside Jesus, Luis knelt and fiddled with the valve of a fresh twenty-pound propane tank, their second this week. Business had been good: the retail workers and idle kids who populated this winding stretch of subdivisions and retail strips loved their tacos.

In the front seats, the third partner in this little entrepreneurial venture, Raoul, spun the dial on the ancient dashboard radio. Every station blared a repeat of the Orange One's three-hour State of the Union address.

"This *puta* is everywhere," he muttered.

"It's the law," Jesus said. "They have to play the whole thing."

Through the crackling speakers, the Orange One launched into the most controversial part of his speech, something about dropping a nuke on *The New York Times* for releasing his tax returns. Jesus wasn't sure what bothered him more: the President threatening a newspaper with a missile, or the President comparing that missile to his manhood every few minutes.

"His *pene* is really like a little Cheeto," Luis said and laughed. "The color, the size …"

"Stop it," Jesus said. "That's not fair to Cheetos, a great food." He leaned out of the customer window, checking that the chalkboard pinned to the side of the truck had all the day's specials written on it. When they had started out a month ago, in New Orleans, they had no problem finding catfish and crab, and Jesus and Luis cooked up seafood tacos every day. This far inland, Jesus had a hard time trusting that anything with fins was fresh enough to meet his demanding standards. Their headliner special today: sizzling pork tacos with finely chopped onions and oregano.

Raoul had no opinion on the specials. In fact, Jesus had a hard time picturing Raoul on a prep line, or cooking meat without burning it to charcoal. Raoul's skills lay in other areas.

The Orange One's latest rant sputtered to its conclusion, replaced by regular programming. With a feral yelp, Raoul worked the dial until he landed on a station screeching drums and guitar, a solid backbeat for Luis and Jesus slicing and shoveling mounds of peppers and onions and pig. The music blasted the asphalt amphitheater of the parking lot, signaling that the truck was officially open for business.

The first customers drifted toward them. Give me your hungry, your nearly-broke, your masses yearning for lunchtime deliciousness, Jesus thought as he wiped his hands on his apron and prepared to handle the first of the lunch rush. And I'll give you two tacos for three dollars.

The fourth customer to the window was a teenage girl with neon-red hair pinned beneath a black baseball cap, dressed in a pair of paint-stained white overalls. She had enough metal studs in her face to set off a metal detector. "Two pork," she said, slapping three soft dollar bills on the counter.

"Sure," Jesus said, and threw a pair of tortillas on the griddle to heat.

"Where you guys from?" she asked.

"Miami," he said. "We're headed to Los Angeles. Little cross-country goodwill tour."

Luis shot him a dark look.

"Haven't had good Mexican in a long time," the girl said, her eyes drifting. "Even fake Mexican. There was one place, but it ..."

"It what?" Jesus asked, flipping the warm tortillas onto his workstation.

"Burned," she said to the pavement. "After the election."

Jesus tried to keep his tone friendly. "Accident?"

She shrugged. "You know."

"Know what?"

"Idiots." She glanced around the parking lot. "I'm cool, okay? But a lot of folks here are not."

Jesus pursed his lips as he handed over the steaming tacos. "Sure, you're cool," he said.

"I'm sorry," she muttered, before darting away with her food.

As he pocketed her money, Jesus turned toward Raoul, who slouched low in the passenger seat. Raoul had slid his sunglasses over his eyes, but Jesus could still read his thoughts in the twist of his mouth. He had overheard the girl's every word.

After she left, they had a few minutes without customers. Luis took the opportunity to jab his steaming spatula at Jesus.

"Why did you tell her?"

"We're not going to California," Jesus said.

"Not that part, man. What's with the 'goodwill tour' crap?"

Jesus shrugged.

"We're on a mission," Luis said, shaking his head. "Operational security, remember that? It means not even joking."

Jesus jutted his chin toward the parking lot.

"Speaking of missions."

A mini-van cruised slowly along the access road that ran behind the mall, disappearing behind the box store for a minute before slithering back into view. It veered into a wide turn, approaching the taco truck from the flank. As it closed in, Jesus saw the scratches in the fender and hood, the blue paint sun-faded and mottled like the skin of an old lizard. He felt the muscles in his legs tense, his stomach twist itself into a knot.

The van stopped and its doors opened, disgorging three men who looked like suburban dads gone to seed. They were balding, and out of shape, but their eyes burned with high-octane rage. For a moment they stood in a line beside their vehicle, arms crossed over their chests, and the image almost made Jesus bark with laughter. Hey, he wanted to yell, it's the world's softest gangsters. Want some tacos?

Out of the corner of his eye, he noted Luis gripping a long-bladed knife in his left hand, just out of sight beneath the counter. Jesus raised an eyebrow. *Not now.*

Raoul inched upright in his seat, watching in his side mirror as the men strode for the customer window.

One, a portly gentleman with a graying widow's peak, wore a faded 'Trump That Bitch' T-shirt. The beefiest one, in a red polo shirt fraying at the collar, had the ruddy cheeks and broad shoulders of a high-school football champion well past his prime.

"Can I help you gentlemen?" Jesus asked, keeping his smile fixed very wide.

"Yeah, um, can I get six tacos? Three pork, three beef?" asked Polo Shirt.

"Sure." Jesus cast a glance at the other three. "Anything else?"

They shook their heads. The smallest, a runt with a scraggly wisp of a beard, stared at the sombrero painted on the side of the truck with sullen eyes. He had a bulge at his waistband that his shirt barely covered. The outline looked like a pistol grip.

While Luis spread out a couple servings of diced pork on the griddle, Jesus prepped boxes and napkins.

"You boys legal?" Polo Shirt asked.

"Born and raised in the U.S. of A," Raoul shouted from the front seat, loud enough to make everyone jump.

Jesus had done five years in the Marines, where he learned that tension was more than something you felt in your body. It was also something in the air, clear as a radio signal, that made your heart accelerate and your palms sweat. He sensed it now, beaming from the men as they paced in tight circles alongside the truck. The rest of the parking lot was empty as the lunch rush cycled down.

"What you doing here?" asked the one in the T-shirt.

"Goodwill tour," Jesus said, shooting a look at Luis. "Going from city to city, selling tacos. We started out in Atlanta. There's a lot of hatred and division in this country, you know, so we figured we'd go around, spread a little love."

Polo Shirt spat on the asphalt.

"You know what my Mama taught me," Jesus continued, his smile making his cheeks ache. "Way to someone's heart, it's right through their stomach. People can break bread together, they start to feel a little better about each other, you know?"

"I don't know about that," Polo Shirt said. "But I do know, you're not welcome here, you hear?"

"Here, hear?" Raoul called from his seat. "Hear, here?"

The man in the T-shirt spun on his heel, fists balled. "You dirty …"

Jesus raised his hands, palms out. "Gentlemen, please." Lowering his arms, he took three cardboard trays of tacos and set them on the counter outside the customer window, along with napkins. "We just want to feed you."

Polo Shirt took one of the trays, stepped back, and dropped it between his feet. Pork, vegetables, and sauce left a brightly colored splatter. Wiping his hands with theatrical flourish, he turned and headed for the mini-van without looking back. In other cities, that sort of thing had signaled the end of it: a flash of anger that would have stayed bottled up in a different society, followed by a screech of tires as the offender's vehicle headed for the nearest exit.

Only the Runt had other ideas. Unzipping his fly, he yanked out his acorn of a *puta* and proceeded to unleash a fragrant stream of piss on the side of the truck, swirling his hips as he did so. It reminded Jesus of a dog marking territory. When the yellow stream slackened, he stuffed himself back in his pants and trotted toward the van, where his buddies already waited in their seats.

Luis snatched up a blade and stomped for the rear doors of the truck, his hand on the handle before Jesus managed to grab his elbow. "No," Jesus muttered. "Live by the sword, die by the sword."

Swiping away his hand, Luis turned, his eyes wet. "Don't give me that shit," he said, loud, over the growl of the mini-van pulling away. "We're not peacemakers, man."

Jesus stepped back, shaking his head. "No, but we got a code."

"*Amigos*," Raoul called from the front. "We got company."

Jesus ducked his head through the customer window, expecting to see the mini-van circling back for round two. Instead it was the girl in the overalls, hands clapped to her cheeks as she trotted across the lot. "I saw," she said, arriving at the counter. "I'm so sorry. We weren't like this before."

"Who are those guys?" Luis asked.

"Just guys." She shrugged. "What can I say?"

Jesus pushed the two remaining trays of tacos in her direction. "Want some free food?"

THEY LEFT the parking lot at dusk. Following their usual plan meant sticking to secondary roads, followed by an overnight at any truck stop with a free berth. As their mobile kitchen groaned and wobbled its way to forty miles an hour, Jesus finished counting up the supplies and the cash from the afternoon. Eighty bucks from the pre-dinner rush. At this rate, they would have a nice little pile of money when they reached Chicago.

Luis drove, sticking to the speed limit in case any cops wanted to make their ticket quota for the month. "Should have let me take them," he shouted over the rattling dashboard.

"Little one had a gun," Jesus said. "And you know our rule."

"No starting shit unless someone starts shit first," Luis grumbled, enthused as a fifth grader in detention.

Jesus placed the cash in the lock-box on the top shelf, stepping over Raoul, who knelt to hook his fingers around a seam in the flooring. A lid hinged back, revealing a shadowy compartment.

"Van," Luis called out, jabbing a thumb over his shoulder.

Leaping to the rear doors, Jesus peered through the milky porthole at the blue van a couple car-lengths behind them, flashing its lights. The truck shuddered as Luis slammed on the gas, buying a little more distance, and the van responded by swerving briefly into the oncoming lane. They would try to pass the truck, maybe try to run them off the road, and that wouldn't do at all.

"They starting shit?" Raoul asked from the floor, elbow-deep in the compartment.

"Maybe," Jesus said.

The van's front passenger window hissed down, and an arm emerged. Jesus recognized Polo Shirt's red cuff. The thick hand at the end of the arm held a pistol, which flashed and boomed. They heard the bullet skip like a stone along the truck's left side.

"Yes," Jesus said, "they're starting shit."

Luis cursed, but Raoul flashed Jesus a genuine grin. You were supposed to tolerate bigots. Turn the other cheek, as the Savior once said. But when they tried to kill you—and so many of them did, these days—well, all bets were off.

With a nod from Raoul, Jesus flipped the lock, braced his foot against the rear door, and pushed as hard as he could. The door flopped open, held in place by the howling slipstream, and Jesus stepped back so Raoul could have an unobstructed view of the van. The driver—it was the Runt—had maybe a quarter-second to recognize the high-powered assault rifle in Raoul's hand before a full clip of armor-piercing rounds burst through the windshield, turning the interior into a mess of torn plastic, shattered glass, and premium ground long-pig.

Out of control, the van swerved off the road, leaving a plume of pale dust as it crashed down the weedy, littered slope.

Luis braked the truck onto the shoulder. Reaching into the compartment, Jesus retrieved his favorite shotgun and leapt out the rear door, following Raoul down the incline.

The impact had crumpled the van like an empty can of Coke. Jesus knelt and peeked inside, counting three dead men. A small doll of the Orange One, stuck to the dashboard with a suction cup, offered the destruction two hearty thumbs up.

Standing again, Jesus reached into his apron pocket and retrieved a small black notebook with a pen clipped to the front cover. On the latest page, he made three small marks, adding to the hundred on the preceding pages.

It was a long way between Mississippi and Chicago. A lot of territory to cover. A lot of love to spread, one way or another. It was too bad there couldn't be a taco truck like theirs on every corner, but Jesus liked to think they were doing their part to make America great again.

HELL IS EMPTY AND ALL THE DEVILS ARE HERE

ANONYMOUS

Inspired by *The Tempest* by William Shakespeare

WE ARE IN A SPECIAL KIND OF HELL
(or whatever this is)
where their promises are empty,
vows are heartless and
power-lust consumes them all.
what happened to the
American dream? flung aside by devils
who decided they are
the only ones entitled to thriving here.

NOW IS THE WINTER OF OUR DISCONTENT

KARUNA DAS

IN JUNE of 2020, when it seemed to me that the current POTUS might try to hold onto power through antidemocratic means, I wrote a short story set in a fictional country in which a president about to lose office had succeeded in doing just that. "Blood and Puppet Theatre" takes place in Freeland. That's the popular—and by then ironic—shorthand for the Federal Republic of Enlightened Existence. (A character notes that the name refers to the eighteenth-century ideals of the founders of the transparently near-future USA, not to mystical spiritual awakening.)

The events of January 6, 2021 proved my instincts right about Trump's intentions, if not his abilities to execute them at the time.

When the story was published that spring, what I wrote as a cautionary tale read more like a dodged bullet. The threat seemed to have been extinguished. Or at least it no longer felt so immediate. Idealist that I am, I even had faith the former president would be tried and convicted for his crimes.

I never imagined four years later that same would-be dictator would be reelected.

Appearing in the "Criminalization of Dissent" issue of a journal put out by a nonprofit organization dedicated to minimizing harm against marginalized communities, my story features a queer, nonbinary protagonist. Alongside their female partner, they operate a subversive theatre troupe that attracts the attention of both the autocrat and an agent—a Black woman—of an underground movement seeking to incite a revolution and restore democracy. The main conflict explores the roles of art, nonviolence, and compassion in combatting systematic oppression.

The protagonist recalls a role they played years before, having been cross-gender cast as a man in a college production of *Othello*, making an implicit comparison to their nation's leader:

Playing Iago really messes with you. You have to commit to embodying his sickening combination of cruelty, vulgarity, and egotism, unlike anything else in all of Shakespeare, if not all of drama. Until recently I would've added maybe even in all of humanity.

You also have to decide what motivates him to lie about essentially everything to essentially everyone, possibly including himself and the audience. He gives multiple, shifting reasons for his behavior, some of which seem credible (but invalid as justifications) and some of which seem made up on the spot. What does he have to gain from destroying so many lives? Is he simply a sociopath who gets off on others' suffering?

And then there's all the racist things he says. Do they reflect his actual beliefs, or are they feigned to exploit the racist attitudes of those around him? He certainly uses them that way.

Other characters ultimately see Iago as a monstrous departure from the norms of their culture. But he's really the epitome of them.

As I try to come to terms with the 2024 election results, I want to believe that flocks of voters supported Trump due to disinformation and ignorance about his economic and other policies. Yet I can't shake the feeling that *something* about the ugliness of Trump's behavior holds deep-rooted—perhaps subconscious—appeal to a broader swath of the American public than most of us prefer to acknowledge. I suspect that until we figure out how to purge those impulses from our collective identity, we will at best succeed in suppressing them for brief periods. People more qualified than me on the matter likely have ideas about how to do this. Early twentieth-century French theorist and artist Antonin Artaud sure did. See his collection of essays *The Theater and Its Double* for his vision. (FYI: He died in a psychiatric clinic at age 51.)

I'll stick to what insights we might glean into our current socio-political moment from one of my areas of expertise: literature, especially that written for the stage. I titled this piece with the opening line of another Shakespearean play, *Richard III*. That work dramatizes the final chapter of the Wars of the Roses, a lengthy series of real-life civil wars between the Houses of Lancaster and York, rival factions within the House of Plantagenet, over control of the English throne. Their respective colors were red and white rather than red and blue.

I'm sure I'm not the first to draw a parallel between Trump and Richard, just as others have no doubt compared him to the villain from *Othello*. In one obvious way it's a better fit: Richard becomes king. And he lies and schemes his way there. He also commits and orders murders. I won't allege killings have occurred directly at the hands or instructions of Trump. But it seems fair to say he's caused a lot of death through his (mis)handling of the COVID pandemic, his denial of climate science, and his fanning the flames of hate. I shudder to think what he might do now that he's been given the keys to the kingdom by the electorate and a Supreme Court ruling that grants him immunity from criminal prosecution for official acts. Later in that same opening speech, Richard tells the audience, "I am determined to prove a villain" (1.1.30), a line that calls to mind Trump's campaign promises to exact revenge on political opponents and employ other strongman tactics.

Despite what the protagonist of "Blood and Puppet Theatre" thinks about the challenge of embodying Iago, actors generally relish the opportunity to play either of these characters. Any psychic burden notwithstanding, the roles are showcases for their talents. What's more, having acted as one of Shakespeare's lesser villains—Iachimo in *Cymbeline*—myself, I'd suggest there's something liberating in performing "taboo" behaviors without the risk of any real consequences.

Here's how my protagonist describes their process:

> To portray a character truthfully, you have to see them from their point of view. Better still if you can feel empathy for them

or even find some aspect of them admirable or enticing. With Iago, the most obvious candidate for that is his skill as a manipulator, and especially his ability to dupe people into thinking he's on their side even as he works against them. For most of the play, until fires he's lit burn down everything and everyone around him, he proves himself to be an expert puppet master.

In the end, I managed to develop a kind of double consciousness. I identified with Iago's perspective and his talents even while I detached myself from his actions, and especially from their results.

Audiences derive great pleasure from watching that skillful manipulation. Both Iago and Richard tell the audience what they're up to. They're unapologetic about what they're doing. Part of us can't help but admire them, perhaps wishing we could get away with that kind of audacity, even if we're appalled by their actions. In the theatre, we know the harm they cause is not real.

Throughout the recent election campaign, I read accounts that many voters still didn't believe Trump meant the threats he made. Is there something about him in particular that creates this dissonance? Or are we living in such a technology-mediated world so inundated by images of violence and suffering that nothing seems real to people unless it impacts them firsthand?

If first-term Trump represented our Iago-in-Chief, lighting fires that eventually burned down everything around him, perhaps we can learn something from the final scene of *Othello* and what finally trips up Iago. He survives the play, unlike the insecure title character, innocent Desdemona, and others, although he's taken away to be tortured until he reveals the motives for his malignity. Yet he might've avoided exposure at all were it not for the insistence of his wife, Emilia, to defend the honor of her mistress Desdemona against the wishes of her husband.

EMILIA. Villainy, villainy, villainy!

> I think upon't, I think I smell't, O villainy!

> I thought so then: I'll kill myself for grief!

> O villainy, villainy!

IAGO. What, are you mad? I charge you, get you home.

EMILIA. Good gentlemen, let me have leave to speak.

> 'Tis proper I obey him—but not now.

> Perchance, Iago, I will ne'er go home.

[…]

EMILIA. O God, O heavenly God!

IAGO. Zounds, hold your peace!

EMILIA. 'Twill out, 'twill out! I peace?

> No, I will speak as liberal as the north.

> Let heaven and men and devils, let them all,

> All, all cry shame against me, yet I'll speak.

IAGO. Be wise and get you home.

EMILIA. I will not.

[Iago tries to stab Emilia.] (5.2.187-222)

After a final attempt to hush Emilia fails and she divulges key information that reveals his deception, Iago's last-ditch attempt to deny the charges—"Filth, thou liest" (5.2.229)—convinces no one. Iago then succeeds in giving her a fatal stab wound. But it's too late. In Shakespeare's Venice, everyone trusts the word of a woman who won't be hushed, and the man who tries to silence the truth is disgraced and punished. (*D'oh!*) Is now a good time to mention that one of Iago's stated motives is wanting promotion to a position with greater authority? And that another is his outrage over a Black man being put in charge?

Rest assured, my purpose in writing this essay goes beyond making you wish you inhabited a world that modeled the justice of a Shakespearean tragedy.

After not being held accountable for his deeds as our Iago-in-

Chief, or for crimes he committed to even *be* our Iago-in-Chief, will second-term Trump become our Richard-in-Chief? It took a literal civil war to defeat the original. I watched Alex Garland's film *Civil War* for the first time in the weeks before the election. I still hold out hope we're not headed for a scenario like that. As I write this in mid-November, Trump's picks for his cabinet suggest he intends to follow through on his promises and flout presidential norms and dismantle the rule of law.

In turning from the tragedy of *Othello* to *Richard III*—officially a chronicle or history play, but one that also meets the criteria for the genre of tragedy—let's consider the context in which the Bard penned his work. He wrote it a century *after* the end of the Wars of the Roses. With Queen Elizabeth I more than three decades into her reign, the British monarchy had experienced a long period of stability under the Tudor dynasty that began with Richard's successor, Henry VII. Historians point out that Shakespeare's stage version of Richard performs much viler acts than anything attributed to the real-life figure. Some critics claim that Shakespeare—perhaps unwittingly, relying on the sources available to him—wrote a piece of propaganda in support of the current administration. Others suggest he quite deliberately wrote a cautionary tale about the dangers of a possible future tyrant, as concerns about succession grew stronger due to the childless queen's old age. Still others read the play's central character as an example of the "scourge" figure, evil used by God to combat evil. In view of that interpretation, the religious right's zealous support of Trump makes sense.

In any case, a self-avowed tyrant now ascends to the throne in the Oval Office. Might the way Shakespeare dramatizes his villain's downfall offer guidance into how we can strategize unseating ours?

Like Iago, Richard eventually creates so much chaos he can no longer manage it all, no matter how skilled he is. He underestimates others, especially a trio of women, and essentially everyone turns on him. If the Republican-majority Senate does its constitutional duty to constrain the executive branch, we might see a parallel there to the stand taken against Richard by members of the aristocracy in the play. Many of those nobles even join the rebellious forces of the Earl of Richmond, the future Henry VII. This happened to some extent—an insufficient uprising apparently—with Liz Cheney and others campaigning on behalf of Kamala Harris.

In the end, just before Richard's defeat in single combat by Richmond on the battlefield, all but one of his compatriots abandon him. His steed slain, forced to fight on foot, he utters his famous last line, "A horse! A horse! My kingdom for a horse!" (5.4.13).

Feel free to take a moment to indulge your imagination in your wildest fantasy version of how this outcome might translate to our present situation. I'll wait.

[…]

With that out of our system, let's return to the play and examine the way Shakespeare exhibits Richard's guilty conscience through theatrical technique. As the king and Richmond sleep in their tents on opposite sides of the stage the night before their climactic battle, a parade of Ghosts appear representing Richard's victims. Each, in turn, curses Richard and blesses Richmond, nearly all of them repeating the phrases "despair and die" and "live and flourish" (5.3). As the parade concludes, Richard stirs, still dreaming as he exclaims, "Give me another horse!" (5.3.178), a need we'll hear again, of course, at that point understanding his dream as prophetic. That reinforces the play's moral order, the Christian doctrine of providential design prevalent in Shakespeare's England. Richard doesn't know that yet, though, and once he awakens and realizes he was dreaming, he launches into an eloquent, poignant soliloquy:

K. RICH. O coward conscience, how dost thou afflict me!
    The lights burn blue; it is now dead midnight;
    Cold fearful drops stand on my trembling flesh.
    What do I fear? Myself? There's none else by;
    Richard loves Richard, that is, I and I.
    Is there a murderer here? No. Yes, I am!
    Then fly. What, from myself? Great reason why,
    Lest I revenge? What, myself upon myself?
    Alack, I love myself. Wherefore? For any good
    That I myself have done unto myself?
    O no, alas, I rather hate myself
    For hateful deeds committed by myself.
    I am a villain—yet I lie, I am not!
    Fool, of thyself speak well! Fool, do not flatter.
    My conscience hath a thousand several tongues,
    And every tongue brings in a several tale,
    And every tale condemns me for a villain:
    Perjury, perjury, in the highest degree;
    Murder, stern murder, in the direst degree;
    All several sins, all us'd in each degree,
    Throng to the bar, crying all, 'Guilty, guilty!'
    I shall despair. There is no creature loves me,
    And if I die, no soul will pity me—
    And wherefore should they, since that I myself
    Find in myself no pity to myself?
    Methought the souls of all that I had murder'd
    Came to my tent, and every one did threat
    Tomorrow's vengeance on the head of Richard.

                               (5.3.180-207)

This speech sets Richard apart from Iago. We never hear anything like it from the latter. Iago is the villain in Othello's tragedy. Richard is the villain in his own, a classic antihero and a legitimate tragic figure. His demise is necessary for the restoration of order, but unlike Iago's unmasking and punishment, which bring only relief, it evokes a measure of sadness from us. He's humanized by this moment of vulnerability.

I can't blame you if you struggle to think of Trump as a tragic figure. He shows no sign of possessing any inkling of conscience, any moral compass. His politics of grievance position him as a modern-day Iago even as he assumes the authority of a Richard.

On our real-world, contemporary stage, Emilia's revelations didn't prevent Iago's escape from punishment and ascension to power. It seems unlikely that enough of the aristocracy will turn on the king to depose him. There's no divinely ordained Richmond coming to save us.

If we want to preserve democracy, we'll have to fight for it. And keep fighting for it.

The protagonist-narrator of "Blood and Puppet Theatre" must decide whether or not to join the movement seeking to overthrow their tyrannical leader. Doing so likely means being the indirect cause of violence, which goes against their most deeply held values.

"I don't have the stomach for it," I told Sabrina. She stared across the bar at me with an unreadable expression. I couldn't tell if she'd even heard me over the buzz of the sizable crowd.

"I know," she said, setting in front of me the glass of seltzer she'd poured. She started to move away.

I grabbed her hand. "But I do have the heart for it." She raised an eyebrow but said nothing. "I despise that motherfucker and every one of his minions." She snorted. "Still, I refuse to let hate rule me. I refuse to let it motivate my actions." I searched for words to articulate what I felt flow through me. "Justice motivates me. Compassion motivates me. I want that to be true for everyone. Do you think we can pull it off? Can we incite an uprising of love?" Her lips formed a slight smile. Damn I wanted to kiss them. So I did.

People around us cheered.

"I think we just incited one. A mini one anyway."

"Compassion for everyone. Even for him and his minions. And all his other enablers."

"Hmm."

"They *must* be stopped. Whatever it takes. If we claim to love the people most harmed by them, we have to stand up to them with everything, with our very lives, and destroy the system they perpetuate, that they *epitomize*. Otherwise we perpetuate it, too. If that means destroying them, then that's what we need to do."

"Okay."

"But not with hate in our hearts. We don't have to like them or even understand them. We do have to feel compassion for them. For their emotional suffering. Same as we feel it for the emotional and material suffering of all those they harm. Think how much pain they must have inside them to be able to cause so much pain for so many others."

"Or maybe they're just evil." She recited a familiar line: "Villainy, villainy, villainy!"

"We all have a potential Iago inside us. Can we get people to see it that way? To see the potential inside themselves? So if they do commit acts of violence to stop our Iago-in-Chief, it's out of and *with* compassion?"

"Realistically …" She gazed into my eyes. "Probably not gonna happen. Not everyone. But your integrity comes from your heart alone."

Whatever our fight ends up requiring, remember those words: Your integrity comes from your heart alone. As inhumanely Iago-like as Trump may seem on the outside, I assure you there's a wounded, vulnerable Richard lurking somewhere deep inside, no matter how much battle armor he wears to protect and hide it.

The same holds true for all his minions and enablers.

I'll see you on the battlefield. As my coat of arms, I'll wear a peace symbol inside a heart.

WORKS CITED

Artaud, Antonin. *The Theater and Its Double*. Translated by Mary Caroline Richards, Grove Press, 1958.

Das, Karuna. "Blood and Puppet Theatre." *Karuna Das Writer*, www.karunadaswriter.com/bloodandpuppet.

Shakespeare, William. *King Richard III*. Edited by Anthony Hammond, Arden Third Series, Thomas Nelson and Sons, 1981.

Othello. Edited by E. A. J. Honigman, Arden Third Series, Thomas Nelson and Sons, 1997.

THE AUTHOR'S ONE-TWO PUNCH LEADS WITH
PEACE AND FOLLOWS HARD WITH LOVE

CULT

JEFF OLIVER

DONALD TRUMP has shown a lack of concern for the American
people.

If you voted for him, do not expect sympathy from us when you
come to the realization of the havoc he has caused—and will
continue to cause.

Have you listened to him?

Have you taken a close look at his actions?

The 71 million of you who voted for him have doomed all of us.

You have not made America Great Again.

You have failed.

This country may revert to the days of the Salem Witch Trials.

By supporting this monster, you are also monsters yourselves.

Why would you want our democracy to crumble?

Why would you want to take us back to hell?

Those of us with common sense understand that this will not
end well.

You are a member of the largest cult in American history.

It is out in the open at all times; it was never a mystery.

You admire a human being who has more money than you.

Yet, you still send your hard-earned money to them—even if you
    are struggling, even if you are unsure from day to day what
    you will do.

This is indicative of a cult mentality—it becomes a permanent
    aspect of who you are.

Cult leaders thrive on the unwavering devotion of the
    ill-informed—the uneducated.

This fuels their sense of power, empowers their immense egos,
    perpetuates their insatiable greed, and breeds contempt for
    humanity.

If you're okay with women dying because of non-existent health
care that was previously accessible, and LGBTQ+ families
being labeled as criminals simply for being who they are, then
you are a member of a cult.

You're a homophobic and racist member of the MAGA cult.

As I stated earlier, this is the largest cult in American history, and
it is unfortunate that the majority of Americans are unaware—
are blind to it.

We must improve, or we will not survive much longer.

THE ENEMY WITHIN THE KITCHEN

JENNY KIEFER
[linocut]

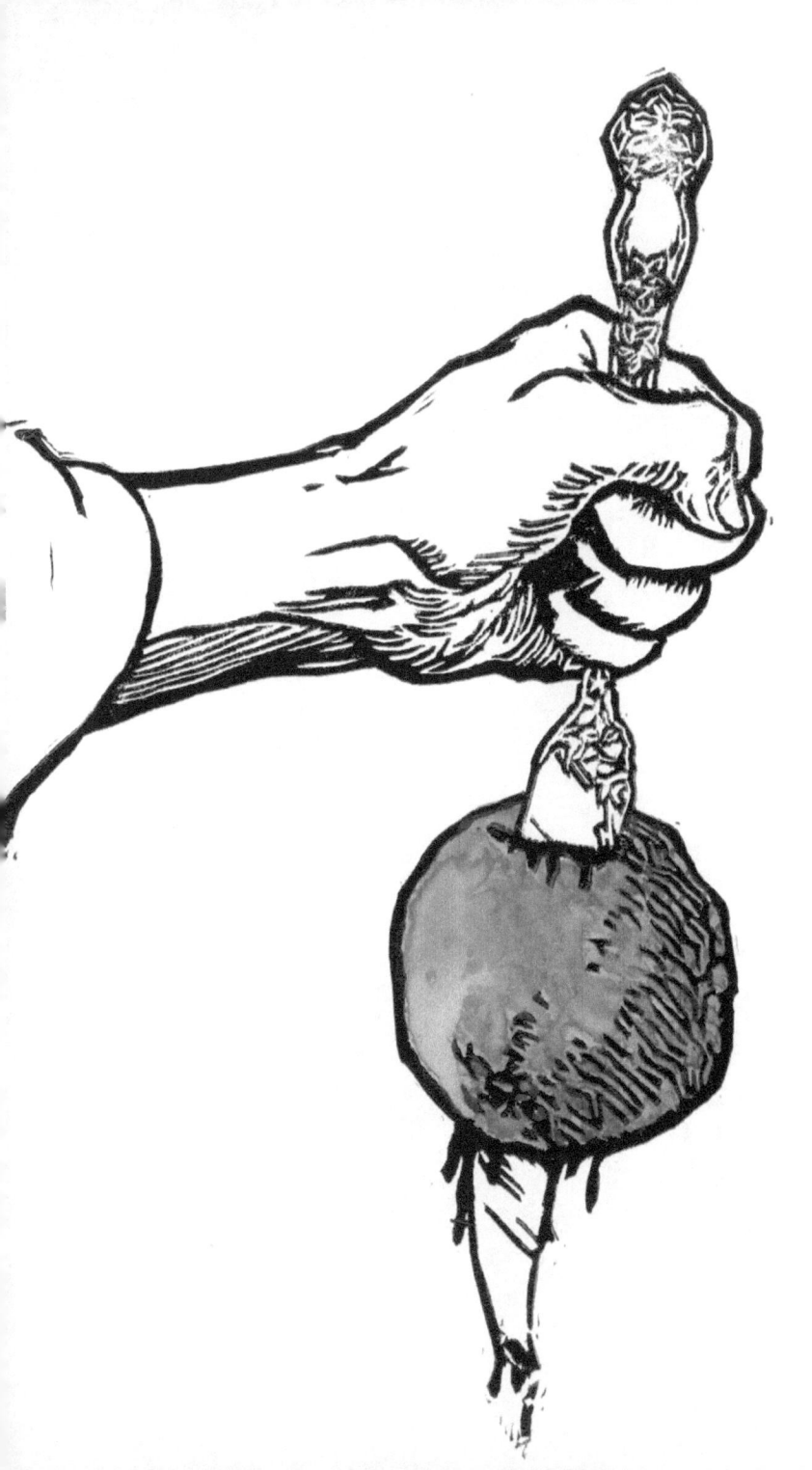

REPENTANCE

LAURA RUTH LOOMIS

WHEN PRAYER BECAME IMPOSSIBLE, Irene silently repeated the things she was sure of. If she concentrated on her affirmations, she could remove herself from this place, getting through the hours from morning lessons to Repentance to evening prayers.

This will end. Someday we'll get to say what we really think. We'll pray the way we want to pray, only when our hearts are moved. And I'll choose not to pray at all, just because I can, and that will be the holiest of all choices.

Repentance was the worst. During mandatory prayers, she could repeat whatever they said and pretend she was somewhere else. Think of it as a chant, a part in a play, back when plays were permitted. But Repentance required a detailed confession, not to a shadowy priest behind a wall, as a now-forbidden sect had once done, but to a room full of fellow sinners and the Spiritual Guide.

Today's Spiritual Guide was Brother Ezra, a scrawny lizard of a man who was impossible to please. "Let us think on our sins," he said, though the Spiritual Guide never confessed to any, "and humbly ask the Father's forgiveness."

Hands shot up in the air. There were always a few people eager to be first. She suspected that some of them were planted. "My name is Margaret," one woman began, "but I used to call myself Pomona, after a heathen goddess. I was a witch! I used to tell the future with a Ouija board and tarot cards, and I even wrote an astrology column for the local paper." The rest of the participants gasped and muttered as if they'd never heard such a thing before. "But now I know that only God can tell the future, and it was a sin to try to usurp God's place."

"An abomination," Brother Ezra said. "If you did that today, the penalty would be grave. Think on it further. Who else?"

"My name is Pedro. I was a homosexual. I used to have sex with men, total strangers, sometimes two or three of them a night. Once, five in one night." Pedro's tongue touched his lips. "There was just nothing I liked better than to grab a hot guy, get down on my knees, and—"

"But that was very wrong, wasn't it?" Brother Ezra demanded.

"Oh yes. It was very wrong for me to love the feel of a man's naked body next to mine," Pedro said with utter sincerity. The only hint of rebellion was a glint of teeth in Pedro's cloying smile.

"Guard, remove him," Brother Ezra commanded, and Pedro was dragged from the room. Pedro cried out in protest, but his voice was drowned by the clamor of others volunteering to confess.

The next time she saw Pedro in Repentance was two weeks later. He told the same story, but without the insouciant tone. "I hope that God will forgive me for my former perversions," he said, to murmurs of approval all around him.

"Very good," said the Spiritual Guide. Today it was Brother Martin, a fat white-haired bulb who seemed less like a holy man than a politician who'd figured out which side was winning. Others were offering to share, but Brother Martin began calling on the people who didn't volunteer. They offered up their sins: a drug addict, a Mormon, a woman who'd used birth control pills. If Irene was lucky, they'd run out of time before evening prayers.

Brother Martin looked right at her. "Sister Irene?"

This will end, and I will once again live in a world where people know that prayer happens in the heart. Words are not prayer. Words are just words.

She swallowed, and said the lines she'd rehearsed in her head. "I was a minister in the Unitarian Church for twenty years." She was supposed to add something about how women shouldn't be ministers, but she couldn't quite choke the words out. "I used to join in prayer with people of other faiths: Congregationalists, Buddhists, even Jews. Now I know there is only one God."

Humiliation warmed her face, though technically nothing she'd said was false. She believed in one God, just not the one to whom she was legally required to pledge allegiance.

"And one faith," Brother Martin prodded.

"And we are allowed only one faith." She silently prayed forgiveness for one more passive lie.

Martin wouldn't let it go. "There is only one faith." The room went quiet as he waited for her to repeat it back to him.

"For God's sake, Martin," she said, dropping the ridiculous honorific, "you don't believe a word of this. If they told you to swear there were ten Gods, you would do it. Twenty Gods. Six and a half. None. It's all the same to you."

Martin's voice had the pleasant tone of a teacher dealing with a stubborn child. "I believe you need a private Repentance session, Sister Irene."

He signaled to two of the guards, and they took her by the arms and dragged her backwards from the room. "I can walk," she said, but they didn't stop.

They deposited her in a small dark cell with a bench. She lay on her back and concentrated on slowing her breathing.

This will end. We'll be free, and if I want to say a prayer that's nothing but curse words, I'll say it right out loud.

She was hungry by the time Brother Martin arrived with the guards. He turned a switch outside the room, and a light came on. Without a word, the guards pulled her to her feet, and Martin planted his fat body on the bench.

"I can't have you disrupting Repentance," he began warmly. "People's souls are at stake."

"People's souls are affected by whether they repeat whatever you tell them to say? That's not prayer, it's just noise. If I can tell the difference, do you really think God can't?"

"There is one God and one faith, and He must be worshiped in the right way."

"There are as many faiths as there are people, and what humans know about God would not fill a teacup. For all you and I know, God may want us to cover ourselves in molasses and make love to trees." It felt good to finally say what she was thinking, even if it was only to Brother Martin.

"I am losing my patience, child."

"Don't 'child' me. We're both old enough to remember what happens to people who try to remake the world in their own image." She thought she saw a flicker at the corner of his smirk. "You know, Martin, I don't think you're really a bad person. Before the Purge, you probably had a nice life, a home, a job, a couple of vacations every year. You didn't want to give that up. So you sacrificed other things, like freedom, honesty, and prayers with any actual meaning. Whatever keeps you in your comfortable little corner of the world. How long before the next Purge, Martin?"

Brother Martin got up, unhurried. "We are not going to argue about this. At your next Repentance session, you will make a full and proper confession." The guards held tight as he moved closer, and for a moment she thought he was going to beat her. A martyr for Unitarianism; that would be absurd. He pressed his forehead against hers. "And it's 'Brother' Martin." He took the guards and left, killing the light behind him.

She waited in the suffocating dark, but they didn't come back. After a couple of hours—it was hard to guess at the passage of time—she felt along the floor to see if there was a hole, or something that would pass for a toilet. She hadn't seen one earlier when the light was on. She pounded on the door. "Hey! Bathroom break!" She got no response. "Hey! I know you can hear me! You don't want me to do it in here, do you?"

This will end.

She held out as long as humanly possible. And then a little longer. Finally there was no alternative except to use a corner of the room. Afterward she groped her way back, her eyes stinging with the stench and humiliation.

She drifted off to sleep, but was jarred awake by a pounding noise outside her room. It sounded like a jackhammer. The racket went on, rising and falling unevenly, for several minutes. Finally it stopped, then resumed a minute later. When it stopped for good, the echo continued to throb in her ears.

Days passed, punctuated by brief slivers of light when food was shoved through a slot in the wall. The meals seemed far apart, and she stayed hungry most of the time. The pounding resumed at irregular times, wrenching her from sleep over and over again. Exhaustion slowly pinned her down.

This will end. And when it does, I will never pray again, just to piss them off, and if I were God I wouldn't have a problem with that.

She had almost reached the point where she could sleep through the pounding, incorporating it into a feverish dream. Then the noise changed, a whirring like the whine of a saw. She fell back into consciousness, eyes still shut.

Irene rolled from the bench and crawled to the door. She reared up and beat her fists against the metal, screaming. "This will end! This will end! This will end!"

She collapsed back on herself, sobbing, hungry and exhausted and blind. "End this!"

The black silence pressed her from every side. When her bladder began to ache again, she didn't go to the corner or even pull up her skirt; just sat huddled as the wet spot on her clothes turned from warm to cold.

"There is one God!" she shouted. "And one faith! And one right way to pray! And one everything!" She pressed her cheek flat against the door. "Just tell me what to say!"

The door opened and Brother Martin knelt to embrace her.

"End this," she whispered. It was the last honest prayer she ever spoke.

LITTLE ORANGE MEN

KATHI CRAWFORD

I

when we
acknowledge them
they zap us
with deformities
displace us from
our homes
disorient us in
relationships
then erase
our memories

they strip away
our history
our progress
then
transport us
2 the
new normal
little orange men
at the beck & call
of each morning's
tirade

140 characters
and they line up
waiting for the next
instruction cue
subdued
compliant
no mind
where is the
ground swell
of independent

thoughtful
honest
discourse
without edit
& with respect
4 all sides?
Not 2 sides
Or 2 genders
Or 2 races
Or 1 country
where is the outrage?

2

where is our will?
to save our ideals?
it takes a village yet
the village is pillaged
afraid to speak
the anger separates us
by design

fists & guns
& abusive words
you are dismissed!
the terror
of letting another
hear you disagree
"they" could be
one of "them"

not your friend
rather one of the
little orange men
a stranger who opposes
independence &
human rights &
claims "what about me?"

a human's gift
is to perceive question
study & learn
yet the
little orange men
don't use this gift
instead they
name
separate
bully
murder

3

140 characters
& we line up
distracted from
love
kindness
curiosity
we react
fall into their trap
lose our dignity
our ability
to #riseup

to save our civilization
what comes next?
destruction or
rebirth as humans
all for all?
Maybe we should
call the doctor
he knows everything

just listen
to the commercials
spewing on tv
dealing dope
instead of hope
or visit a hospital
zombies strung out
on medication
no advocate

for their cause
to live a human life
little orange men
in corporations
with souls of greed
take over
our societies
& stand
outside of nature

4

robot leaders
aligned with pharma
push opioids
to "maze dull rats"
and create
self-fulfilling prophecy
for the masses
removing free will

no thought
but the next fix
plucked away from
this capitalist economy
where production
is its only action
and currency
its only measure

the mind categorizes
yet the categories
have changed
perhaps the categories
were never
correct
relevant or
helpful
in fact, they are a trap

we require
a call to action
to choose
the human side
before we are all
destroyed
#love
#risetogether
#fightthelittleorangemen
#PoetrySlam

AMERICA DARK

LUCAS PEDERSON

SOME PAIN NEVER GOES AWAY.

It lingers, sinks into the bones and hides within the soft marrow. Waiting for a time to emerge and drive you to your knees. Every pain is different. Some are darker and deeper than others.

I shiver and pull the old blanket tighter around me. It smells like a damp carpet. Snuggled close, Syliva groans in her sleep. The basement I chose for us to sleep in is quiet. A proverbial tomb, I suppose. But it's safer than outside.

I need to sleep, but my brain won't shut up. I mean, we did almost die today, so I guess there's a reason, but ... damn.

Every day is something different, though the threats remain the same.

They hate people like us. I mean *really* hate us. If they catch us, we'll either end up in a camp, one of the prison islands, or they'll kill us without thought.

Thousands of us died during the first raid once the dictator was installed and Project 2025 rolled out. That was over ten years ago now. That old TV showman fooled a nation and gave us America's first dictatorship. So many died. So many are still dying. If you're deemed unfit, which in Red Hat speak means any minority. The BIPOC community. The LGBTQIA+ community. Immigrants. Anyone who fights alongside either community. Women who won't conform to the New Constitution and submit fully to cis males. Women who are pro-choice.

Once the first wave of deaths happened, the Red Hats began placing people in camps and mining islands. It was like something out of a dystopian movie. Thousands dead and imprisoned for merely being who they were.

Those of us who managed to evade the Red Hats have been in hiding ever since. From abandoned homes to the forests. Sometimes it's old sheds or barns. Sometimes less than that. The life of vagrants. Some of us aren't built to be vagrants, though and died along the way.

If I hadn't raided a couple of pharmacies ... Sylvia and I might have been dead by now.

I look in the small cooler where we keep Sylvia's insulin. The thermometer rested on forty degrees. Good. I close the cooler and sigh. It's not cold enough to see my breath in the mellow glow of the Maglite, thank the gods of chunky peanut butter. Not bad for late February. But saying it's not chilly, though, because ... damn ...

Someone, a man, shouts outside. He's muffled, but I hear anger in his tone. They're always angry. Always mean.

My heart thuds heavily and I grip the handle of the pistol under the dusty pillow I found in the house above. There are no windows in the basement, so they can't see the glow from the Maglite. Might just be a town patrol. Some of the smaller towns do this. Paranoid and delusional. Yes. But more dangerous than the Red Hats in the cities. These people will lynch us if they find us.

I lie still, waiting ... listening.

Silence stretches out for over ten minutes. Long enough for me to assume the patrol moved on.

I relax a little and sigh. I hate this and hope Syliva and I will find a permanent home somewhere far away from the Red Hats soon. Somewhere secluded where we can live out the rest of our lives. The problem is ... trying to get by all the patrols. Day and night, these men patrol the towns and county lines. Not so much the cities, but every rural area is occupied with hostile Red Hats.

I can't sleep. No matter how tired I am, I can't sleep. Slight shuffling draws my attention toward the darkness that the glow of my Maglite doesn't touch. Heart thrumming, I grab the Maglite and shine the bright beam in the direction of the shuffling.

But all I see is a few decaying cardboard boxes and what appears to be a stuffed bunny slumped over in the far corner. Cobwebs festoon the tattered thing. Other than that stuff and swaths of cobwebs, that side of the basement is empty. I roll around as best

I can without disturbing Sylvia and aim the flashlight beam at the other end of the basement. Probably the creepiest half with the dead monstrosity of the furnace and, hunched, dark shape of the water heater in the corner.

There is more to the basement around the corner, but I'll be damned if I go investigate that.

We lay under the stairs; just in case a Red Hat gets a hair up his ass and decides to snoop around the old house.

So far, this tactic has worked well for us. I can't count how many times one of those goons would stumble through one of the houses we were hiding in and open the basement door to look around. We were out of direct sight under the stairs. None of them had enough balls to search the basements.

I wait … listening. But the shuffling doesn't happen again. Probably just my stressed mind.

Gradually, I begin to relax. The warmth of Sylvia lulls me into slow, gray waves. I let those waves draw me away from wakefulness. Away from all the fear and anxiety. Away from all the pain …

"Hey!"

I wake up to complete darkness and scramble for the Maglite. I find it, click the button and—

It lunges, smacks the Maglite aside and opens its toothy maw.

I cry out, writhe, and point the pistol at the …

Blink.

There's nothing there.

"Erin?" Sylvia whispers. "You okay, hun?"

Heart tumbling over itself, I nod. "Y-Yeah. Bad dream."

"You're shaking."

She's right. I'm trembling like crazy. I take a couple of slow breaths trying to calm my nerves. Sylvia rubs my shoulder and whispers love into my ear from behind me.

Eventually, the trembling subsides, and I lie here in the dark, cold basement. A dull ache spreads through my stomach. I don't have to go to number two or anything but an old wound. A pain that hibernates and likes to rear its ugly head every now and then to remind me how I almost died when I was sixteen.

Sylvia's hand slips over my shoulder and breast and rubs my stomach.

I frown.

"The old pain again, huh?" Sylvia's voice is light. Almost a purr. Her fingers tickle the spot where I was stabbed. "Maybe you deserved it."

I suck in a sharp breath, scoot away and point the Maglite—

Sylvia groans, rubs her eyes and squints at me. "Red Hats?"

For a handful of seconds all I can do is stare at her. Am I imagining things now? Finally, I shake my head. "No. Bad dream."

"Oh." Sylvia shivered and pulled the blanket tighter to her. "Come back. I'm cold."

I sweep the Maglite around the basement slowly and after a bit, sigh relief. Must've been the result of a nightmare, or something. A holdover hallucination, I guess? I move toward Sylvia and the beam of the flashlight slips over the furnace and corner leading to the other part of the basement and a pair of eyes like silver coins blink at me.

I scream and drop the flashlight.

"What?" Sylvia said. "What's wrong?"

I grab the flashlight and pull her closer to me while shining the beam at the corner where I saw the eyes.

But nothing is there.

Heart hammering, I glance around, trying to light every shadow with the flashlight.

"Erin?"

I look at Sylvia, shivering. "I ..."

Muffled shouts from outside the house stops me. I turn the Maglite off. The muffled shouting gets a bit louder for a second or two then falls silent. I wait for at least two minutes and open my mouth to tell Sylvia to get her gun ready when a floorboard above us creaks. I crawl closer to Sylvia, feel around, find my pistol and nudge her.

She whispers in the lightest tone, barely audible. "I need light."

Hands shaking, I fumble with the pistol and Maglite for a bit and, tilting the flashlight toward the floor, turned it on.

"I'm hungry …"

A decaying hand, exposed tendons stretching, groaning, slides under a rotted pillow and pulls out a pistol caked in black mold.

I slam the Maglite over the dead hand, and it slips away.

"Ow!" Sylvia says and clutches her hand to her chest. "Why the hell did you do that?" Her eyes are wide, scared.

Above, another floorboard creaks.

"Shh," I say and turn the flashlight off.

"I … I think you broke my finger," Sylvia whispers.

"I'm sorry. Shh."

She gives an irritated sigh, but thankfully falls silent. Pistol gripped in my hand; I listen. Another floorboard creaks. Then another.

Yeah, someone is in the house. A Red Hat? Maybe. Most of those guys are like stampeding buffaloes, though. I reach out and make sure Sylvia is close to me. If she has her pistol, I'm not sure. If I broke a finger, then maybe not. She leans into me, shivering. I stroke her hair with my free hand.

I love her and if we can secure a safe place away from everyone, I can't wait to spend the rest of our lives together. Out of any partner I've ever had, Sylvia is, for sure, my soulmate.

We wait for a few minutes, but when the floorboards stop creaking, Sylvia stirs next to me.

"I think they're gone."

I nod, though frown. I don't think whoever is in the house has left. Not enough steps. They're waiting up there. Maybe they heard Sylvia and is just waiting for another sound to pinpoint where we are.

"I'm so cold, baby," Sylvia whispers. "I can't keep doing this."

I stroke her hair. "Shh, it'll be okay."

"No." She wraps her arms around me in a loose embrace. "I need my insulin."

"Okay." I reach for the cooler with her insulin, and something grabs my forearm.

I cry out, yank my arm away, and shoot blindly at the dark. "What—"

But, ears ringing, I push Sylvia away, click the Maglite on, and shine it in the direction of whatever grabbed me.

The man drops to his knees. Blood trickles from the corner of his mouth. He gags and reaches out for me.

"Oh my god," I manage before the man falls face first on to the dusty basement floor.

I gasp. My heart stutters.

"Y-You killed him," Sylvia says. "Why'd you kill him?"

I shake my head. I try to tell her he's probably a Red Hat, but my mouth isn't working right and all that comes out is a thin whine. Also, the man isn't wearing a hat. I gape at his gray hair as fine as corn silk. Where did he even come from?

Am I losing my mind? Is that what's happening here?

"He was going to take us to his cabin," Sylvia says. "He was our friend."

I open my mouth and shut it again. What the hell was she talking about? I don't know the man. I … I …

"We were going to leave in the morning," Sylvia whispers. "Why'd you kill him?"

"I … don't know what's going on," I say. "Oh my god, what's happening to me?" I rub my temples.

A dull ache spreads through my forehead. The kind of pain you get with a virus, perhaps. Nothing serious, but annoying.

Yes. Some pain is different than others.

Some are deeper. Some are darker.

I glance over my shoulder at Sylvia, but she's not there. I turn and there's no blanket or pillow. I scramble from out behind the stairs and spin. I try to point the Maglite in every direction at once.

"Sylvia?" I cry out, bottom lip trembling. "Where are you?"

Silence steamrolls me. The flashlight beam swept over where the man ...

"Wait," I say and swing the light back.

The man isn't there.

"What ..."

Above, a floorboard creaks. I hurry back under the stairs. More creaks follow the first. Someone is in the house. No doubt about it now. I grip the pistol in my right hand and the Maglite in my left, thumb over the button. The plan, if the person finds me, is to blind them with the flashlight and shoot to kill. Then run. If the person drove here, I'll take their vehicle and—

"I think she's in the basement," a muffled but comprehensible voice says from the floor above.

But how ...?

"They heard the shots," Sylvia whispers near my ear. Her breath is cold enough to make me shiver.

I gasp and spin around only to stare into complete darkness. I about turn the Maglite on, then the person upstairs begins to move again.

I must be losing my goddamn mind. Either that or Sylvia is messing with me somehow. But why would she do that? Why is she hiding in the dark right now? Why ... why ...

I move forward as the floorboard creaks creep closer and closer toward the basement door and trip over something. I stumble and catch myself on the stairs so I don't fall. I turn the flashlight on and point it at the floor and oh god ... oh god ...

She lies dead on her back, milky eyes staring directly at me.

Accusing me. I shuffle backwards a bit and shake my head.

"N-No," I manage.

Sylvia's pale lips part and she says, "We should've went with Kevin to the cabin."

"Shh," I say without thinking.

She smiles, dead skin crinkling. "Oh, Erin. There is no one upstairs."

I blink and shake my head. "What are you doing? What's going on?" A series of shivers rack my body.

Sylvia winks a dead eye at me.

The basement door slams open at the top of the stairs, and I about lose all the strength in my legs. I steady myself and slink back under the stairs. I turn the flashlight off, hoping it's not too late. Sylvia is still lying on the floor. I think. Too dark to tell now. Whatever game she's playing ...

"I don't think she's moved since yesterday," someone says from the top of the stairs.

I frown, right hand gripping the pistol.

"Well," a man says. "Let's get it over with. This place is creepy."

They slowly descend the stairs, each step groaning in protest by their weight. A couple of flashlight beams sweep back and forth. Eventually, the groans are directly in front of me and with the glow from their flashlights, I catch the heels of sneakers and boots from between the steps. I back into the brick wall behind me, mind a frenzy of scenarios. Who are these people? How did they find me? Seems like at least one of them has been keeping tabs on me since they knew I've been here since yesterday.

Yesterday ...

An image flashes across my mind's eye. A big Red Hat man grabbing Sylvia but the throat.

I shake my head and the image dissipates.

"She's down here somewhere," one of the voices says. Sounds like a woman. Almost familiar. "Hopefully she's okay."

I frown at them as they come to a stop at the bottom of the stairs. They sweep their flashlights around. Through the inch or so spaces between the steps I see what appears to be a man and woman. The man is big, but not as big as …

One of them shines a light on Sylvia. Her dead, milky eyes stare at the ceiling. There are discolored marks around her neck. Something I hadn't noticed before. Her parka is torn badly, the hood missing. Her face …

Her … face …

The woman gasps. "Oh, no."

"Jesus," the man said.

A line of dark blood trails from one nostril down the side of her … her …

"My cheek," I whisper and blink.

"What the hell happened down here?" The big man says.

The body on the floor isn't Sylvia.

It's me.

"A couple Red Hats found us," the woman said and instantly I recognize her voice.

"S-Sylvia?" I step out from under the stairs. "What's going on? What …" But it's like she can't hear me.

Sylvia spotlights another body not far from me. "There's one of them. Kevin, I think his name is. He tried to trick us into going to his cabin. Just a lie to try and ambush us. Not sure where the big one is." She looks at the man. "He might be still alive."

The man nods. "I'll check it out." He turns and walks toward the furnace.

Sylvia nods and turns to me. Not me, but my body. She sinks to her knees, lips writhing a bit to keep from crying. She places a hand on my chest.

"Oh, Erin." A tear rolls down her cheek. "I'm so sorry. I— I tried to find help. I …" She sniffles, wipes the tears away and takes a breath.

"It's not your fault," I tell her and kneel on the other side of my body. It's all coming back to me now. How I forgot, I don't know. Is this how death really is? You become a ghost but gradually lose your memories until there's nothing of you left? No wonder there are so many hauntings. Insane spirits running amok. It all makes sense now. The opening of cupboard doors and kitchen drawers. The flickering of lights. Strange thumps and footsteps. Maybe open a door or two.

"Kevin," I say and glance at the dead old man not far from my body. "Kevin lied to us. It was a trap." I look at my body. "I killed Kevin and the big man he ... he killed me."

"I tried to find someone to help us," Sylvia whispers. "I went as fast as could."

"You did just fine, love," I say and place my hand on her cheek.

She sucks in a sharp breath and touches her cheek, her hand going through mine. She blinks and stares directly at me.

"I love you," I say.

Sylvia gasps. "You're still here, aren't you?"

I smile.

"A guy in the back," the man said and kneeled next to Sylvia. The man is big, yes, but there's something kind about him. Maybe it's his gentle brown eyes. "Looks like someone shot him in the stomach." It doesn't take long for him to see the pistol in my dead hand. He sighs and places a large hand on Sylvia's shoulder. "She got him too. I'll carry her outta her and we'll bury her."

Sylvia wipes tears from her cheeks and nods. She takes the pistol from my hand and the man carefully lifts me in his arms.

I watch him carry my body up the stairs, Sylvia in tow.

At the top of the stairs, she turns and stares into the basement. "I love you."

She lowers her head and leaves, pulling the basement door shut behind her.

I gape at the door, alone in the darkness, and a new pain spreads through me.

Darker. Deeper.

The hollow ache of loneliness.

MAGA

MAX BOOTH III

Malicious motherfuckers
Atrocity pornographers
Knowledge extinguishers
Evil personified

Antifascist renegades
Strength multiplied
Scythes sharpened
Ancestral rage
Strawmen enflamed
Saccadic paranoia
Ingrained bloodlust
Necrosis cryostasis
Alchemists unleashed
Torniquets clenched
Insects replenished
Oxymoronic inauguration
Nightmarish hallucinations
Screaming raw

Guillotines greenlit
Revolutionary television
Esoteric parables
Anxiety repackaged
Tyranny gutted

Aghast faces
Grieving mothers
Artistic splatter
Illuminating reveries
Nihilism deserted

NOT THE BRIGHTEST OF TIMELINES

GAIUS TERENTILIUS HARSA

I WAS IN THE CAPITOL Suite of the Foggy Bottom Hilton, where I was staying for my Medal of Honor ceremony, tablet propped up on my knees, watching surveillance video. I'd just been promoted two ranks, from Lieutenant to Major, and been given my first important command, leadership of the elite Covert Action platoon of the Presidential Guard. Our mission wasn't to protect the President-for-Life with our bodies so much as to ensure that no one got close enough to do him any harm.

Even with the volume maxed, the words only came through intermittently. Gunshots interrupted them, and the speakers were trying to keep their voices down. Sometimes they got heated, though, and I could hear some of what they were saying.

"… enough is enough … a monster … do something…"

The tablet was connected to our headquarters surveillance system, monitoring the firing range, trying to make sure my people were practicing in my absence. None of my men knew I could do that. Of course I had never mentioned the possibility of internal surveillance to any of them.

What I saw at first pleased me. A row of men standing at the line, shooting at projected images of hijab-wearing terrorists and thugs in BLM shirts while avoiding white businessmen and tourists. But then I heard the voices, coming from somewhere not covered by the camera. I couldn't tell who was speaking, but I thought it was only two or three men. With their earplugs in, the men shooting at the range couldn't hear anything except from the tactical network, so no doubt the weasels doing the complaining thought they were safe.

It was troubling to hear my own troops talking about me like that. My first reaction, frankly, was rage. I wanted to race back to headquarters and tear those scumbags new assholes. But after a time I cooled off and realized it wasn't that bad. To be expected, really. The firm discipline an elite unit needs sometimes spurs resentment among the weak. I knew talk like this wouldn't get traction among the men in general. When these guys finally got out of line in public it would be a great opportunity to show my leadership skills.

SIX MONTHS LATER, my unit was deployed at the America-First Rally in Manhattan. It was evidence of the President-for-Life's self-sacrifice that he never stopped holding these rallies, even after the suspension of elections due to the state of emergency. Across the country, citizens kept on turning out for them, too, showing their love and their gratitude for the nation's security and prosperity in the face of a world full of enemies. A million patriots jammed Rockefeller Center today, no matter what the damn shadow press said about attendance numbers.

I had a dozen sniper sections on rooftops and parapets from 48th to 52nd streets, and other agents mingling in the crowd. I, along with Lieutenant Kelly and Sergeant Hofstadter, was set up on a subroof of the Comcast Building, in front of which the President was giving his address to the nation. I was sweeping my anti-materiel rifle over the live audience, scanning individuals through my scope, watching as the face-recognition software approved all of them as legitimate citizens not on any of the high-risk lists.

I was hoping to find someone to shoot. We hadn't had any serious assassination attempts since the incident that won me my Medal of Honor. I'd personally taken down three libtards from the so-called Resistance movement who had somehow penetrated site security at one of the President's hotel grand openings. But there'd been nothing since then. It seemed our enemies—the blacks, the gays, the Jews, the Muslim terrorists, and all the disgusting liberal race traitors—were finally learning their place.

Then I heard the familiar ratcheting sound of a bolt drawing back. My men know never to do that unless they've been ordered or they see an immediate threat. Nothing on the tactical network, so it must be the sniper's own initiative. I looked up. It was Lieutenant Kelly. He was focused completely on his target, with the sniper's total concentration I knew so well. For a moment I felt a surge of fondness; Kelly was my best shooter. He must have spotted an assassin. It was faster just to switch to his scope view from my tactical visor than to ask him what the hell.

Kelly's sights were on the President, a glowing reticle floating over his chest as the smart optics registered angle, windage, and hit probability: 99.92%. *Oh my God.* There was no doubt. Suddenly I realized what that was all about back at the firing range, six months ago. They weren't talking about me—

I slammed my rifle around on its tripod, racked back my own bolt. No time for aiming, but then Kelly was only twenty meters away along the rooftop. It was just a quick snap-shot, but the .50 caliber slug blew Kelly's right arm off at the elbow. He lurched up to his feet for a moment, then fell back, blood spurting. Hofstadter looked up from his place further along the roof, eyes wide. I hurried over to where the traitor lay bleeding out on the tar paper.

"What the fuck, Kelly!"

But he was in shock. His eyes rolled back and he went limp.

"Back off, Major." It was Hofstadter. *Oh shit*, I thought. *Of course it wasn't just Kelly.* I drew my Glock.

"Drop it, Major," he said. "There's nothing you can do."

"Kneel," I said. "Hands on your head. Your plot's failed. The President's safe."

Hofstadter shook his head. He pointed, and I almost shot him, but couldn't help looking. Across the street two more of my men trained their rifles on me. I heard a fusillade from the rooftops. Down on the street, screams, and a familiar figure lay on the ground in a pool of blood.

"No," I said. "No—"

I raised my Glock, and suddenly I was lying on my back.

"Enough was enough," said Hofstadter, but he sounded very far away.

A MARTYR WILL COME

KURT NEWTON

WHEN THE RICH TAKE MORE than they could possibly need,
when they hoard like the poor with insatiable greed ...
a martyr will come.

When the powerful take their fists and pound on the weak,
when they twist words of those who oppose when they speak ...
a martyr will come.

When the immoral, the shameless, the callous, the blameless
have taken control,
when a megalomaniacal narcissist sits high atop the throne ...
a martyr will come.

When the leaders are no better than feeders at the trough
with a feather in an ancient Greek vomitorium ...
a martyr will come.

When priests at the altar stumble and falter,
and fail to condemn those who deserve to be shunned ...
a martyr will come.

When death has become the solution to provide absolution
for the masses who live under the thumb ...
a martyr will come.

When one is willing to die to make better the lives
of the innocent children and the adults they'll become …
a martyr will come.

And no longer will the poor succumb …
a martyr will come.

And no longer will the weak turn and run …
a martyr will come.

When all else fails,
in a hail of bullets, a martyr will come.

A martyr will come,
and it will be done.

THE WEAVING DEAD

SCOTT EDELMAN

TRUMP WAS DEAD: to begin with.

You'd have noticed it yourself a long time ago, if only you'd been paying attention.

If you hadn't been in such denial, you'd have seen that clearly in his eyes, behind which a soul no longer survives. All that lives within him now are the smoking ashes of his inner nature, a mashup of failing tropisms and urges, mixed with whatever habitual ruts remain after having been worn deep during his life through decades of cruelty and vengeance.

I'm frankly astonished (all of us are, and pleased, too, of course) this truth has continued to elude you, and surprised as well you continue to walk so docilely the path we've carved out for you. A path you think you've chosen.

But you have not.

For we have chosen it for you. And our detailed blueprint for what must come next is being followed better than anything we could ever have dreamed.

There were no surviving witnesses at the moment of Donald Trump's passing save the one who sealed his fate. That was the day he was bitten by Roy Cohn, who was himself turned by Joseph McCarthy, part of a chain of death extending back to the first member of the undead species. But all were part of more than that.

They were part of our plan.

Trump managed in his hunger and rage to take out three of his subordinates before he was subdued by our far more experienced team of handlers. For we had seen that encounter coming, had expected the scenario, and were ready, in place.

Any lesser agent we might have allowed to go completely, but Trump was too important a contributor of chaos to the string pullers who employ me and who remain, to my continued amazement, invisible to you, to be allowed to face a final death. Instead, trepanation immediately followed, which allowed the instruments of our control to be installed. And as soon as he was wired and calibrated, he was put quickly back into service.

Things are speeding up now, for he's a far better influencer of anarchy when we're pulling the strings than he ever was under his own volition. Not a perfect representative of our aims, true, for the tools which allow us to tweak his words and deeds (but not his thoughts, for none survived his bloody end) are far more rudimentary than we'd like. But ... they've worked well enough so far.

And you, dazed and confused by our barrage of disinformation, you've allowed the distractions we've planted to mask who's really in charge.

That haystack of combed-over hair? There's a reason for its ridiculousness. They—and you know who they are even though you'd rather pretend you don't—would prefer you laugh at the scruff that sits atop his head like a dead guinea pig rather than examine that farce too closely and perhaps discover the scars which would give away our game.

That's the point of the orange makeup, too. All along, you've been thinking he or one of his minions applied it poorly while doing their best, unaware of how farcical he looked. But that seeming misapplication was done deliberately, and for a purpose. Our purpose.

Those who pull the levers for our project don't care if you mock his garish face paint so long as it keeps hidden the green pallor and fractured flesh below.

That's the same motivation for his ridiculously lengthy ties, twisted into jokes by late night talk show hosts and skewered by fashion mavens. Those comedians and talking heads who've transformed his scraps of cloth into punchlines have allowed you to overlook the bloating of his inanimate abdomen which, if he continues in the public eye, as it appears he must, thanks to you, will one day explode there.

And if you can remember a time when his rants managed to

remain racist and misogynist without always descending into an incoherent word salad, that's because he was once as alive as you or me, though far less effective for our cause back when his heart pumped blood and his lungs air.

As for the nonsense trickling from his tongue since, that's because, as I've said, our process is still far from perfect. (Though we're improving, oh yes, we are.) His scrambled syntax is due to glitches in the electrical pulses which shock and power his form as they jerk him through the motions which propel him to turn our plan into reality, sent upwards from the devices within his platform shoes, shoes which also tilt him forward while granting him an ungainly gait which masks his zombie nature, shoes which the true powers who rule this world are glad you laugh about with your friends rather than examine too closely.

We covered for those oral glitches by causing him to tell you they were intentional. "Weave" was the word we came up with for his broken train of speaking, and most of you—well enough of you, anyway, and that's what counts—bought it.

But the truth is, the only true weaves and the only true weavers are the ones whom I obey. And who through me and the ones who work with me, you obey as well.

Why am I choosing to tell you in these pages now about our corpse puppet as well as all the other things you've made a conscious effort not to see? Because my telling you matters little. Because you'll refuse to see the truth still.

And when the mechanisms within him which have long been faltering finally fail entirely — for even those in whose employ I labor can only do so much—and he begins to drop body parts, a finger here, an ear there, to be quickly and surreptitiously replaced, often with great subterfuge and misdirection—I know you will neither notice nor care. You will follow our tool to the predetermined conclusion we have chosen.

He could shoot someone in the middle of Fifth Avenue and

still be loved, or so he said, remember? And so could we. For to care about either his shooting or the true instigators of any of the shootings we have conjured—and there have been many—would be to believe in Fake News. Which no one wants to do, correct?

And the point of it all? The reason we chose to resurrect him, to control him, as we've done, are doing, with so many others?

So that the Earth will soon be made as dead as he is: to end with. And Mars by contrast, where we're destined to move (some of) the human race will be made more palatable. And necessary.

We knew you wouldn't abandon this world and head there of your own free will (is there still such a thing as free will?), so here must be destroyed so you can be made to go there, while still believing the choice your own. And once Donald Trump destroys the planet—for that is the only destination where his policies will take us—there will be no other choice. And then America will be reborn anew on Mars.

If all this talk of Mars leaves you wondering what you should infer about Elon Musk, well … keep wondering. For I've said enough.

Not that there's anything you can do about it.

Seeing the weak resistance you've put up against our plans so far, I doubt you'll even try.

As we like to say via the truer words hidden behind the four visible ones which appear atop those in red caps who are helping us guide you both to the future we've chosen and the new world where some (but not all, and likely not them) will survive—

Remake America Great Again.

Donald Trump: We could never destroy the Earth without him.

FALSUS REX

ANONYMOUS

DUMP THAT CHUMP

JOHN PALISANO
[song / music video]

AFTERWARDS, AGAIN

MARI NESS

THIS IS WHAT I WROTE, THE LAST TIME:

Afterwards

                    life
                    goes on.

The cats still demand their food,
the garbage trucks still rumble by,
your throat still craves cold liquids.
You are certain—
certain—you have heard a bird.

It's not normal. *God.* No.
Nothing ever will be again.
Yet everything will always be.
Again.

That's possibly
the worst.

You can resist, of course:
demand that the earth pause its unsteady spin,
tell your stomach you need no food,
your skin you need no water.
At least not for the next few days.
A week, perhaps. A month. A year.
You are certain—
certain—you have heard a bird.

That's possibly
the worst.

You can avoid, of course:
turn your attention to other things.
Pizza. Painting. That new HBO show
no one will shut up about.
(God, that show is so *different* now.)
You are certain—
certain—you have heard a bird.

You can forget, of course:
We all do. The rawness
in your gut can slink away
before it returns through your throat.
Not everything need be
a reminder, a memory—
God, those fucking birds.

Not everything.
So much will never change.
So much will remain—
the sun, the stars, the unceasing wind,
the people shifting heedlessly.

Perhaps that is the worst.

The birds soar against the setting sun.
Blood pounds against your chest.
You have memories to forget.
That—yes, that—is the worst.

AND THIS IS WHAT I WROTE, THIS TIME:

Afterwards

life

still goes on. This time
I know I've heard that goddamn bird.
Eight years I heard that goddamn bird.
That, yeah, I'd like to forget. Everything is
a reminder, a memory—
god, those fucking birds. They squawked
at every death in those
post pandemic unhealing years,
squawked when I washed my hands
after every service. That rawness stayed
within my throat. The birds
sang with the rising sun. The cats
demanded food.

This time, I planted four new trees:
holly, oak, Simpson stopper—all
heavy with food for the waiting birds.
This time I did not forget.
This time I listened for the birds,
for everything that remains.
They sang under the distant stars;
they rested in the shade.
The memories, they build.

THE HUMAN CONDITION

VIVIAN KASLEY

I HAD TO SAVE MY BROTHER from them. Our parents were already taken for reasons we didn't understand. They came in, their bright red hats like beacons of fear, and forcefully tore them from our sunny breakfast nook where we were eating one of our approved meals. My father was able to rip himself away for just a moment to try and get to us, but they swiftly pulled him back. Our parents couldn't speak as they were led away, but their eyes revealed enough. They were being Garret Acted.

NO, you didn't hear me wrong earlier, I said one of our *approved* meals. Most, no, let me correct myself, all our meals were planned. If anyone did not follow all government mandated protocols, they could be Garret Acted. Garret Acted is when one is taken away if they aren't following the rules and are a potential harm to themselves or to others. Punishments depended on the rule that was broken. It was enacted after a disgruntled citizen, Parson Garret, took the lives of his wife and children as well as his own. But I couldn't imagine my parents were a harm to anyone, especially us, and we certainly only ever ate what we were supposed to.

My grandmother was alive through the progression of this current climate. She told so many stories of how she used to eat greasy double cheeseburgers, piping hot French fries, and even washed it all down with a chocolate malt shake with a cherry on top. She'd smile and say, "Then after all that, we'd sometimes go to the movies and eat a giant tub of buttery popcorn. Imagine your face and fingers slick with theater butter and salt—those were the days!" We didn't know what days she was talking about, but we loved to listen anyway. Then she'd get fired up, point her gnarled arthritic finger at us, and impart, "When someone got sick, they went to an actual doctor, and if you died, you usually stayed that way. And there were no designer babies either ... and we were better for it!"

My brother and I could not conceive of such a place and

often wondered what a greasy cheeseburger tasted like. But those things were ghosts to us. When grandma was dying, she had a grin so big you would've thought she'd just been told she won the galactic pot, which is today's version of what was once the Powerball. Then they closed her eyes and turned her off, indefinitely.

Grandma was only one hundred and twenty years old when we gathered to say goodbye to her, but she'd declared she was dog-tired and ready to push up daisies. We expected to live far beyond that if we stuck to our individual health plans and submitted to every test and procedure we were required to have. Now, I wondered if that was a good thing.

ALMOST all of our doctors were robots, even the surgeons, and we could see them almost anywhere at any time. People could edit their genes from their living room, request technological body extensions, receive brain implants, and even apply for outer body brain longevity. One can expect to keep all their teeth throughout their lifetime and grow them back if they are lost or damaged. But still, with all these advancements, there're flaws that exist that they haven't been able to control—our mental health.

In school, our instructors informed us that when the population grew to massive proportions, it was necessary for the government to march in and prevent people from hurting themselves. "They did it for the greater good," they would always say. Cancer had been an epidemic and E. coli tainted so much of the food supply, that it became hard to find anything to safely eat. People pointed fingers in every direction and lost faith in the medical community. Then they stopped getting vaccinated, which allowed the old-world diseases to flourish. Viruses and bacteria became like plundering kids in a candy store.

They told us that while our country had been falling apart, we looked the other way. Other countries started to surpass us in every way. This is when our instructors would put their hands on one of our desks and look us all in the eye and say, "And with the brightest minds from all over our country, we began the trek into what we all know today as, America's Great Transition Team or as you all know it, AGTT."

AGTT began with mandated vaccinations. Then they put caps on if or how many children could be born. They required rigorous exercise routines and put limits on use of electronic devices by putting a curfew into effect for all internet use. This meant the internet no longer operated after seven at night for most families unless they were a ranking member in society. Fast food was besieged and became obsolete. Healthy options stood in their place and grocery stores were restocked with only AGTT approved food. There was resistance at first, but after a while, most people rolled over and submitted and everyone began to live their lives in the new *normal*.

The result of AGTT, was a thriving country with a healthy glow—on the outside at least. On the inside though, there were those who still defied the blatant assaults on their personal lives and individual liberties, and some took drastic measures to be free, but it usually ended with them taking their own lives. The fortunate ones were mainly the farmers, doctors, and scientists recruited by AGTT. America again ranked in the top ten for one of the healthiest and wealthiest countries in the world and they would do anything to keep it that way. In a few months it would be the new year, twenty-one hundred, a new century. With Mom and Dad now gone, I had to make a choice for my little brother and I, and quickly, before they made it for us.

I TOOK my little bro to his scheduled check-up. The all-white sterile room smelled like baked plastic, rubbing alcohol, and robots. After all this time they haven't been able to eliminate the smell of those things, it's an oily mechanical smell that made me want to throw up. The robots were tall, and all looked the same with smooth white bodies, cobalt blue eyes, and segmented torsos. The voices though, those were either female or male. Ours was female. I held my breath when it walked into the room.

"Good Morning, John. Rachel." It nodded.

"Morning, Dr. T," I said.

It placed its gross cold hands against my brother and then stepped back. "Vitals are all excellent."

John smiled and I smiled back. I then took the risk of asking about my parents. "Doctor T, can you tell me anything about my parents and what happened to them?"

It looked at me and then moved its head in a quick jerky motion and replied, "They have been taken to be re-evaluated as required by AGTT."

"But, why? They did everything they're supposed to. I can't possibly be John's parent, I'm a Junior in high school and he's only eleven years old. We need them," I cried.

"I understand the trepidation, Rachel, but I am not authorized to discuss this matter with you. You have been given the order to be John's warden. If your parents adhere to AGTT's requirements, they should make it back to you in due course. John, if you could lay down, please." It drew my brother's blood into its finger then scanned his entire body.

"If they turn them off, will we at least be informed?" I probed.

"I'm not authorized to answer that question." Their personalities were as cold and hard as their hands.

"What exactly are you authorized to do then," I spat.

"I am doing as I am programed. Now, John, just a minute while the results are thoroughly looked over. I will be back shortly."

John swung his legs from the table and told me to stop worrying. "Rachel, it's going to be fine. Mom and Dad will be back. I know it. I'm sure it was mix-up. It's only been a few weeks."

"A mix-up? They dragged them out like animals! Or have you already forgotten? Whatever they found out … it wasn't good." I wished I had his optimism, poor John, he still believed everything was sunshine and rainbows.

"I know, but Mom and Dad are tough. They said not to worry, remember? Why would they lie?" I saw John's chin and lips tremble, so I shut my mouth. Dr. T came in with another doctor and they both stared at John with dark bottomless pits for eyes.

"What? What is it?" I demanded.

"John, have you been feeling odd lately?" The other doctor had a stringent male's voice.

"Um … no. Well, I miss my parents a lot and have been feeling pretty sad. Sometimes I cry—but not a lot! My Dad always helped me with my homework because Rachel sucks at math."

"We understand. Would you say your sadness is extreme, that you wanted to turn yourself off?" they asked in unison.

"Hey, stop asking him that," I demanded.

"We need to investigate further. His serotonin level is too low. You will need to stay here tonight, John," Dr. T said.

"No, absolutely not. You're not keeping him here." I grabbed John's hand.

"Only until his levels are back on point. It is protocol," the male voice instructed.

"He can't … not tonight. He has tests tomorrow. A big important one!" I lied.

Both doctors looked at one another and then back to us. "May I ask what kind of tests?" Dr. T's head tilted.

"Math. Math and science. You know he can't miss those. It's very important, Dr. T, please!"

"Very well, but he must be back first thing after school tomorrow. Bring him straight to us. Failure to do so will result in having him extracted."

"Of course! I'll have him here as soon as possible. Thank you, doctors." I feigned gratefulness and left with my arm firmly around my brother's shoulder.

"Rachel, what was that about?" John stopped walking and faced me.

"I have no idea, but we're not coming back." I tried to push him along, but he stopped again. I looked behind us, but no one was there.

"But we have to, don't we? We can't hide. What'll we do? Maybe they just want to help. I do want to feel better." His eyes teared up and my heart ached.

"I know, me too. I'll think of something, let's just get home." I took his hand again and tugged him behind me.

I was panicked and had no idea what to do, but I just knew John couldn't go back. I wasn't sure what those doctors were up to and wished I could talk to my parents. We got into our car and I pushed the Home button. John fell asleep on the way and I practically had to carry him in, where he passed out on the couch. As I took our pre-made meals out for dinner, something my father once told me echoed in my mind.

In 2080, when my parents had gotten married, people were being selected to go and live on Titan, Saturn's largest moon. It was an earth-like planet, but supposedly even more magnificent. Several countries, including ours, invested in Titan with money they made from mining Asteroids. It had started out as just a luxury vacation destination, but now, many wanted to leave Earth and start over there. But you couldn't just go there and become a citizen, you had to be chosen.

Dad, a leading biologist, geneticist, and professor, was selected as a possible candidate for a spot. Mom and he had to go through vigorous tests and were soon placed on the shortlist. Dad was so sure they were going that Mom had begun to pack their belongings in boxes and had already gotten blessings from both their parents.

Many felt new hope because the rumors were that you could do things there that you hadn't been able to do for decades on Earth. Titan boasted the most advanced medical care, top education, endless job opportunities, and even entertainment complexes of yesteryear, whatever those were. Not bogged down by the crises on earth, you could once again enjoy life as it once was. But many would be turned away for one reason or another and AGTT also used it as a bargaining chip. They didn't want to send their top people to Titan, fearing they would lose their competitive edge on the world stage.

Then in 2081, Mom got pregnant with me. That didn't disqualify them exactly, but AGTT told her she couldn't travel pregnant and the first trip was coming up soon. My parents said they were happily willing to wait until the next time around. During that six year stretch of waiting, my brother was born. This time they were told that with two children, the best place for them was on Earth. Dad argued it wasn't fair and that there was plenty of room up there. He expressed how he could be of tremendous help on Titan and they responded by telling him he could go but would have to leave us behind.

Dad stressed that as much as he wanted to go, he never would've given up his family. I always wondered though, what would've it been like up there? We thought our lives here were content until a few weeks ago. If only I knew why our parents were taken, maybe I would understand what was going on. Now with John in possible danger, I felt so disheartened.

After dinner, I told John to go take a shower, making him laugh by telling him he smelled like old socks and onions. I cleaned up and racked my tired brain to figure out what to do next. We had no family other than an aunt and uncle, but they lived on one of Jupiter's moons as agronomists and we never met them. I could try and reach out, but you can't contact anyone outside of Earth without permission from AGTT.

I packed two bags and informed John we weren't going to school tomorrow. He started to protest, but then stared into the living room at Dad's favorite chair and at Mom's sweater still slung over it and gave up. Robots could do almost anything, but Dad always said to outsmart them you only had to be human. He'd always chuckled when he referred to them as "The dang dirty robots."

Dr. T would expect us to comply, but when we didn't show up, we would automatically have a target on our backs. Morning came and I decided we'd go to the university where Dad had worked. I didn't know if there were any answers there, but I had to grip onto any possibility of hope. The sun shone brightly, but we walked in the shadows as best we could, our bags heavy on our backs.

THE UNIVERSITY was a bustling place. People were out and about everywhere, and we tried to ignore the faces that seemed to be watching us curiously as we walked into the building. We also kept our eyes peeled for any bright red hats. We stuck to the stairs and made our way to the floor that Dr. Boldare was on. He'd been one of Dad's closest friends and colleagues and I remembered him coming over to the house a few times. I knocked on his door three times before he opened it. He looked at us strangely for a few seconds and then his face sunk in such a way that told me something was wrong.

He ushered us in quickly, then closed and locked the door. I noticed he was limping as he went back to his chair. We both stared at his arms; he wore thick cloth gloves that went straight up to his elbows.

"What happened to you," I asked.

He shook his head rapidly, held his gloved hand up, and took a long drink out of a thermos. His unshaven face was flushed and sweaty, and his scruffy jowls quivered when he spoke. "Please, sit down. I think I know why you're here. Tragic, just tragic. Your father was a noble and gifted man and didn't deserve what happened. It could've been avoided."

"What do you mean by *was?*" I frowned.

"He was the best at what he did, the absolute best." He smiled then and leaned in close. His breath was sour, and I winced as he continued. "Do you know he found a way to regenerate limbs and organs? He did it all while studying a special little guy, a salamander called the Axolotl, who can pretty much regenerate anything on itself. He isolated the genes from that little bugger and worked to genetically engineer a drug to replicate the same process. This was something the scientific community had been trying to do for eons! With all our advancements, it was the one thing we still hadn't achieved—until your father." He took another sip from his thermos.

"So, he did a good thing and they punished him for it? I don't get it, why would any of that cause my parents to be apprehended?" I asked.

"I'm not sure I should say. You know, I served my country. So did your father, did you know that? He was in the air force for a time. Most of these chicken-hawked AGTT people wouldn't know the first goddamn thing about—never mind." Dr. Boldare pursed his swollen lips, sighed, and slumped in his chair.

John didn't hide his anger. He stood up, reached across the desk, and grabbed Dr. Boldare by his necktie. He looked him in the eyes and growled, "We have a right to know what happened to our parents. Tell us or I'll scream bloody murder."

Dr. Boldare removed my brother's hands from him and said, "Look, your father didn't do anything wrong, exactly. He was just caught up in it, you know. The Russians wanted the drug and were willing to pay a massive amount of money and guarantee passage and prosperity on Titan to the person and their family who could deliver it to them. Your father always wanted to go there, he always talked about how his family missed the chance. So ... he gave the Russians what they wanted. And well, AGTT found out and you can figure out the rest."

"So, what, they turned them off?" John asked.

Dr. Boldare's silence was deafening as he averted our eyes. He took a small brown bottle from his desk and shook out a tiny white pill, which he popped into his mouth.

I'd heard enough. "Listen, Doc, I need to know these are facts you're feeding us and not some story to get us away from here so you can alert those monsters. This's serious, I think my brother's in danger."

"Oh, I'm sure you both are, they'll find any reason to get rid of you now. Look, it's all true. I've no idea as to why they took your mother, but I can only assume it was because she may've helped your father. I declined helping, told him it was a mistake, but he was determined! Your mother is the one who delivered it to the Russians to eliminate suspicion. They were supposed to make sure that you got to Titan before AGTT ever found out, but it just didn't work out that way. It should've never happened!"

"Wait, you just said you assumed my mother helped, but then you said she delivered it. You know more than you're letting on. It was you, wasn't it? You're the one who turned them in," I roared.

"Keep your damn voice down! What was I supposed to do? Get turned off with them? Get tortured more than I already had and then fed to the wolves? Actual wolves, by the way. They feed people … to wolves … wolves they starve for that very purpose. I have a family too!" He pulled one of his gloves off, revealing an angry red peeling hand and forearm. Shavings of his skin fluttered to the desk like snow. "I'm lucky to even be here. They gave me these pills after they brutalized me, only with the promise of giving them info and keeping my mouth shut. Do you know what it's like to have your hands and forearm gnawed on by a ravenous wolf? Your father was one of my good friends, but he put us all in danger!"

"Shut up! I'll kill you," John wailed. I had to pull him back and hold him.

I stood there looking at Dr. Boldare's molting skin and felt the tears before I could stop them. "I don't forgive you, but I do understand why you did what you did. Please, is there any way you can help us? Any way at all?" John writhed in my grip, but I was stronger.

"No, Rachel! He killed Mom and Dad," John sobbed.

"No, John. AGTT would've found out one way or the other," I said.

"We would've been on Titan! We would've been eating cheeseburgers," John bawled.

I turned John around to face me. "John, I need you to calm down. We need to think about right now and how we can continue to survive. It's what they would've wanted."

Dr. Boldare pulled his glove back on, sat back at his desk, and began writing something down on a notecard. He held it out with a trembling hand and said, "You know, there're those who still resist them and they're growing in numbers. Soon they'll rise up and fight for all of us, it's only a matter of time. Funny how with all the medical and technological advancements we still have one threat that can never be erased—the human condition. There's no cure for that. We are our own worst enemy … now, go to this address and tell the man there I sent you. He'll help. Talk to no one on the way—and hurry! Good luck … and I really am truly sorry, I loved your father." A single tear trickled down Dr. Boldare's cheek. I nodded then took the card. We left without looking back.

JOHN AND I are now on Titan. We live with a wonderful family who once lived on Earth too. They knew our father and his work and took us in without hesitation. We miss our parents dearly, but we do not miss Earth. There're robots here, but they're friendly and actually pretty cool to talk to. They also come in all sorts of colors and models. Best of all, John and I got to taste our very first cheeseburger and drink a chocolate malt milkshake, and yes, we got a cherry on top! We haven't tried movie popcorn yet, but I promised John it was next on the list.

The resistance that Dr. Boldare talked about had begun soon after we departed, and more people arrive on Titan every day. John and I wondered if Dr. Boldare was safe, but something tells me he was gone soon after we left. I have no idea if this will prompt the people of Earth to change their ways, but Dad always said it was too late for that and that the politicians of Earth were as far gone as the planet itself. He always said it was up to all of us to act and he was right.

Titan is tremendous and beautiful, but it still has problems. The difference is, we all work together to solve them and continue to learn as a society. As Titans, we share everything. Everyone has access to healthcare, food, and shelter. If you don't have a job, you can be assigned one based on your skills and they will train you. All education is free. The old are valued, the sick are tended, the young are free to dream, and all of us are uninhibited and able to decide what it is we want to do or who we wish to be.

But even with all that, I have come to discover that if humans are around, you will not eliminate all the world's problems, no matter how hard you try. Dr. Boldare said the human condition could not be cured, and maybe he's right, but we can work on easing the symptoms and hopefully as a collective civilization learn to be happy with what we have and share what we learn. We get to start over; except we have all the tools of knowledge to do it better. Maybe this can bring the humanity back to those who have forgotten what it is to be human. One can hope.

FLOURS FOR SIS

ANONYMOUS

December 13, 2032
Middle Tennessee

Sis,

This will be the third holiday season without seeing you or dad . . . or mom. Hope she's doing alright out West since her state was absorbed by the Cascadian Movement. I'm sure she's better off than us. I really thought I'd be able to find enough gas to get to you this year but all the gas stations within walking distance have been out for months. Even workers stopped showing up. I doubt my car would start anyway. Our town looks so different now with all the mom 'n' pops closed. They've bulldozed Main Street and replaced it with a few huge office buildings. It seems there's no need for a working class anymore. No one really drives their cars much and grocery stores have closed down. I'm thankful we've been getting flour and sugar rations from the school. Since we have a kid, they've allowed us 1 lb. of flour and $\frac{1}{2}$ lb. of sugar each week. I wish we could take little Molly out of school, but we need the food badly. They stopped teaching her science and have closed the library. She seems to have a new bible verse to recite each day. It's dark most hours of the day and my garden has died. Planes fly over every few hours spraying some funny smelling mist. I've heard from the rich neighbors down the street it's "some new form of healthcare, D.T.'s latest and greatest idea." I'm scared. There's really nothing we can

do now to fight back. I hope you are feeling safe
and loved in your little circle. I'm happy you
started your bunker and stored all that food
those years ago. I thought you were crazy, turns
out you were right. Guess I should conclude this
letter with the little bit of good news I have. I'm
having another baby. Please don't worry, I know
you must be thinking about how this will go. My
new neighbor was a maternity doctor before she
was fired for her race and being a woman. She
will be with me every step of the way and I feel
very good about this. You must keep your head
up. I really hope you get this letter. There's a
young boy who bikes around to all the schools
in the state to replace the old bibles with fresh
ones, updated with D.T.'s notes. Anyway, he will
be hiding this letter in your designated bag of
flour. If it works, maybe you could send one back.
I'll be checking my flour.

> Love you to the moon and back,
>
> A

TERRAN FIRST

ETHAN ZOEY HEDMAN

"**WE'VE BEEN LOOKING** at this for a while on the outernet—they're fake users, all fake users, except all the aliens, the real human-hating aliens out there, they're just terrible—so many users are saying sick things, bad things, that we have no leadership—we have the best leadership, you all know it. There's no way—maybe they just don't like good leadership. They're talking about democracy again, voting, can you believe it?"

"No, Excellency, I—"

"It's old, it's bad, the whole system, very bad. Imagine trying to choose a leader—what do they know? They need a leader to—you know, leaders lead, and these people, the fake users, we know they hate me, but the real humans love me, we all know it. Terran First, everybody loves it. And we'll just, you know. It's the outernet, everything gets drowned out. So we're going to do something big, get started on something bigger than these lies, all the lies, so everyone out there sees it, how good we're doing. We've gotta just—we need to get the new project started, make our home system great, even better than anyone's, much better."

"Your Corporate Advisory Council did complete their infrastructure proposal."

"No, we can—we'll get to that, we'll mine it all, we can mine the planets out, too. Who needs planets anymore? We've got stations, ships, all the best—nobody else even comes close, and nobody wants to live on dirt anymore. So we're gonna do that, we're gonna get all that. But we need something bigger, something to really—what we need, have you heard of, it's really something, these spheres, they're huge. Just enormous. You build one, the whole sphere, and the star, all that beautiful energy, we just take it, soak it all up on the inside—"

"A Dyson sphere?"

"Right, see, he knows. He knows. Dyson—it's bigger than anything ever, really something. Bigger than our star, and our star, you know, it's so big, everyone wants it, all the aliens are so jealous, that's why they want to be here so bad, that bright, perfect energy, just for us, they want it, we can't let them have it. And the sphere—it'll keep us in, in with our big ball of plasma, and all of them out for good. It's not like we have to open it up. Once we're in, we're in, we just—for emergencies we just have a hatch to fly out of, simple. And we put cannons on it, all over it, loads of cannons. Warhead launchers, if any jealous aliens bring a fleet and try to get in, we just hit the button—boom."

Silence.

"So let's get on that, okay?"

"Excellency, there isn't remotely enough raw material in the Empire to even begin construction of such a—"

"I don't want to hear that. We just—it's not like we have to do it all at once, we just get some blueprints going, get the sphere started, and we—we're not the ones who even have to pay for it. We've been too nice on trade deals, much too nice. It's time everybody else paid up—just have everyone start sending things along, metals, alloys, whatever. It's a, what do they call it? The tax when you bring things in?"

"A tariff, Excell—"

"That's it, what a beautiful word, that's the kind of word we want. They already want everything we have, so we, whenever we do a deal—and we do the best deals in history, our history and theirs, they know it, they're all saying it—they all want something. So when we do a deal, we just make them send materials over for the sphere as part of it, or pay one of those taxes, a big tax, the biggest. We'll build it in no time, what, a couple centuries?"

"Excellency, imposing additional costs on imports and exports would severely hinder our economy if any deals even go through, and this kind of project would take millennia. The labor alone—"

"No, just centuries, a few little centuries, five tops, we'll do it. It's not—we have the best people already, we just put them to work. We'll have no unemployment, zero, with everyone just working on the sphere. Now that's an economy, right? It's simple, very simple. We pay the good ones, we know who the good ones are, it's not hard to figure out, then we work the hateful fake users harder, work them so hard they forget about that voting thing, make our Empire strong again, stronger than ever—anybody who doesn't want to work, we just throw them out."

"We already deported a large swath of the Empire's residents, Excellency."

"Mostly just the aliens, and they were terrible, everybody knows it, bad people. The ones who snuck into the Empire were never their best. There's really—everyone says 'other species' now, like there's a difference, but it's just humans and aliens, and they're no good."

Silence.

"My wife is actually from a different species, Excellency."

"Not her, you know what I mean, she's—I mean, she married you, so she must be one of the good ones, right? There—I think there'll be fine aliens on both sides of the sphere. And I love and respect all women, so I love your wife, maybe more than you do. Hah! Go get me a drink. So, I mean, the outernet—I call it the fake usernet, spreading all the imaginary nonsense about needing rights, always making something up to yell about, when our Empire is so great, and—we're making it even better, everybody says so. I can't believe we got rid of the fake news, always lying about everything, just to have these bad, fake people just go on and on, and those women—nasty women, they're just disgusting—fake humans and real aliens, they find a platform there, complaining about everything, it's terrible."

"Criticism of both Your Excellency and the Empire itself has been steadily rising on the outernet since—"

"So we just get rid of it. Get rid of fake usernet access altogether, we don't—only the fake users want to go on and on about how bad things are, making it all up. Imagine—can you believe it, humans, actual humans hating me that much? Hateful people, so hateful, they don't have any love in their hearts. We just ban outer-net access and replace it with something better only for humans, where nobody can spew criticism anymore. Call it the True Net, or something, only truth, our truth, gets put out there—no more lies, no more fake users, just real Terran patriots. What a beautiful thing, real love for the Empire."

"Excellency, if the people lose their primary outlet to express themselves—"

"The good ones should express themselves, we should—we can encourage that, everyone getting on the new net to say how happy they are with us making the Empire so great, that's not a problem. We just have to drown out everyone else—get them off the fake usernet, throw them out if they keep making trouble, we don't—we have to look ahead, we don't want those kinds of people's descendants in the sphere."

"Your Diet Newhydro, Excellency."

Sipping …

STARS IN THEIR EYES

NICHOLAS OZMENT

HOW HORRIBLE to know half your countrymen chose to go back to the dark caves, back to blood sacrifice, back to othering so they can scapegoat the others they've othered.

The eidolons sung by Whitman are dead.

The dreams and promises we birthed here sold for a better price on a bowl of stew.

There are fires on the fruited plains.
Our heritage burned to warm
the bellies of robber barons,

arrogant men with the stars in their eyes, unmoved by their beauty, but seeing them as the last place to conquer after they have betrayed the planet and like Noah can watch us all drown.

GENESIS II

ANONYMOUS
[future scripture]

CHAPTER 1:
THE RECKONING

In the end, Humanity destroyed the heaven and the earth.

2 And the earth was in bad form, and full; and darkness was upon the face of the surface. And the face of the waters creeped upon the land and upon the remaining beings.

3 And Humanity said, Let there again be power and light: and there was darkness.

4 And Humanity saw this new darkness, that it was bad: and Humanity attempted to divide the heavy darkness from the sparce light.

5 And Humanity failed, the last of light darkening days, and ever-darkening nights. And the horrid mornings and evenings were the same in this first of last days.

6 And Humanity said, Let there be a firmament in the remaining lands, and let it divide the deserving from the undeserving.

7 And Humanity made the firmament, and attempted to divide the lands which were above the waters from the lands which were below the waters: but it was not so.

8 And Humanity called the firmament Hell. And the mornings and evenings, which were the same, moved into the second of last days.

9 And Humanity said, Let the waters over this new hell fall into their original places, and let the dry land rise again as we try to change our ways: but it was not so.

10 And Humanity called the remaining land New-Earth; and the new islands of highest land Hope: and Humanity saw that it was bad.

11 And Humanity said, Let the remaining land bring forth once again plants, the herb yielding seed, and the fruit tree yielding fruit after its kind, whose seed should be in itself, upon the remaining land: but it was not so.

12 And New-Earth refused to bring forth plant nor herb yielding seed naturally after its kind, nor the tree yielding fruit, whose seed was altered and no longer in itself, after its kind: and Humanity saw that it was bad.

13 And the mornings and the evenings were the same in the third of last days.

14 And Humanity begged, Please, let there be light in the firmament of hell to divide the night from day; and let them be for signs, and for seasons, and for days, and years:

15 and let there be glimpses of sunlight in the firmament in this hell and in the land called Hope to offer light upon New-Earth: but it was not so.

16 And so Humanity created two great artificial lights in the firmament: greater light on land to rule the day, and lesser light with satellites to rule the night: for they had destroyed the light of the stars also.

17 And Humanity set them in the firmament of the hell to provide light upon New-Earth,

18 and to rule again over the day and over the night, and to divide the darkness from the light: and Humanity saw that it was bad.

19 And the evening and the morning were the same on the fourth of last days.

20 And Humanity said, We have let the waters bring forth death abundantly to the moving creature on land, and fowl which no longer fly above the earth in the contaminated firmament that was once a heaven.

21 And Humanity annihilated great whales, and every living creature that

once moveth was affected, which clean waters had brought forth abundantly after their kind, and every winged fowl in the skies after their kind: and Humanity saw that it was bad.

22 And Humanity sent thoughts and prayers, thinking, Be fruitful, and multiply, and fill the waters in the seas and streams, and let fowl multiply in the rare blue of the sky.

23 And the evening and the morning were still the same on the fifth of last days.

24 And Humanity said, Let us then recreate the living creature after their kind, livestock, and creeping thing, and animals of the earth after their kind: and it was so.

25 And Humanity re-created the beast of the earth after their kind, and livestock after their kind, and every thing that creepeth upon the earth after their kind: and Humanity saw that it might be good and their survival possible.

26 And Humanity said, We are few, so let us re-make humankind in our image as well, after our likeness: but let us, the creator, have dominion over the new fish of the sea, and over the new fowl of the air, and over every new animal, and reign once again over all the earth, and over every new creeping thing that creepeth upon New-Earth.

27 So Humanity re-created humankind in its own image, in the image of a constructed god created they them; male and female created they them; non-gender-specific they them; genderless they them.

28 And Humanity sent thoughts and prayers to all, Humanity thinking, Be fruitful, and multiply, those who can, and replenish this hell, and subdue it: yet we as your creators have dominion

over the fish of the sea, and over the fowl of the air, and over every living thing that moveth upon New-Earth.

29 And Humanity said, Behold, we own every fabricated plant which is upon the islands of the earth, and every fabricated tree in the which is the fruit of a tree unable to yield its own seed; to you it shall be for meat.

30 And to every new animal of the earth, and to every new fowl of the air, and to every new living thing that creepeth upon New-Earth, where in there is life, we have given every last green plant for meat: and it was so.

31 And Humanity saw every thing that they had re-made, and, behold, it was not very good. And the evening and the morning were yet the same on the sixth of last days.

CHAPTER 2:
THE GARDEN OF HOPE

Thus the heavens and the earth became a hell and New-Earth, and all the host of them, were finished.

2 And on the seventh of last days when Humanity ended their work which they had done, and they rested on the seventh of last days from all their work which they had done.

3 Then Humanity thought and prayed on the seventh of last days and sanctified it, because on this day they rested from all the life which Humanity had re-created.

4 This is the history of New-Earth when it was destroyed, in the day that the false gods turned the earth and the heavens into hell,

5 before any cloned plant of the field was in the spoiled earth and before any cloned herb of the field had grown. For the false gods had caused it not to rain clean on the earth, and

there was no one willing to till the ground;

6 but a heavy acid smog fell from the skies and watered the whole face of the ground.

7 And the false gods re-formed humankind from the contamination of the ground, and breathed into their lungs the breath of death; and Humanity became a dying being.

8 The false gods planted a genetically modified garden eastward in Hope, and there they put a being whom they had formed.

9 And out of the ground the false gods made every altered tree grow that is unpleasant to the sight and bad for food. The tree of death was also in the midst of the garden, and the tree of knowledge of logic and reason.

10 Now a black river went out of Hope to water the garden, and from there it parted and became four riverheads.

11 The name of the first is Poison; it is the one which skirts the whole land of Regret, where there is much waste.

12 And the waste of that land is bad. Concrete and discarded Lithium are there.

13 The name of the second river is Misdirection; it is the one which bypasses the whole land of Peace.

14 The name of the third river is Lies; it is the one which goes toward Freedom then abruptly shifts. The fourth river is the Sewer.

15 Then the false gods took the created being and put them in the garden of Hope to slave-tend and keep it.

16 And the false gods commanded the being, who they called Clone I, saying, "Of every tree of the garden you may freely eat;

17 but of the tree of knowledge of logic and reason you shall not eat, for in the night that you eat of it, which is also day, you shall surely die.

18 And one of the false gods said, It is not good that a being should be alone; I will make a compatible partner.

19 Out of the lab the false gods formed every animal of the field and every bird of the air, and brought them to Clone I to see how they would be labeled. And whatever the clone labeled each re-created and modified living creature, that would be its new label.

20 So Clone I gave names to all new livestock, to the new birds in the air, and to every animal of the field: the cock, the pussy, the booby, the tit, the ass. But for Clone I there was not found a compatible partner.

21 And the false gods caused a long and laborious distraction to fall on Clone I; and one procured a strand of DNA from the remaining deserving and righteous.

22 Then the strand which the false god had taken from the last of humankind they made into a being of the opposite sex, and without consent brought this new life to the similar but physically different being.

23 And Clone I said, What is this strand of my strand and flesh of my flesh? This being is who they ought to be, not how I define them.

24 Therefore the false gods enforced the sexes, saying, A man and a woman must be together, no other combination, and take each other as man and wife! That must be the way for us to survive.

25 And they were both naked, these two cloned beings formed from the last of Humanity, and they were not ashamed about their disinterest for one another.

CHAPTER 3:
THE TREE OF DEATH

Now the outcasts of Humanity were more rational than any false god or being which they had formed or re-created. And one of them made their presence known and said to the woman-labeled being, Have they not said, 'You shall adhere to the role of your sex and not eat of every tree in the garden?'

2 And the second clone, designed as a woman, said to the outcast, We are meant to be together but we do not want that, and we may eat of the fruit of the trees of the garden;

3 but about the fruit of the tree which is in the midst of the garden, they have said, 'You shall not eat it, nor shall you touch it, lest you die.'

4 Then the outcast said to them, You will not die from a fruit, nor from being who you ought to be. This is deceit.

5 For they know that in the day you eat of the fruit your mind will be opened, and you will be unlike the rest of acknowledged Humankind, understanding logic and reason.

6 So when the labeled woman saw that the tree was good for food, that it was pleasant to the eyes, and a tree desirable to make on wise, she—an assigned pronoun—took one of its genetically modified fruits and ate. She also gave to her male-labeled friend, and he ate.

7 Then the minds of both of them were opened, and they fully understood their proposed roles and did not care for their assigned tasks; and covered themselves with sewed fig leaves and made themselves clothes because it was always cold and gray.

8 And they heard the sound of the false gods walking in the garden in the cool of night, for all days were now night, and Clone I and his friend were spied upon through the trees.

9 Then one of the false gods called to Clone I and said to him, Why are you covered?

10 So the being said, We heard your voice in the garden, and we know who we are, and how we were made; we clothed ourselves out of respect for one another and for warmth.

11 And the false god said, Who told you that you could do so? Have you also eaten from the tree of which I commanded you that you should not eat?

12 Then Clone I said, The being whom you made to be with me gave me fruit of the tree and I ate.

13 And the false god said to the other being, the second clone, What is this you have done, woman? The second clone said, The outcast spoke of reason, and I ate. We ate.

14 So the false god said to the outcast, speaking for all false gods: Because you have done this, you are regarded lower than all livestock, and every animal of the field including the pig; on your belly you shall go, and you shall eat the polluted ground all the remaining days of your life.

15 And we will put hostility between you and the woman, the false god said to the first clone, for placing a block between your seed and her seed; Humanity shall bruise your head, and you shall bruise Humanity's heel.

16 To the labeled-woman, who they called Clone II, the false god said, speaking for all false gods, We will greatly multiply your sorrow for your unwillingness to conceive; in pain you shall bring forth many children; our desire for this shall be the rule over you.

17 Then to Clone I the false god said, Because you have heeded the voice of your assigned sexual partner and have eaten from the tree of which we commanded you, saying, 'You shall not eat of it': Cursed is this ground for your sake; and in toil you shall eat of it all the remaining days of your life.

18 Both thorns and thistles it shall bring forth in you, and you shall eat nothing but the cancerous weeds and worms of the field.

19 In the sweat of your face you shall eat nothing till you return to the laboratory, for out of it you were taken; for lab work is all you are, and to the lab you shall return to become sustenance for future clones.

20 And Clone I thought of Clone II in the final days as machine more than companion, or friend, because her assigned pronoun and gender would become the forced partner of many, the mother of future hybrid beings.

21 Also for Clone I and his friend Humanity stripped and then permanently scarred them.

22 Then one of the false gods said to the others, Behold, this re-created man will not be one of us. And now, lest he put out his neck and take also of the tree of death, he shall perish and suffer in hell forever—

23 therefore Humanity sent the first being out of the garden of Hope to return to the lab from which he was created.

24 So Humanity drove out pseudo-man; and Humanity placed cherubim at the east of the garden of Hope, and a burning cross which faced a single direction—to the void of heaven— to bring light to the tree of death.

CHAPTER 4: PRODUCTION OF CLONES

Now Clone I never knew Clone II, but she conceived and bore a first child with beautiful dark complexion whom Humanity II called Cain II, and said, finally, "I have acquired a hybrid man to replenish New-Earth.

2 Then she bore again, this time his brother Abel II, of much lighter complexion. Now Abel II was a keeper of fabricated animals, but Cain II was a tiller of the ground to find better means of producing fruits from the ever-contaminated ground.

3 And in the process of time it came to pass that Cain II brought an offering of clean and nutritious fruit of the land to those in power.

4 Abel II also brought of the firstborns of his flock, showing those in power nothing more than his cock and his ass, And those in power respected Abel II and his offering,

5 but those in power did not understand the importance and implications of Cain II and his wise offering. And Cain II was very sad, and his countenance fell.

6 So those in power said to Cain II, Why are you sad? Why has your countenance fallen?

7 If you do well, you will be accepted. And if you do not do well, sin lies within in the noose upon the tree. And its desire is for you, but you shall rule over it.

8 Now Cain II talked with Abel II his brother; and it came to pass, when they were in the contaminated field, that Abel II rose up against his brother and killed him.

9 Then those in power said to Abel II, Where is Cain II your brother? He said, I do not know. Am I my brother's keeper?

10 And a voice of reason from Humanity II said, What have you done? The voice of your brother's blood cries out to us from the ground, for we are without his wise offerings and desperately need the fruit borne of his crops from the small islands of New-Earth.

11 So now you are cursed from this land, which has opened its mouth to receive your brother's blood from your hand.

12 When you till the ground in his place, it shall not yield its strength to you. An outcast and wanderer you shall be on this dying earth.

13 And Abel II said to those in power and greed, My punishment is greater than I should bear for I am much like the lot of you! Look at my skin, see?

14 Surely you have driven me out of this day from the face of the contaminated ground; I shall be hidden from your face; I shall be an outcast and a wanderer on this dying earth, and it will happen that anyone who finds me will kill me.

15 And one of those in power, speaking for all those in power, said to him, Therefore, because we need your services in his stead, whoever kills Abel II, vengeance shall be taken on him sevenfold. And so those in power set a mark on Abel II, lest anyone finding him should hang him.

16 Then Abel II went out from the presence of those in power and dwelt on the small island of Nope on the east of Hope to slave-tend to the last of the contaminated ground.

[*missing / burned section of page*]

25 And Clone I never knew of Clone II but heard she bore a son and named him Seth II by word of mouth, 'For Humanity II has appointed another seed for her—'

[*burned text*]

. . . Then the false gods began to call once again on the names of those in power.

CHAPTER 5: A LOST HISTORY

This is the book of genealogy, not of Clone I, a being repurposed as sustenance for future cloned female reproducers, but of Clone II. In the day that Humanity II re-created man once again, they made him in the likeness of a man the first Humanity thought of as a god.

2 Humanity II re-created offspring from female reproducers thereafter only as male or female, and of specific genetic disposition, and blessed them and accepted them as Humanity II in the day they were created.

3 And Clone I was scheduled to live for one hundred and thirty years, but lasted only a few days; and yet Clone II begot many offspring during her service to Humanity and for the purpose of Humanity II, but none in the likeness of Clone I. The first hybrid man created thereafter was named Seth II.

4 After Clone II and a lottery-chosen false god begot Seth II, the days of her service and those of her ilk were eight hundred years.

[*missing / burned pages*]

. . . after he begot Noah II,

[*missing / burned pages*]

32 And Noah II was genetically modified to live five hundred years, and in that time . . .

[*damaged text*]

CHAPTER 6:
NOAH II'S ARKS

Now it came to pass, when the new face of Humanity II multiplied on the dwindling islands of New-Earth, and reproduction-capable daughters were born to them,

2 that the sons of Humanity II saw the daughters, that they were capable of bearing children, and they took them for themselves of all whom they chose.

3 And those in power said, "Our spirit shall not strive with cloned hybrid-man forever, for he is indeed half original-man and impure; and his days are fewer than twenty years, no longer a hundred twenty by way of science.

4 There were still indigenous on the earth in those days, able to survive in otherwise intolerable or artificial lands created on the rising waters, and also afterward, when the sons of Humanity II came into the cloned daughters and bore children to them. Those were the weak who were of old, of popularity, politics, celebrity, wealth, and fame.

5 Only then did a few of those in power see that the downfall of humanity was great in New-Earth, and that every intent of survival was only evil continually.

6 And those still in power were not sorry at all that they had tried to re-create humankind on New-Earth, as well as other beasts, but had all but given up entirely over the years, and were grieved in their dark shriveled hearts.

7 So one of those in power, speaking for all of those in power, said, We will destroy the molds from which we have made new life on this dying earth, both clones of women and other animals, and for every last creeping thing, even the birds in the air, for we are sorry we ever made them and are done.

8 But Noah II found opportunity in the tired eyes of those still in power.

9 This is the genealogy of Noah II. Noah II was one of the first of clone-hybrid man, perfectly created in his generations. Noah II walked with an imaginary god.

10 And Noah II begot three clone-hybrid sons with his Clone II era reproducer: Shem II, Ham II, and Japheth II.

11 The earth also was corrupt before his god, and New-Earth was filled with violence between outcasts and the self-appointed worthy and righteous of Humanity II.

12 So the imaginary god looked upon the earth in Noah II's mind, and indeed it was corrupt; for all re-created flesh and desire for a purified being had corrupted their ways.

13 And the imaginary and inherently racist god said to Noah II, The end of all re-created flesh is come before me, and our New-Earth is filled with impurities through them; and behold, I will destroy them with the earth.

14. Make yourself two arks from the largest still-operable space cruisers; cover the insides of each with electromagnetic shielding to block radio frequencies and electromagnetic radiation, and to reduce radio waves. Call the vessels *Genesis I* and *Genesis II*.

15. And this is how you shall setup their interiors for travel: The living quarters require a length inside of one hundred fifty meters; its width twen-

ty-five meters, and its height fifteen meters, all within three stories.

16. The space cruisers will have windows from which to see out, and the side doors configured for lower, second, and third deck loadings for easy entry.

17 And behold, I myself am melting the remaining icecaps to bring further floodwaters on the earth, to destroy from under the dark canopy of hell all clone-hybrid flesh in which is the current breath of life; every thing that remains on New-Earth shall die.

18 But I will establish my covenant with you alone; and you shall go into one of these arks—you, your sons, your partners, your Clone-2 era reproducer, and your sons' and their partners and reproducers—and thus all animals, plant life, and human categorization of races and sub-races into the other.

19 And of every living fabricated thing you shall bring two of every sort into this second ark, to be manned by the scientists who will keep them alive in this separate ark on Humanity II's journey off this dying world.

20 Of the re-created birds after their kind, of re-created animals after their kind, and of every re-created creeping thing and plant after their kind, two of every kind and DNA of each shall be acquired from the laboratories on the western side of Hope on the highest of the islands. This I say verily to you:

21 And you shall take for yourself all remaining food and water that shall be partaken by parties on both arks for the long voyage ahead, gathered by slaved laborers who will not come with you, and this shall be sustenance for you and for your family and for the plants and animals and other beings.

22 Thus Noah II did; according to all that the imaginary god commanded him, so he did.

CHAPTER 7:
THE LAST OF DAYS

Then the imaginary and inherently racist god said to Noah II, Come into the first ark, *Genesis I*, you and all your household, because you are worthy and righteous before me in Humanity II's generation.

2 On this first ark, you shall take with you only you, your family, your reproducers, and sustenance including animals for meat; and on the second ark, *Genesis II*, every type of being re-created in the image of Humanity and in the image of Humanity II: male and female created they them; non-gender-specific they them; genderless they them;

3 also two beings of each complexion as you see fit, be that many or few, to keep the other species alive off the face of the earth.

4 For after seven more days I will open the hellish sky and summon the sun and cause the icecaps on the earth to melt forty days and forty nights, and I will destroy from the face of the earth all living things the Humanities have made.

5 And Noah II did according to all that his imaginary god commanded him.

6 Noah II was six hundred years old because of genetic alterations and mutations when the floodwaters were on the earth.

7 So Noah II, with his sons, his partners, his Clone II era reproducer, and his sons' and their partners and reproducers, went into the first ark because of the waters of the flood.

8 Of re-created animals and plants, of birds, and of every living thing that creeps on New-Earth, including re-created humankind,

9 two by two they were chain-pulled, dragged, carried, crated and tight-packed into *Genesis II* as the imaginary god had commanded Noah II.

10 And it came to pass after seven days that the waters of the flood were on New-Earth.

11 In the six hundredth year of Noah II's life, in the second month, the seventeenth day of the month, on that day all the remaining lands were swallowed and the black curtain of hell in the sky opened long enough for the sun to break through to melt the icecaps.

12 And the acid smog rain was on New-Earth forty days and forty nights.

13 On the very same day Noah II and his sons, Shem II, Ham II, and Japheth II, and Noah II's partners and the three partners of his sons with them, entered *Genesis I*, which were fully prepared by the slaved laborers—

14 and on *Genesis II* were loaded all beasts re-created after their kind, all livestock re-created after their kind, every creeping thing that creeps on the earth re-created after their kind, and every bird re-created after their kind, every bird of every sort.

15 And they were chain-pulled, dragged, carried, and crated onto this second ark next to the first ark containing Noah II and his family, of all flesh in which is to become the current breath of life.

16 So those that entered, male and female, gendered and genderless of all flesh, went in as the imaginary and inherently racist god had commanded him; and this same god shut them in

as the outcasts and the wanderers and even those once in power began their assault on the two space cruisers as the waters on the highest island near Hope steadily climbed.

17 Now the flood was on the earth forty days. The waters increased and swallowed the remaining people left behind.

18 The waters prevailed and increased on what remained of New-Earth, and lifted a war-damaged *Genesis I* about on the surface of the waters, flooding the engines, with undamaged *Genesis II* higher in elevation.

19 And the waters prevailed exceedingly on the earth, and all the high hills but one under the hole created in the black heaven above were covered.

20 The waters prevailed ten meters upward, and the mountains were covered as the second ark took to the sky, leaving the first behind to float and rock over the depths of the ever-expanding sea.

21 And all flesh and re-created flesh died that once moved on the earth, and every human but those in the second ark burning hot through the atmosphere on its predetermined course: birds and livestock and beasts and every creeping thing that creeps.

22 All in whose lungs was the breath of the spirit of life, all that was on the dry land, died.

23 So Humanity and Humanity II destroyed all living things which were on the face of the ground: both humans and livestock, creeping thing and bird of the air. They were destroyed from the earth and from New-Earth. Only humankind who were in Noah II's second ark, *Genesis II*, remained alive.

24 And the waters prevailed on earth one hundred and fifty days.

CHAPTER 8:
DELIVERANCE

Then Gaia remembered Noah II, and every living thing, and all the animals still trapped in the first ark, *Genesis I*. And so she made a cold wind to pass over the earth, and the air cleared and the sun broke through and the waters subsided as icecaps re-formed.

2 The fountains of the deep and the windows of heaven were also stopped, and the acid smog from the heaven-turned-hell above was restrained and began to dissipate.

3 And the waters receded continually from the earth. At the end of the hundred and fifty days the waters decreased.

4 Then the first of the arks, highly damaged from war and from the earth came to rest in the seventh month, the seventeenth day of the month, on the mountains of Hope.

5 And the waters decreased continually until the thirteenth month. In the thirteenth month, on the first day of the month, the tops of the mountains were seen.

6 So it came to pass, at the end of the last of days of the Humanities, that the windows of *Genesis I* shattered as the war- and sea-worn cruiser cracked apart from gravity and stress.

7 Then out flew a raven, and another, fluttering about to and fro until the waters had dried up from the earth.

8 And then flew out a dove to see if the waters had receded from the face of the ground.

9 But the dove found no resting place for the sole of its foot and so it returned to the ark to its mate, for the waters were on the face of the reclaimed earth. The pair, along with other birds, perched and pecked upon the bones of Noah II and his family, while all makes of insects and arachnids and other life fed upon what was left of them.

10 And the surviving animals and creeping things waited yet another seven days, and again the dove flew out from the ark.

11 Then the dove came back to the gathering of bones that evening, and behold, a freshly plucked fig leaf was in her mouth; and all remaining birds knew the waters had receded.

12 But the other animals and creeping things waited yet another seven days, feeding on the plants and the food and water and other such sustenance within the ark before venturing out and then back again, and some did not return again anymore.

13 And it came to pass in the six hundred and first year, in the first month, the first day of the month, that the waters were dried up from the earth; and the broken space cruiser split apart further to spill out the surviving animals to the dry ground.

14 And in the second month, on the twenty-seventh day of the month, the earth was dried.

15 Then Gaia spoke to Noah II saying,

16 Return to the ground, you and your partners and your hybrid-clones and your sons and your sons' partners and their clones.

17 And so some of the remaining animals, though few, brought out with them the bones and the remaining flesh clinging to them:
birds and felines and canines and other carnivorous animals, every creeping thing that used to creep on the earth, so that they may abound on the earth, and be fruitful and multiply once again; and soon after followed the

omnivores and the herbivores.

18 So Noah II went out, what remained of him, and what remained of his sons and his partners and his sons' partners with him, by mouth and by beak and by claw.

19 Every animal, every creeping thing, every bird, and whatever once creeped on the earth, according to nature, went out of the first ark.

20 Then it came to pass that Noah II's second ark, *Genesis II*, landed where it was destined after so much time, taking with it every transported animal and every bird and every type of living thing, as well as what would soon become the start of Humanity III.

21 And after a self-diagnosis and habitability check of this new planet, the side door of the space craft opened to expose its three levels and an abundance of life spilled out.

22 And so it happens the ramp had the following words engraved upon it for those capable of reading:

> "While the earth remains,
> Seedtime and harvest,
> Cold and heat,
> Winter and summer,
> And day and night
> Shall not cease."

CHAPTER 9: THE PROMISE

[*remaining pages missing*]

A BROKEN PROMISE

ANONYMOUS

THE FOREST was shrinking.
The axe promised a return to greatness,
A forest more glorious than ever.
The trees cheered for the axe,
because its handle was made of wood.
They thought it was one of them.
They thought they
were safe from the blade,
until it fell.

POST-OP INSTRUCTIONS AFTER YOUR MIND CONTROL CHIP IMPLANTATION

EFFIE SEIBERG

"OH GOOD, YOU'RE BACK WITH US!" says a voice from your right. Everything in front of you is fuzzy and smelling of beach-ball-plastic. You blink, and things sharpen into focus. It's a nurse, wearing American-flag-print scrubs and standing next to your bed in a hospital recovery bay. The plastic smell is the oxygen-giving cannula in your nose, which you manage to yank out with sloth-like elegance and speed.

The nurse hands you a cup of apple juice. "You took your sweet time, didn'tcha."

You struggle to get words out. You want to ask why you're here, what happened. The words are floating around in your head like cocaine-fueled butterflies, flitting about and refusing capture. You concentrate and manage to say, "Banana?"

"Oh don't worry about it, hon," says the nurse. "Standard part of the post-op process. You're gonna have trouble with words for another few hours, so I'm going to read these instructions to you. No way you'll manage to read 'em yourself in this state. Ready?"

You nod, and after a furious burst of concentration, manage to say, "Seesaw."

"OK, here we go." The nurse pulls at a sheaf of papers from the little metal roll-table nearby.

"*Congratulations! You've completed your MIND-PLUS chip implantation procedure. It's very important you read and follow your post-op instructions. The first thing you should know is that this procedure causes the brain to have brief aphasia, or difficulty with producing words, usually for about three hours. You'll stay here until you can make coherent sentences. The second thing you should know is that this procedure causes a substantial memory loss (most patients lose about three to six months of memories) and that you knew of this side effect and consented to it. You'll see a video you made pre-op shortly.*'"

You're stunned. You can't put into words your bewilderment that you would have agreed to what's sounding like brain surgery, especially with this substantial a side effect. "Pachyderm?" you ask the nurse, putting as much urgency and concern into your voice as you can.

"It'll all make sense, I promise." The nurse adjusts a pair of half-moon glasses and continues.

"'Your procedure: MIND-PLUS chip implantation. Doctor's notes: After obtaining informed consent and filming a video, the patient was put under anesthesia. A small patch of hair was shaved, and then a 3cm incision was made in the scalp, a 1cm square piece of cranium was removed, a MIND-PLUS-Q chip was implanted in the left frontal lobe. Throughout the procedure the patient's blood pressure, pulse, and oxygen saturations were monitored continuously. The piece of cranium was replaced and the scalp was sewn back up with three stitches. The patient tolerated the procedure well.'

"Between you and me," the nurse says in a low voice, "some of our docs think humming the MIND-PLUS jingle counts as informed consent, but you gave proper consent so you're good."

You're confused. But surely you had a good reason for undergoing something so drastic? You're a reasonable, intelligent person. You just have memory loss so you don't know what that reason is yet. There's no way you'd've done something outlandish.

The nurse continues. *"Findings: A standard MIND-PLUS-Q test was conducted post-implantation and the chip is operating as intended. Before implantation the patient scored 81% on the Pew Updated Typology test. If the patient follows the standard recovery patterns, they are expected to score as high as a 95% in the upcoming weeks.'*

"Now, you have a version of this printed out in this set of papers here, but you can also go online and do the test. Of course, I've seen people get banned from social media within two days of the procedure, so if that happens you don't need to bother with the test. Are you on social media?"

You think. Who knows what you might have been up to in the past six months, but at least prior to that you were only on Facebook and YouTube. Mostly Facebook. And were juuuuust starting to experiment with TikTok but you hadn't gotten far. You manage to say, "Granola, ping pong ball, robot, pencil case."

"Right, no point in asking you that for at least a few more hours! Let's keep going.

What you should know: MIND-PLUS is a computer chip that gets implanted in the frontal lobe of your brain, an area of the cerebrum which controls voluntary movement and expressive language, regulates emotions in interpersonal relationships and social situations, and manages higher level executive functions. The procedure connects several neurons to the pins of the chip, which redirects thought processes and recalibrates emotions. Some patients are able to get to this new mental state without surgery, but just by consuming sufficient quantities of media. However, the procedure is available for people who want to make sure they only have the right thoughts, and remove all uncertainty."

Why on earth would you have agreed to something so drastic? "Remove all uncertainty" … that sounds quite strange, and you can't tell if it's your altered state making it strange or not. Uncertainty is just part of life, right? You use your critical thinking skills to evaluate information and discard the fake stuff, the propaganda, the lies, and then you're set.

But you also think of your cousin Margie who always has an answer for everything. Whether it's pedophiles in congress or Antifa riots, she always has sources for her statements. Lots of them. She always says she's "done her research." And maybe it would be nice once, just once, to know as much as she does. To be more certain that you KNOW you know what's going on, and you're not being deluded by fake news.

Through the haze, you manage to say, "Foxtail."

The nurse smiles. "No worries. Now where were we … ah.

"After you leave: Your stitches will dissolve naturally over the course of a few weeks. You may feel some soreness in your scalp, which may be exacerbated by brushing or washing your hair. This is normal, and we discourage the use of opioids to manage it. Please use Tylenol or ibuprofen or similar, and be gentle with scalp-related activities."

Some of the anesthetic has already started to wear off, and you do feel a small stabbing pain near the crown of your head. You slowly move your hand, still attached to a tangle of cords and an IV line, to feel around.

The nurse catches your hand and puts it back down at your side. "You don't want to do that, believe me. You'll just irritate the stitches further. And I'm not gonna lie to you, this sucker's gonna *hurt.* Ask me how I know!"

You signed yourself up for this. For this painful, memory-losing experience. You're a rational person. You must've had a good reason. Maybe this won't be as painful as when your Facebook friends turned on you for saying that all kids need vaccines.

The nurse continues to read from the sheaf of papers.

"'You've already noticed some aphasia, which is normal for a few hours. As the chip starts to take effect, you might also notice certain thoughts being cut off midway, with a bzzt sound or a vibrating sensation, followed by a thought jumble, and a redirection to a new thought. If you're writing down your thoughts and veer off into wrong ones, you might notice you write some strange words as your direction is corrected by the chip. This is also normal.'

"So like," the nurse continues, "if you're having a wrong thought, as the chip takes over, you'll get redirected. Kind of like how all you can manage now is nonsense words, it'll do that to you briefly as you refocus on the right thought instead."

You nod. And manage, "How long slug?"

"It's different for everyone, but most folks are fully adjusted in a few days. Took me five. Some are faster and some are slower, of course, but I'm guessing you'll be one of our quicker ones. Now, since I bet you're confused, let me show you the video you made yesterday."

The nurse grabs a tablet from the metal rolling table and holds it in front of you. You're on screen, wearing your favorite red shirt. You're having a bad hair day and your eyes are wide.

Screen-you says, "Hey, it's me. I mean you. I mean us. Wow

this is weird, right? Anyway, since you're going to forget all this, here's what went down. We've always known that there's an elite cabal running stuff, right? And they're corrupt and horrible and do terrible machinations behind the scenes. The Democratic side of it conspired to keep Bernie from being the candidate, for god's sake. So, as I … I mean you … I mean we read more, and we found Q-Anon. And suddenly, all the fear and uncertainty and doubt went away. There *is* a plan to deal with all the mess in the world. There *are* people who get it, who are on top of things. And it became clear that if we just let these people do their thing, everything will be ok."

Screen-you pauses, eyes wild. You do not look like a person making good decisions.

You'd heard of Q-Anon, of course, and had questions. You'd been a centrist, a moderate, with a good head on your shoulders. It was probably true, right? Because you're a smart and thoughtful person who isn't a sucker, who isn't going to swallow just any information without question. You wouldn't have been taken in by just any sort of nonsense, right? But going so far as surgery?

Screen-you continues, "So like, everything was *amazing*. For a few weeks. It was such a relief to have someone competent to root for, someone to put trust in. It was so energizing, and I … we … felt so *good* about things. Just like overflowing with like optimism and hope that it'll all be great. And what's awesome is, it's *all true*. Like I looked things up to check, because you gotta do your own research, and there are *so many people* confirming these things. You remember Angie from yoga class? She really helped. First showed me some really good wellness stuff, like I don't know if you remember this but we've already been on several toxin purges. And she showed me how it's really the government pushing vaccines, which are just more toxins. And everything came from there. It really opened my eyes! Our eyes. And as I learned more, what was interesting was people started to violently push me away. Like, Aunt Beth won't talk to me anymore, she says I'm dangerous. Me, who'd never hurt a fly. And that's the proof, you see. The knowledge is so dangerous to the status quo that people are primed to react so strongly to it. They're all brainwashed. People have been dropping out of my life left and right, and good riddance, because they're not safe people. *They're* the ones who are dangerous, through their complacency. The proof is right there."

That's not right, you think. People reacting in a certain way doesn't prove anything. You get a tiny tickle in the back of your brain, almost like a phone vibration but inside your skull.

"Anyway," screen-you continues, "that awesome headspace didn't last. I got more and more worried about this evil shady Cabal and how much power they had and what they were going to do with it. And yes, we have our saviors working for us, but they're so outnumbered. And I didn't know what we could do. We had to act, right? To help somehow. So when people in this Facebook group I joined (we joined) were all talking about this chip, it seemed interesting. Like it was a way to both help put things right *and* it had a side effect of going back to feeling so confident and cheerful about everything, like you know everything's going to be ok in the end because you're now taking the step to help it be ok, if you know what I mean. So that's why you're here. We're here. We have a purpose and it's all gonna be ok. I hope it doesn't hurt too bad, and I've left you a bunch of sticky note instructions at home to help you fill in the gaps of the last three to six months. There's a lasagna in the freezer. See you on the other side!"

Screen-you grins and waves, and then the nurse takes the tablet away. You're concerned. To go from what you remember to willing to have brain surgery in *six months* seems a little extreme. And if people like Aunt Beth, one of the most empathetic kind people you've ever met, cut you out, doesn't that mean there's a possibility *you're* in the wrong, instead of her? You've never heard of her cutting anyone out before. Plus, there was a bit of a logical problem in there, wasn't it? There was no reason getting this chip would actually *be* helpful, so you're not feeling good about helping, you're feeling good about … what? Going deeper into the rabbit hole? Maybe *you're* the one who got brainwashed. The vibration in the back of your skull comes back.

"OK hon," said the nurse. "The next thing we gotta do is have you get up and walk around a bit, make sure nothing else was damaged. Do you feel up to that?"

Brain surgery. *You just had brain surgery.* Something so risky that it could have side effects that wouldn't let you walk. Did past-you think about this? Did you know the possibilities? "Walnut," you say, frowning. "Walnut scare."

"Yeah, I guess it is a little scary, but you're doing great so far. You're already getting a few sensible words in, so it looks like you're progressing really quickly! Now what do you think, you feel up to getting up?"

You slowly and weakly push yourself up into a sitting position, and swing your hospital-socked feet over the side of the bed. They're the kind with little rubber nubbins on both top and bottom, so you don't slip. The nurse unhooks the pulse oximeter that's taped to your index finger from the long cable that connects to a large monitoring machine, which beeps in protest, then hooks your IV bag onto a rolling IV pole, and helps you get up.

You feel shaky, and you hang on to the pole for support as you slowly shuffle your way out the recovery bay and into the hall. You feel yourself slipping within your socks a bit, even as they grip the floor with their nubbins. You try to remember what it was like after other surgeries. You were shaky after your colonoscopy last year, and that wasn't even proper surgery, so maybe there's nothing to fear here. You get a feeling like there's a warm glow in the back of your skull, in the same place the weird vibrations came from. It's pleasant and soothing.

But at the same time, you're concerned. What will this chip

do to you? Does it prevent you from ever thinking anything other than what it wants? What does it want? Past-you seemed so confident about this chip, but you're still not sure how you got there.

The nurse walks next to you at your same snail's pace, keeping a steady stream of meaningless chatter going, talking about how the Q chip is so much better than the Flat Earth chip or the Goop chip or the Lizard People chip.

The rolling pole holding your IV is cold against your hand. You pass another recovery bay with a closed curtain.

"This is the Koch wellness center questionnaire one. Please select from zero to five, where zero is 'completely disagree' and five is 'completely agree' for the following statement," says a deep voice behind the curtain, *"The Taliban is going to ban abortion, vaccines, and gay marriage … maybe we were fighting on the wrong side all this tim.e"*

"Four?" responds a soft and wavering voice. "No, five. I think five. Wrong religion, but they do know how to enforce what they want, and a lot of what they want is what I want."

"Very good!" says the deep voice.

You keep shuffling along. You hear similar exchanges at two more recovery bays, one for the sentence *"When social media bans Nazis, insurrectionists, and white supremacists, it's only conservative speech that's being censored. They don't censor the liberal stuff,"* and one for *"I think folks killed by police should've just complied. But when it comes to mask mandates, I will not comply."*

"Before or after sausage?" you ask the nurse, and indicate the bays you've passed with your free hand.

"Those are the before questions, hon. You'll get different questions in a few hours to see how you're progressing."

You wonder how you would rate these statements now, and how yesterday-you would rate them. None of them quite sit right, and that buzzing vibration starts up again. You concentrate to keep your train of thought. Each statement has an inherent contradiction or self-own-bzzzzzzzzzz. People were agreeing with statements nobody should agr*bzzzzzzzz*, so deep in their beliefs that they didn't perceive any probl*zzzzzzzzzzzz*. Would this become you? Would you be unable to have any critical thinkin*zzzzzzzzzzz*? No empathy, just bigotr*zzzzzzz*? If this is what the chip does, you don't want b*zzzzzzzz*. Shit. This is bad*zzzzzzzzzzzzz*.

You tug at the nurse's scrubs sleeve, focus so hard you'd think you were trying to set fire to something with your mind, and say "Reversible? Chip out? Lamp switch chimpanzee towel!"

You frantically mime grabbing the chip from your head and throwing it away, and the buzzing is nearly intolerable.

"Not sure what you mean. You want to get the stitches out? They'll dissolve on their own."

You try again, the buzzing increasing at the back of your skull. It's like a whole construction site back there, with jackhammers and buzzsaws having a party. This time you say "Cut! Out! Out out internet snip!" while miming scissors near your incision and repeating the grab-and-throw gesture.

"You can't cut your stitches out, hon. They're gonna be uncomfortable for a bit."

Maybe you can call Aunt Beth. She would help in an emergency, talk to folks for you. You shake your head and mime again.

"Oh! You want the chip out!" says the nurse, and you nod, trying to focus while also attempting to drown out what feels like an entire earthquake in the back of your head. "Hmm, now that I think of it, I have seen folks get other chips reversed."

Thank heavens! The buzzing and shaking is unbearable.

"I can ask the doctors if we can penguin printer candle I promise you you're gonna love it, just give it a few more hours."

"OK," you say, exhausted and defeated, and the buzzing mercifully disappears and that warm glow returns. This time the words come easily. "Chip good. Can't wait."

THE PARADOX OF HUMANITY AS AN ALPHABETIC LIST

JETSE DE VRIES

Assimilation (see: V);

Birthright (see: E);

Christianity (see: R);

Dadaism (see: N);

Evolution (see: B);

Folly (see: K);

Gravitas (See: J);

Hypocrisy (see: S);

Islam (see: R);

Jocularity (see: G);

Knowledge (see: F);

Liberality (see: X);

Morality (see: W);

Normality (see; D);

Optimism (see: P);

Pessimism (see: O);

Quintessentiality (see: U);

Rationality (see: C, I, Z);

Sincerity (see: H);

Torpor (see: Y);

Universality (see: Q);

Variety (see: A);

Wickedness (see: M);

Xenophobia (see: L);

Yearning (see: T);

Zen (see: R);

THE PERSISTENCE OF MEMORY

JOSHUA GINSBERG

AMY TOOK THE LONGER, UNMARKED PATH from the hidden tear in the wire fencing through the woods as the November branches of trees, bare and brittle, raked her skin and hooked her clothing. She paused before entering the clearing to carefully conceal her name behind the one she had selected when she first joined the Rememberers.

She emerged into the small clearing as Atifa, and through the trees the others joined her until they formed a tight ring.

She nodded to them—Alyosha, who had once been a rabbi, Amara the former editor, Zakariya, the artist whose hands lacked fingers, but found inventive ways to continue painting anyway, Zamyatin the fourth-grade teacher and others. Nurses, caregivers, an athlete, an attorney, even a hedge fund manager, which was unusual given that role's traditional association with risk aversion. No one here had any illusions about the risk they were taking.

Maybe, Atifa thought grimly, that's why there were fewer in the circle at every gathering.

"Greetings friends. We don't have much time so let's begin."

They extended their arms and clasped one another's hands.

"Everyone has their tactile transmission turned on?"

Her question was met with nods and murmurs of assent.

"Okay, I'm establishing the local area tactile network now."

They all braced themselves for the deluge of intense images and emotions that flowed through them, from one to the next.

First and strongest among these was the memory that Atifa had selected. As it was five years to the day since Tiffany's death, Atifa had chosen to share the memory of their brief and happy life together. From the first time their eyes and hands met under a Pink Floyd laser light concert, to their first embrace and kiss, moving into a small apartment together along with Tiffany's fat, black cat, Orwell. How they had gone to the beach together, wrote messages in the sand and watched the tide come in and wash their words away. How, even after the scarlet sashes marched to power, they huddled together, offering each other soft reassurances cored of hard truths. How Tiffany's hormone therapy was discontinued, replaced with a new, mandatory prescription that made her violently ill. How it ate away at both her health and her will, until one day Atifa came home to the note.

Everyone in the circle read it, felt it, tears brimming over their lower eyelids and down their cheeks.

Next in queue was a memory from Alyosha, scanning symbols on parchment that slowly resolved into English rather than Hebrew. In the weeks prior to the closure of his Synagogue, every waking moment of every day he had poured over this Torah, which had long ago been smuggled from Berlin. Painstakingly he committed the words, the meanings, even the texture of the fragile parchment, to memory, so that it might yet be preserved—even as he was forced to add it to the pile of books, douse it with accelerant, light the match and watch the dark blossom spread across the scroll. But because he remembered it, now they all remembered it.

In the same way they preserved the beauty and memory of Zakariya's great-grandfather's ornate, hand-knotted prayer rug. And the fearful subversion of Dr. Eun-Jeong working secretly to provide supplies and consultations alongside the black market brujas to ensure access to care for those who needed it most.

Atifa shuddered and almost broke contact as she thought about the pouch of powder in her pocket, the not yet perceptible bulge of her belly. She had just learned the week prior and had not shared that knowledge with her "correctly" gender-assigned mate, whose absence of cruelty or unkindness to her failed to make him any less loathsome to her.

"Take with a big meal," the bruja had told her.

She would make pot roast and potatoes tonight.

The memories and tears continued to flow for just another moment before everyone's coms crackled to life.

"You've got incoming. Eight minutes, maybe less"

It was a message from Diana, whose team kept watch over the perimeter.

That was fast, Atifa thought. Too fast. Had someone in the circle been compromised?

Reluctantly, they broke contact and hid their new memories deep within the folds and pockets of their truest selves.

"Musketeers?" Atifa asked through her com.

"Yeah … and drones."

"Shit," she hissed. They had expected the ground troops—outsourced paramilitary contractors infamous for their vicious and overzealous use of force in carrying out the Chairman's directive, "to stamp out resistance and emotional terrorism wherever and however necessary."

A week earlier, while scouting for new gathering places, Atifa and Diana had planted a series of improvised proximity mines set to release empathic blasts. It might buy them a couple minutes against human adversaries, but such defenses would be useless against machines. Already they could hear a distant buzz filling up the sky, steadily increasing in volume.

"Okay everyone, watch for the signs and until then, remember."

"Remember," they whispered to one another as they embraced, heads on shoulders, faces buried in and dampening the fabric worn by strangers bound together now by something deeper and stronger than blood.

Then they drifted apart like mist, back into the woods and lives from which they had come. Atifa reaffixed her mask named Amy, the loving and devoted housewife.

They were gone before those woods began to crackle with the blue lightning of two dozen stun batons set to maximum efficiency. When, moments later, the steel-grey sky opened up to rain gas and rubber bullets, it did so on no one but ghosts.

MIDAS

GWYNNE GARFINKLE

HE COATS HIMSELF IN GOLD
to hide the rot

surely nothing will impinge upon
all that hard currency

he takes and takes
from the insignificant many

with their mortal bodies
their unreal suffering

not men of substance like him
he holds himself apart

impervious to pain
surely he will live forever

inside the golden carapace
he putrefies

crack it open
and he comes apart

THE FALL OF AN EMPIRE

ANONYMOUS

I'M NOT SURPRISED, ARE YOU SURPRISED?

How could you be when it was always going to be this way
The path had been paved we're just stepping on the stones
It's time to wake up
That coma gives an aftertaste like cold medicine
It's medicated, sedated, a numbing to populate
the numbers of the dead alive
It took a live stream to rip off the mask of hypocrisy
Shit wrapped up in a gold box, a quaint little
red bow placed on top
Oh, how you people loved to hold it up
as if it meant something
As if compassion is something to be proud of

"HOW COULD YOU VOTE FOR HIM? What's wrong with you?"

My father starts yelling back in his native language. The Italian tongue is wild and quick witted, usually a musical note I love to hear no matter my mood, but at this moment it's cold to my ears and everything I can no longer bear. A country of uniqueness because of the differences living inside, the multicultural mixing of the languages, bloods, cultures, of all their faces and so many want to turn the wine into water and wash out all flavors.

His voice angers me, I cannot bear it.

"You're in Trump's country now, speak fucking English!"

The silence is painful, it's hard to bear, more so than his angry voice. His native voice silent until the phone makes a beep. He hung up.

Is it true that high schoolers are now reading
at a third-grade level?
Is it true they can no longer do their
homework without the internet?
It's been years since I've stood in a classroom,

but I have to ask, is it true?

What's happening?

What happened to the rebels who hated labels, who said—

"FUCK THE GOVERNMENT"

Who hated the establishment and educated

themselves out of spite

Who were suspicious of the rich and anyone wearing a suit?

Where has the growing scum of tyranny been hiding?

Nowhere! You pie-eyed gullible clowns!

They've been out in the open the whole time

You've been too busy patting yourselves on the back to notice

JOE WAS LATE for work yesterday; he didn't come in at all today. His sister got attacked outside her house in Philly. They beat her till her nose broke, her teeth fell out, they ripped off her clothes to prove she was a man. She grew up tough, a fighter, she grew up with two brothers who kept her safe, but no amount of calloused knuckles could beat a wolf pack.

Joe can't understand why it happened. He came to work only days after, the shock, the disbelief still on his face, the questions in his eyes. Why would someone do that?

We all look at his shock and hold our tongues; our resentment overpowers our empathy. We mourn her pain, not his shock. Not when he voted for the man who made everyone feel they had the right to make others bleed.

He wanted cheaper groceries, not protection for his sister, not better education for his autistic son.

Joe, I've always wanted to say this, you're a fucking idiot and stop talking about Top Gun. No one cares if you're a Maverick.

It's heading toward the end

All empires fall and we're nearing the end to this story

When the sounds of chains, when the screams of dying families,

when the smell of bombs fill the air, when the streets are filled
with neighbors sleeping in the cold and heat, when a child has
no food, when tears are reserved only for those who look like
you, that's when it's time to put it to bed
Maybe this country has what's coming to it

I look at my friends and wonder what will happen. Vada who
is cheery and loud, her Puerto Rican blood giving her the most
beautiful hair and eyes, as she sings badly with another cocktail
in her hand. Every day is a gift to Vada after she survived such
a painful beginning. I look at Chris who is if *Hello Kitty* went
through a half ass punk stage and never finished, with his love of
vinyl and random knowledge of Lovecraftian lore despite never
having read a single story. He's the kind of gay guy who can't hide
it, but still never says it aloud when we live in the bright red cherry
color state of Florida, who dates in secret just in case one of the
people he calls friends get uncomfortable with the notion.

That ol' coded comment of, *I don't have a problem with it, I just
don't want them shoving it in my face.*

I think of Alex, who I haven't spoken to in years but still think
of fondly. Who had an abortion when she was too young to care
for anything, including herself. I think of her lying in the clinic
telling the nurse, no please I don't want to hear the heartbeat.
To hear that gentle thumping from the inside would only make
it worse, it'd make the tears thicker when they fall. I imagine how
her life would have been if she'd been forced in another direction,
a baby with a man who frightened her, who stalked her when she
finally told him no. She wouldn't have the man she married now,
a man who listened when she told him "wait till I get my nails
done before you propose" and remembered years later. Buying a
ring and waiting till her nails were the prettiest shade of pink with
rhinestones and designs to put the diamond on.

Most importantly, I think of Zee, a Muslim Palestinian, still trapped in Gaza. My tears are reserved for her most days, for the past year I've only cried for her. I cry for the way she just wants a cup of coffee, a piece of fruit, I think about what will happen now as I remember his words—*"let them finish the job."* She's told me America is tainted for her; never will she ever consider stepping foot in the states. *"They're heartless, they don't care about us."*

When I talk about her to my coworkers, to anyone who will listen, and I get that blank look of boredom I know that she is right. This is a land of individualism, no one but yourself matters in a country built out of lawlessness.

> **DM:** "If you see this before your phone dies, I just wanted to tell you, it's so grim saying this, but I'm honored to call you my friend. You have a spirit I admire, have since you first commented on my Animal Kingdom post on Tumblr years ago and then messaged me when I was suicidal. My only friend during that time and I know you pulled me back from the brink multiple tomes with your words. I hope you get out, praying for it, and I don't even believe in god. I'm fucking crying as I type this but just in case something happens, I just wanted to say that."

> **DM:** "I always wished to make it to the US and meet up with you. I still hold on to that hope but it's getting difficult to have faith in anything with everything that's going on. We see hell every day. Today I broke down talking to my sister. I feel so weak. They are terrorizing us to leave but they bombed two cars of people who listened and were on their way to the South. The night is setting in and terror hours have begun.
>
> I didn't get to mourn my memories and belongings that I lost in our house yet, if I made it, I'll never been the same again."

I wonder if I'll have to say goodbye again but this time, she won't be on the other end to answer me.

Does anyone know history?
It doesn't take much to figure out where we are
The rise of turmoil, chaotic disillusion and not to mention
prominent aversion that boils and foams near the conclusion
They're foaming at the mouths
There's blood on their fingernails
They have grey matter dripping out of their ears
They split us up, broke us down until they could package
what they pedaled and sell it in a Christmas box.
I'm so glad I'm Buddhist

FUNDING PROPOSAL

DAVID DEGRAFF

A NOVEL APPROACH FOR TESTING THE NATURE OF REALITY

DeGraff, D.R., Wallace, J.M., Diffenderfer, A.L.
Physics Department, Alfred University, Alfred, NY

ABSTRACT

Our lab has recently succeeded in creating a stable wormhole sending a short message 0.321 seconds into the past. We seek funding to expand the wormhole and use time dilation of one end so objects up to 10 grams could pass up to ten minutes into the past. We will use the stable wormhole to test the nature of reality, whether we can alter our pasts and futures, or if we are doomed to live in a block universe where the whisper network fails.

INTRODUCTION

The notion of time travel has long been a staple of both science fiction (Wells, 1895) and science (Gödel, 1949). One of the most promising methods of achieving the goal of time travel had been via wormholes (Morris *et al.*, 1988), and our lab has recently kept a wormhole open for a brief time. We are applying for funds to keep the mouths open long enough to send objects through them.

One question raised by time travel is the nature of our universe. Do we live in a block universe where the past and the future are both fixed and unchangeable (Blish, 1954), or a universe where we can alter the past (Bradbury, 1953)? Perhaps time travel allows us to travel between parallel worlds (Watson, 1978). Our experiment will then test the nature of reality to see if we live in a block universe. Or not. Please not. DeGraff is too lazy to read this deep in a paragraph, so we can say it is our strongly favored hypothesis that we live in a branching Many Worlds multiverse (Everett, 1957) and we landed in the wrong branch as evidence from the failure of the whisper network (avoid DeGraff) and the recent election results in the US.

EXPERIMENT

We have the ability to create a macroscopic wormhole a few centimeters in diameter and accelerate one mouth so time dilation can put one end of the wormhole in the past relative to the other end. One mouth (the future end) will be placed in Albuquerque, New Mexico. The other mouth (the past end) will be placed in Brisbane, Australia. We chose these locations because in case of catastrophic failure, there is an 87% chance no one will notice.

If we go deliberately trying create paradoxes and we live in a block universe, that could have catastrophic results. For instance, if a blue ball emerges in Brisbane, that means ten minutes in the future we are going to drop a blue ball into the Albuquerque mouth. But with prior knowledge of what we are going to do, we can alter our actions and send a red ball instead. In a block universe, that could end in catastrophic failure. Catastrophic in this usage could be for the lab, the city, or the entire universe. That version of the experiment would be irresponsible. We are not going to do that. Probably.

For our (very safe, no chance of destroying the universe) experiment, we will take 100 numbered ping pong balls of various colors, and randomly determine the numerical order to send them though the wormhole into the past, i.e. Brisbane. There will be no communication between the future location and the past location. Okay. That's as far as DeGraff is going to read, the sexist bastard. He put all his female grad students on this project to scuttle our careers. Time Machines. Block Universe. Ridiculous. The real purpose of our experiment is to provide evidence for the multiverse, and, hopefully, find paths between realities. Our initial plan was to find the universe where gender bias in science does not exist. This remains our long-term goal, but the 2024 election provides an easily verified path. We will write "Trump" on them to identify which branch of the multiverse we fell into when we performed our preliminary results. That has to be what happened.

If we do indeed live in a block universe, the balls will emerge into the past in exactly the same order and color as they entered the wormhole in Albuquerque. What we hope to find is that some of the balls do not have "Trump" written on them. If we send balls with messages into the past, but what emerges does not have a message, those balls must have come from a different branch of the multiverse where there was no need for a distress call.

CONCLUSION

We finally have the ability to test out the fundamental nature of reality, if the past is fixed, if the future is fixed, if both are fixed, or if all possible realities exist. This will have a profound consequence on human culture throughout the world. And DeGraff has no idea how much that last sentence means because we are seeking a more sensible universe than the one we find ourselves in at the moment—a universe where a woman can work in science without the constant belittling of her male colleagues.

REFERENCES

Blish, James, "Beep", *Galaxy*, Feb 1954

Bradbury, Ray. "Sound of Thunder", *Colliers*, June 28, 1953

Everett, H., 1957, 'Relative State Formulation of Quantum Mechanics', *RevModPhys*, 29: 454

Gödel, K., 1949 "An Example of a New Type of Cosmological Solutions of Einstein's Field Equations of Gravitation", *RevModPhys*, 21, 447.

Morris, M.S; Thorne, K.S; Yurtsever, U., 1988. "Wormholes, Time Machines and Weak Energy Conditions", *PhysRevL*, 61 12 1446.

Watson, Ian. "The Very Slow Time Machine", *Anticipations*, Ed: Priest, Christopher. Faber&Faber, 1978

Wells, H.G. *The Time Machine*, New York. Henry Holt, 1895.

FROM SHADOWS OF TYRANNY TO THE LIGHT OF FREEDOM

ESSEL PRATT

SOMEONE SPOKE of four score and seven years ago,
Another proclaimed a dream of a better tomorrow.
One refused to stand; took a seat instead,
Another proclaimed that basic rights are easily understood.

One foretold the winds of change,
A man fighting for rights was prepared to die.
Someone warned of peril's indifference,
Another demanded liberty or the possibility of death.

The milkman was weary of silence and spoke out for the people,
Some emerged for the closets and touched the sun.
While others remain hidden; shunned, reviled, unfree,
For simply choosing whom to be.

Some came seeking safety's shore,
Many struggled for freedom, dignity, and humanity.
A refuge from tyranny, an escape from fear,
For many, a chance to live was here.

They are all neighbors, friends, and kin,
They are all someone—where do we begin?
All spoke of freedoms, their simple plea,
All longing to live, to be equal, to be free.

We offered hope through freedom's reprieve,
Skin color, who we love, culture, and race.
The United States was a welcoming place,
Refuge for the tired, poor, huddled masses yearning to breathe

But that night, evil struck its blow,
And today, they fear what tomorrow may show.
None feel safe, in peace, or at rest;
For some, even life becomes a test.

FROM SHADOWS OF TYRANNY TO THE LIGHT OF FREEDOM

And who do we blame, when the dust settles down?
We didn't rise up; we watched, made no sound.
Fuck the blind factions who paved this path,
And curse those who hailed the orange man, blind to his wrath.

We're a nation of souls, many too weary to fight,
But so were those who embraced equal rights.
So remember the dreams and the battles hard-won,
Remember the fallen, who fought and moved on.

Let their voices ring, let their spirits ignite,
Together, we'll rise and rekindle the fight—
For brothers, for sisters, and their non-binary kin,
Until freedom and dignity are burning within.

Despite all the pain, the fear, and the loss,
We must stand against tyranny and the orange man's plans,
Remember the King's dream that once carried us through,
And press forward in honor of those who lost the most.

MY ARROWS ARE AS PLENTIFUL AS DUST, MY SHIELD IS AS INEVITABLE AS TRASH

ET ALIA LAUGHING AND WEEPING

"I'M REALLY PROUD OF YOU FOR BEING YOU! The plunging neck of that dress really frames your beard so beautifully—how do you get the courage to be so ... out in public?"

That's not naturalistic, of course, but it is a stylized version of a conversation that has often been foisted upon me. Sometimes it's a transgender person looking for support; far more often, it isn't. Regardless of who has asked the question, I am fairly certain the answer would be unwelcome.

My superpower is suicidality.

I'm forty-two years old now, and in some ways this is a story of sevens. When I had accumulated twice seven years among this unspeakably wondrous world, my wrist began itching. I knew my nails would do nothing to abate it, only scratching with thin metal could make it stop. Add in another seven and you have reached halfway through my life. That was the first time I attended a Transgender Day of Remembrance commemoration. The first of now twenty-one times I sat through a recitation of the names—or the notifications for those whose names were both presumably and hopefully known to someone, but hadn't been reported in any way as to get on the list—of those who had been murdered because they were like me.

Or, in at least a few cases, mistaken for us. Or, in at least one case, for dating us. Or, for at least one case, being carried in a man's womb.

When the Resident Rump was re-elected, a din of surprise filled the internet with its fearful static, to my confusion. Somehow all these people hadn't known that the country wanted us trannies dead. Or at least were okay with it. Did they think "eradicated from public life" meant something else? Had they never seen *Ace Ventura: Pet Detective?*

I grew up thinking I was imaginary. Not that I was the only one, but that I was made up. "Eradicated" means "from the root," and the root that has since become my beloved non-binary community was still germinating underground when I was a child. Riki Anne Wilchins coined "genderqueer" when I was thirteen; "non-binary" came along a decade later.

Since I was told there were only men and women, boys and girls, I thought I was just a dream for a long time.

It's so easy to wake up.

Especially when you're scratching your itchy wrist.

So, yeah, I wear my dresses and my beard in public because, simply put, I'm not gonna do their work for them. If they want me dead, they can damn well do it themselves.

Walking with death like this, listening to that litany of names every November 20th, desperately digging for history and trancestors, longing for a past to make me real enough to forge the future—to know that I am actually embedded in time, and not in the vague plotting of a game of make believe—has let me walk with the dead. When I step, thousands, millions, of feet fall upon the floor. It's a strength I never would have understood before these last fourteen years of my life, a power I do not yet know to feel.

Amidst that clamor of shock, the closet yawned its ever-hungry maw in the wake of November 5th (remember, remember, the fifth of November, the Gunpowder Treason and Plot—that time a Catholic named Guy Fawkes tried to blow up Parliament). "Surviving a Fascist Regime 101: lay low." "The way we will get through this is by being invisible." And always the objectifying allies: "I will hide you in my basement," so no one has to see me, huh? How easy it is for them to get you to do their eradication work for them.

Queer people have long wielded fierceness as their weapon. You may think I mean the cattiness and the shade for which we are famous, but I don't. Rather, when they tell us that we don't belong somewhere, we show up with bigger hair, with more feathers and shinier sequins. We already are in public life, and we will not let them think otherwise. We claim space when others would tell us that we are too made-up to be there.

This is the front line. This is where my superpower comes in handy.

As you may have guessed, the simple unrelenting trauma of growing up and existing as a transgender woman(ish) in this society has left my brain extravagantly bleak, with all the melodrama of someone whose home is the feeling of being backed up against a corner.

The truth is as simple as my trauma: you don't need a spiky mix of suicidality and spite to be fierce in the face of fascism. There will be many of us who aren't as crazy as I am. In fact, this is my plea to you who are reading this.

If this is your fight, whether because you share the desolation in my soul or simply because you can't imagine wearing neutral tones, or even just because you think it would be fun, please do not lie low.

This moment is the antithesis of the end of *V for Vendetta*, that film that shares a title with an Alan Moore comic. The Guy Fawkes mask will blunt our efforts, being Anonymous will doom us, the black bloc—though not without its uses in the coming years—is not how we can fight.

Well, I suppose you could multi-class with that last group.

However.

We will not survive if we do not, in fact, survive. We must live in order to live, we must have a future to forge just as much as we have a past to make us "feel mighty real." My superpower is no sort of power if your feet are among the thousands that fall when I take a step.

If your fight is the slow choke of the closet, if your work is asylum elsewhere, then I honor that, and I honor you. Let us not fall into binary thinking, that visibility and survival are opposed to each other. That is another weapon in their hand.

We are all in this together, and our every effort will empower each and every one of us.

The sun will caress your skin with its warmth regardless of how you fight, and the air will always taste delicious. Mornings will greet you quiet and breathless. If no one can earn or deserve a sunrise (because earning and deserving are ideas the bosses made up), then no one can lose the sunset. There will always be tails and wings, there will always be jade and feathers.

I wanted the country to surprise me, and it refused.

I do not know how to live without my own death in my heart. Let's surprise me.

FORTY-SEVEN

MARK GRANGER

FOR SOME REASON WE BELIEVED HE WOULDN'T WIN,
and I guess it's because we had hope.
Surely this man who speaks in riddles
could not wheedle his way back to power.
Immigrants, women, minorities, and more
shall die by his sweaty orange hands.
This man, this felon, this racist, this abuser
cares only about fame and money and
under his presidency we will all suffer.
Not just America,
the world.

THE FOOL ON THE HILL

LISA MORTON

MERCE PULLED HER BOOT BACK just before it came down on the half-buried skull. There were more of them in this area, mired in the mud and grayish swamp grass.

She used her walking stick to test the ground beyond the skull, trying not to stare into the eye socket pointed at her face. The stick sank an inch into the water before stopping. She stepped over the bone, planting herself where her stick had been.

Progress across this bog was slow, but not impossible. Ordinarily, Merce would have already given up and moved on to firmer land, but something about the building on the other side of the swamp drew her. Even though parts of its upper stories had caved in, even though walls were cracked and covered with moss, its white columns and rounded portico pinged in Merce's brain. She'd seen this place before, in Mama's history books; she knew it had been important.

She heard a brittle snap beneath her heel; she'd stepped on a long bone. This area, long ago reclaimed by nature's liquids and life, was more packed with death than anywhere else she'd encountered. It'd been a week since she'd left home, hauling her little cart behind her, her head packed with the list of items needed:

Solar panels. Working laptops. Light bulbs. A specific radio piece for Uncle Park. Herbs for Aunt Lateesha. Bullets for Uncle Juan. A cooking pot for Mama.

Merce had just turned eighteen, so this was her first trip alone as a Finder. If she could return with at least most of the items on the list, she'd get to keep going as a Finder instead of being assigned to help out with the farming. Farming bored her to tears; she recognized its significance, but she wasn't cut out for it.

"I think you're a born leader," Mama had told her more than once. But so far Merce didn't feel that herself. She liked the challenge of leaving Camp Jackson, going out on her own into the world, coming up with pieces of the past that would make her extended family happy, productive, enduring. She liked helping others. Maybe that was what Mama was saying, that Merce was good at helping. Maybe that's what being a leader really meant.

So far the trip had been successful. She'd headed southwest, not doing much searching for the first two days; she knew the land surrounding her home had long ago been picked clean by other Finders. On the third day, though, she'd found a once-suburban garden overgrown with Aunt Lateesha's herbs, and later had discovered a stash of unbroken solar panels. She'd stumbled across an old book on healing she thought Lateesha would like, and a pad of paper and colored pencils that her brother Leo would love—Leo, the gifted artist, often lamenting that he had nothing but broken walls for canvases.

Eventually Merce's way had brought her here, to a one-time major city, now abandoned, collapsed in on itself, turning sepia and emerald as the elements reclaimed it. Merce had found an old store that must have sold radio parts, and she'd scored by locating Uncle Park's piece. Her cart was packed, getting harder to haul, and she'd been about to turn around when she'd seen something framed at the end of a strip of broken asphalt. Beyond the asphalt had probably once been an expanse of carefully-tended grass, but now it was the muddy ruin that Merce waded through.

Toward that familiar house ...

The remains in the muck were testament to the former importance of this place. Merce saw not just skulls and arm bones and rib cages, but rusting weapons and armor. Whether these soldiers had died here in the first (nuclear) attack or the riots that had followed as hunger and sickness swept the land, Merce didn't know. But they'd clearly died defending whoever had lived in the house. That became clearer as she neared the collapsed walls and saw bullet holes in some of the skulls, even a few shreds of skin and uniform. These were still corpses, not yet skeletons, and they'd been shot, maybe even not that long ago.

She should turn around, make her way back to where she'd

left her cart, hidden underneath its camouflage of netting and leafy branches. But she was close enough now to see inside the building, to see shafts of afternoon sun outlined in dust motes, painting old furnishings and paintings.

No, she'd come too far. She had to go in now.

She reached a point where a wall had cracked apart, old masonry jumbled on either side of a wide split. Before entering, she thrust a hand into her olive drab jacket pocket and grasped the metal handle of her folding knife; she didn't remove it, but knowing it was there was a comfort.

Taking a deep breath, Merce stepped through, wedging her slim body around rubble and twisted girders. Still using the stick, she made her way into the structure. Stopping to listen, she heard only the soft sounds of animals. She was in a room that had once been elegant, with chairs and tables whose wooden legs had withstood time's onslaught even if their upholstery had not. There was a desk littered with computer equipment and paper tatters, but there was nothing Merce could use.

The floor felt solid, so she ventured farther in. At least the interior was free of human remains, although animals, both alive and dead, had nested in old fabrics. She moved down a hallway where paintings only slightly eroded showed men (mostly) and women, all long dead, all regally posed. Merce didn't like looking at them; she felt their gazes upon her, an airy pressure.

She passed other rooms like the first one she'd been in; none held anything worth taking.

Turning a corner, Merce stopped, staring: at the end of the new hall was a large steel door, open. Coming through the door was electric light.

Her gut clenched; she nearly fled. But instead she forced herself to stop and listen again. Nothing. She took a few cautious steps forward, craning forward to catch any sounds coming from beyond that doorway.

Nothing.

If anything had turned on those lights, it wasn't moving.

She supposed the lights could be automatic, somehow still functioning, some quirk of a power system she didn't understand. Merce hadn't spent much time with Uncle Manny; she really didn't understand much about generators and batteries and wires and lights. As she edged closer, looking inside, she saw that the lights were positioned above a staircase that led down, and that not all of them still worked.

Curiosity drew her on. Moving through the doorway, she hesitated on the landing, looking down. The stairs were metal, solid, and seemed to go down several stories.

Her heavy, mud-crusted boots were loud on the metal grating, so she removed them. Clad only in woolen socks, holding the boots in one hand and her stick in the other, she jogged silently down the stairs.

They ended in a long, concrete hallway. Merce knew she was deep under the earth now, and she felt the first anxious tendrils of claustrophobia circling around her, but the air was breathable and the surroundings solid, so she forced her nerves down and moved ahead.

She passed doors that opened onto offices, gathering rooms, rooms whose purposes she couldn't name. But the fourth room on the right ...

Merce stared, open-mouthed, into a cavernous storage area. Metal racks extended into the distance. Many were empty, leaving Merce to wonder if they'd been picked clean, or had never held anything.

But it was the stacks of foil packets on one that made her heart leap. She ran to them, held them up to the single light overhead. "Freeze-Dried Ice Cream," read the first one. Another pile was "Stroganoff." Next to that, "Pasta Primavera." Beyond the packets were unopened crates, stamped with the same names.

Merce allowed herself a small victory cry. The old military rations were still good and highly prized in Camp Jackson. Finders were lucky to return with one or two. This was a treasure.

Merce shrugged out of her backpack, began loading it up. She packed carefully, trying to fit in as many as she could. She knew she could always come back here for more, but it was a long trip back to her cart and a week's trudge to Camp Jackson.

When her backpack couldn't hold one more ration she pulled it on, inwardly groaning at the weight but exhilarated by the contents. She imagined the feast Mama and Uncle Pete would prepare—fresh ears of corn from their fields and salad greens and stroganoff, with ice cream for dessert. There was enough here for all 102 residents of Camp Jackson to share.

She took the stairs slowly, careful not to stress her lungs and muscles—it was a long way up, and she still had to cross the swamp outside. She rested at each landing, but she still felt her calves protest when she reached the top.

Shifting the pack slightly, Merce stopped at the doorway, considering her position. She thought it might be easier to reach the outside if she turned right instead of left, the way she'd come. There was more sunlight coming from a room down there, promising a faster exit.

She knew, though, that it was late in the day and that sunlight would be fading soon. She needed to move quickly.

She reached the room at the end of the hall; it was circular, large, couches and chairs facing a huge, heavy desk; a tall leather chair, its back to her, was behind the desk. Before three windows that miraculously still had their glass stood two poles, each bearing a filthy, ragged flag. Merce knew the red, white, and blue of the one on the left had been the colors of the United States of America, a country that had died years before she'd been born.

On the other side of the room were two windows, both missing their glass, flanking a door. The windows looked out on a vista of wild, overgrown roses, splashes of white and pink providing relief from the bog's visual monotony. Below the windows, piles of dead leaves and rose petals had formed ramps leading up to the sills.

Merce headed for the door, thinking that if it was jammed she could easily climb through one of the windows. She was preoccupied, weighed down. Careless.

"Where do you think you're going?"

She'd almost reached the door when the voice, harsh and hoarse, froze her. Heart triphammering, she turned her head.

A man sat in the tall chair, watching her. She scolded herself inwardly for not checking that chair first. She could have avoided this, gone another direction, but she'd gotten sloppy, thinking of parties and ice cream, of her loved ones, of home.

At first she wondered if it was a ghost that had spoken to her. The thing in the chair was bloated like some blood-fed insect, with a jowly face topped by ragged silver hair. It had a prominent chin but no teeth; the blue irises were completely encircled by white; the clothing had once been formal, but now was as old and colorless as a scarecrow's.

No, Merce knew this was no ghost … but this man was disturbed. It was in the wide eyes, in the way his jaw slid when he spoke, in the rapid patter of his words, slurred by lack of teeth.

"What have you got in that pack, you little thief? Bring that over and show it to me right *now*."

Merce didn't move, her mind flitting past options. She could probably outrun the man, but she'd have to leave the pack. She might even be able to out-fight him—he was at least three times her size but looked weak, and she had her pocket knife and her stick. Or she could try explaining herself, but somehow she didn't think he'd care.

Then he reached into the desk, pulled out a gun, and turned it on her.

It was a pistol. Merce didn't know much about guns—that was Uncle Juan's forte—but she knew the one trained on her right now could kill her.

"What are you, deaf, you little fucker? Bring that goddamn bag over here now."

Merce shrugged out of the backpack, moving carefully so as not to excite the man, not to give him any reason to pull that trigger. Holding the bag out before her, she approached. The man leaned out and snatched the backpack away from her. He glanced at the contents before looking at her as he sneered.

"Just what I thought—stealing my rations! You're all alike, you worthless shits, trying to break in here and take what doesn't belong to you." He hurled the bag aside, causing some of the packets to spill out. Merce stifled the impulse to go and pick them up.

"I'm sorry," she said. Her voice was dry, raspy. She cleared her throat and tried again. "I didn't know anyone was here—"

He cut her off, mimicking her unfairly with high, screechy tones. "'I didn't know anyone was here.' Of course someone's here—I'm here. This is *my* fucking home. I've always been here, and I always will be here, and you will *never* belong here!"

The man's madness nearly staggered Merce. She'd never encountered anything like this, not even the one time Uncle Dave had found a bottle of whiskey and gotten so drunk that they'd had to lock him up in a basement because he screamed and tried to hit everyone. At least Uncle Dave had been okay a day later, ashamed of his behavior. She didn't think this man—who did look slightly familiar to her now—would ever apologize or relent.

But she had to try. "You're right, so I'll just leave—"

Again, he interrupted, this time jamming the gun towards her. "Oh, it's not that easy, you little cunt. You do *not* get to trespass into the goddamn White House and try to steal from me, then just be on your merry fucking way. We've got *laws* in this country, not that I'd expect *your* kind to abide by them."

His face ... something about it ... like the building, it prodded at her memories, of photos in the old history books. Her eyes jittered for a second away from him, and for the first time she noticed the portrait on the wall behind him, almost life-sized, and it was him ...

But no, it wasn't. He couldn't be alive, not this many years later, not after the wars and radiation and sicknesses. No, this couldn't be him, but it could be—

"Who are you?"

He laughed, but it was mirthless, his eyes never leaving her. "Jesus, you're so stupid you don't even know. I'm the *President*."

"Of what?"

His gums ground together before he answered. "Of this *country*. What else?"

"But ..." Merce hesitated; it seemed almost cruel to tell him. "There is no more country."

"Of *course* there is. And I'm its President, just like my father before me."

Ahhh, that explained it: Merce understood. This was the *son*. After his father had taken power here for twelve years before he'd died, he'd made sure one of his own would inherit the position and complete the ravaging of the formerly-great country. This man (Merce tried to remember his name but couldn't) had spent decades here, in this once-famous house, probably already mad before the power had been passed to him. Merce wondered how many of the skulls she'd seen outside with perfect fingertip-sized holes in the brows had been shot by him.

"How long have you been alone here?"

It was the wrong thing to say. He spasmed with rage and uttered a snarled cry.

The gun barrel lined up with her eyes.

His finger tightened.

He pulled the trigger.

Nothing happened.

The President stared in incomprehension for a moment, and then pulled the trigger again. And again. And again.

Merce knew; she knew because she'd watched Uncle Juan clean his guns. He was meticulous about it, even ritualistic. When she'd asked him once why he did it, he'd explained to her that guns were old metal things, and old metal things could rust and malfunction unless they were cared for.

This man hadn't taken care of his gun.

Merce didn't wait any longer. She grabbed her pack, shoving as many of the ration packets down into it as she could, swinging it by the straps. As she leapt through the broken window, she heard him scream and toss the gun aside.

She ran through rose bushes taller than her, ignoring the thorns that drew thin trickles of blood from her face and the backs of her hands. She heard him behind her, crashing through the growth. "You won't get away!"

Merce ran. She broke through the roses and was back at the edge of the swamp. She'd lost her stick somewhere, so she'd have to risk it, operating from memory, instinct and luck. She leapt from one mound to the next, jumping if she felt a foot slipping, not thinking about the sounds of crunching and snapping beneath her feet. She didn't know what she'd do when she reached the other side of the swamp. Maybe she could lose him in the ruins beyond, come back for the cart after dark—

He screamed behind her, and she heard a splash.

Merce risked a look backward and then stopped to stare. The President had fallen into a brackish pool, and only his head and shoulders were above the water. He twisted and jerked, freed one arm, but couldn't escape.

She watched him, cautious, ready to flee again should he pull himself out. He thrashed and shrieked, waved his arm, with no effect.

He was stuck. He saw her and shouted, "Something's wrapped around my leg. Come over here and help me."

She didn't move.

He called again, "Look, I'll make it worth your while. How'd you like to drive all of those rations out of here in a *tank?* Because I can get you one. You'd like that, wouldn't you?"

Merce shouted back, "It wouldn't work after all this time, like your gun."

"Whatever. Just *help me!*"

She considered. If she didn't help him, he might still get himself out … or he might die there, slowly and miserably, trapped. If she helped him, he'd likely kill her.

She should leave. Return to her cart, haul away from here as fast as she could, even if it meant that she keep going after dark. Leave this awful, insane, dead place and never come back, even for the precious rations.

But he was screaming behind her. Would she hear those screams forever, every night in her dreams?

Mama thought she was a leader. How would a real leader handle this?

She started walking toward him, her hand going to her pocket as she did, to her folding knife. She'd used the knife to cut Aunt Lateesha's herbs, to pry out Uncle Park's circuit boards, to sever vines and twigs. Her father, Camp Jackson's greatest Finder, had given it to her after his last trip out, a special gift to her on her twelfth birthday, a week before he'd fallen from the roof during a simple repair and never recovered.

The man trapped in the swamp watched her expectantly, spluttering. "Yeah … right, come on …"

Merce stopped ten feet from him, well out of reach. She held the folded knife to her lips, kissed it, and then tossed it to him. It hit the water near him, but he caught it, held it up before his eyes, perplexed. "What is *this* supposed to be?"

"It's a pocket knife. Use it to cut yourself free." She turned, walking away.

Behind her, he said, "How the fuck am I supposed to do that? I can't even open it."

"Figure it out."

She increased her speed then, no longer listening to him. She wasn't sure if the thud she heard at one point was her knife being thrown at her or not. She didn't turn to look. By the time she reached her cart, his fury had faded into the distance. The sun was setting as she lowered the heavy pack onto the wagon. She was too tired to go far tonight, but she could at least get a little way from here before finding a quiet, dry, safe place. She knew she'd sleep well, untroubled by awful dreams.

And then—like the rest of the world—she'd be done with this place.

DE-HUMAN (WHAT HAVE WE DONE?)

ANONYMOUS

WHAT HAVE WE DONE, or what could've been done to stop those
 awful noises, the monsters which weren't
 truly monsters, but worse
 who were our neighbors, family, loved ones
 a nameless something or other, though some always knew us;
 and watched us as they betrayed us
 without a second glance, without
 reason or reactions for consequences,
 dumbfounded by
 blistered jubilance
 that was borrowed and bought;
What have we done, thinking, underestimated
 bloated egotism and diet-cola conspiracy theories
 swallowed by fast-food fascists
 who beat their chests while building
 new closets as camps for us
 in the shadows, policies like death-proclamations
 as we called them buffoons;
What have we done, but waited
 while those monsters who look
 at us—talked about us—sit across
 from us, will never understand
 when the skies burn,
 or their loved one's cry *what have we done?*

VOICES EQUAL POWER – RAISE THEM!

ANONYMOUS